MANAGING FEAR

Managing Fear examines the growing use of risk assessment as it relates to preventive detention and supervision schemes for offenders perceived to be at a high risk of reoffending, individuals with severe mental illness, and suspected terrorists. It outlines a number of legislative regimes in common law countries that have broadened "civil" (as opposed to criminal) powers of detention and supervision. Drawing on the disciplines of criminology and social psychology, it explores how and why such schemes reflect a move towards curtailing liberty *before* harm results rather than *after* a crime has occurred. Human rights and ethical issues concerning the role of mental health practitioners in assessing risk for the purposes of preventive detention and supervision are explored, and regimes that require evidence from mental health practitioners are compared with those that rely on decision-makers' notions of "reasonable belief" concerning the risk of harm. Case studies are used to exemplify some of the issues relating to how governments have attempted to manage the fear of future harm.

This book aims to:

• educate mental health practitioners in the law relating to preventive detention and supervision schemes and how the legal requirements differ from clinical assessment practices;
• examine the reasons why there has been a recent renewal of preventive detention and supervision schemes in common law countries;
• provide a comparative overview of existing preventive detention and supervision schemes; and
• analyze the human rights implications and the ethics of using forensic risk assessment techniques for preventive detention and supervision schemes.

Bernadette McSherry, BA (Hons), LLB (Hons), LLM (Melb), PhD (York, Canada), Grad Dip Psych (Monash), is a Professor and Foundation Director of the Melbourne Social Equity Institute at the University of Melbourne, and an Adjunct Professor of Law in the Melbourne School of Law and the Faculty of Law, Monash University. She was previously a Professor of Law, an Australian Research Council Federation Fellow, and Director of the Centre for the Advancement of Law and Mental Health at Monash University. She is a Fellow of the Australian Academy of Social Sciences and a Fellow of the Australian Academy of Law. Professor McSherry is a legal member of the Mental Health Review Board of Victoria and has acted as a consultant to government on criminal law, sentencing, and mental health law issues.

INTERNATIONAL PERSPECTIVES ON
FORENSIC MENTAL HEALTH
A Routledge Book Series
Edited by *Ronald Roesch and Stephen Hart*,
Simon Fraser University

The goal of this series is to improve the quality of health care services in forensic settings by providing a forum for discussing issues related to policy, administration, clinical practice, and research. The series will cover topics such as mental health law; the organization and administration of forensic services for people with mental disorder; the development, implementation and evaluation of treatment programs for mental disorder in civil and criminal justice settings; the assessment and management of violence risk, including risk for sexual violence and family violence; and staff selection, training, and development in forensic systems. The book series will consider proposals for both monographs and edited works on these and similar topics, with special consideration given to proposals that promote best practice and are relevant to international audiences.

Published Titles

LEARNING FORENSIC ASSESSMENT
Rebecca Jackson

HANDBOOK OF VIOLENCE RISK ASSESSMENT
Randy K. Otto & Kevin S. Douglas

DANGEROUS PEOPLE: POLICY, PREDICTION,
AND PRACTICE
Bernadette McSherry & Patrick Keyzer

RISK MARKERS FOR SEXUAL VICTIMIZATION
AND PREDATION IN PRISON
Janet I. Warren & Shelly L. Jackson

HOW TO WORK WITH SEX OFFENDERS: A HANDBOOK
FOR CRIMINAL JUSTICE, HUMAN SERVICE, AND
MENTAL HEALTH PROFESSIONALS, SECOND EDITION
Rudy Flora & Michael L. Keohane

MANAGING FEAR: THE LAW AND ETHICS OF
PREVENTIVE DETENTION AND RISK ASSESSMENT
Bernadette McSherry

CASE STUDIES IN SEXUAL DEVIANCE: TOWARDS
EVIDENCE-BASED PRACTICE
William T. O'Donohue

Forthcoming Titles

FORENSIC PSYCHOLOGICAL ASSESSMENT IN PRACTICE
Corine De Ruiter & Nancy Kaser-Boyd

HANDBOOK OF FORENSIC SOCIAL WORK
WITH CHILDREN
Viola Vaughan-Eden

SEX OFFENDER RISK: AN INDETERMINATE
PREOCCUPATION
Robert Prentky & Howard Barbaree

MANAGING FEAR

The Law and Ethics of Preventive Detention and Risk Assessment

Bernadette McSherry

NEW YORK AND LONDON

First published 2014
by Routledge
711 Third Avenue, New York, NY 10017

Simultaneously published in the UK
by Routledge
27 Church Road, Hove, East Sussex BN3 2FA

Routledge is an imprint of the Taylor & Francis Group, an informa business

Library of Congress Cataloging in Publication Data
McSherry, Bernadette.
  Managing fear: the law and ethics of preventive detention and risk assessment/
  Bernadette McSherry.
    p. cm.
  Includes bibliographical references and index.
  1. Detention of persons.   2. Detention of persons—
  Moral and ethical aspects.   3. Detention of persons—
  Government policy—History.   4. Risk assessment—
  Moral and ethical aspects.   5. Risk perception—Social aspects.
  6. Mental health personnel—Professional ethics.
  7. Mental health personnel and patient—
  Moral and ethical aspects.   I. Title.
  K5437.M396 2013
  345'.0527—dc23   2013006684

ISBN: 978-1-138-00073-5 (hbk)
ISBN: 978-0-415-63239-3 (pbk)
ISBN: 978-0-203-09565-2 (ebk)

Typeset in Garamond
by Keystroke, Station Road, Codsall, Wolverhampton

Front cover image: excerpt from a mosaic mural, "The Canning Dragon",
by Carolyn-Noel Vincent, art therapist, and the Canning Unit patients and
staff, Thomas Embling Hospital, Melbourne, Australia. Photo: Lliam Murphy

Printed and bound in the United States of America
by Edwards Brothers, Inc.

CONTENTS

TABLE OF CASES

AUSTRALIA

CANADA

ENGLAND AND WALES

EUROPEAN COURT OF HUMAN RIGHTS

GERMANY

NEW ZEALAND

UNITED KINGDOM

UNITED STATES

UNITED NATIONS HUMAN RIGHTS COMMITTEE

TABLE OF STATUTES

AUSTRALIA

EUROPEAN UNION

GERMANY

INTERNATIONAL COMMITTEE
OF THE RED CROSS

INTERNATIONAL CRIMINAL COURT

LEAGUE OF ARAB STATES

NEW ZEALAND

SCOTLAND

NORTHERN IRELAND

ORGANIZATION OF AFRICAN STATES

ORGANIZATION OF AMERICAN STATES

UNITED KINGDOM

UNITED NATIONS

UNITED STATES OF AMERICA

ACKNOWLEDGEMENTS

I would like to acknowledge the research assistance provided by Liz Richardson and Sarah Lenthall throughout the writing of this book. I also thank Jacinta Efthim, Kathleen Patterson, and the editorial staff at Routledge, for their invaluable assistance in editing and formatting the manuscript as well as Sandra Pyke for her work on the references, tables, and index. Emeritus Professor Arie Freiberg suggested the title, *Managing Fear*, and I thank him for his guidance and support over the past decade. Most of all, I thank John Murphy for his forbearance, dependability and amity during the writing process and beyond.

Part I

INTRODUCTION AND THEORIES OF RISK AND PRECAUTION

1

INTRODUCTION

INTRODUCTION: FEAR, RISK, AND PUBLIC POLICY

Jacob Rangaita Peta from Manuwatu Wanganui in New Zealand, Kenneth Donaldson from Erie in the United States, Joseph "Jack" Thomas from Williamstown in Australia, Sean, Joseph, and Michael McCann from Manchester in England, and Robert John Fardon from Murwillumbah in Australia share one thing in common. They have all been the subject of legal schemes that have enabled their preventive detention or continuing supervision on the basis that they pose a risk of harm to others. These individuals may be viewed as representatives of specific groups of people singled out for legislative forms of control: those viewed as at a high risk of committing crimes such as sex offenders, those with severe mental illness, and those suspected of terrorist activities. Their stories will be outlined throughout this book.

The title, *Managing Fear*, has been coined to highlight public policy responses to certain groups in society. Through enacting legislative regimes that enable preventive detention and supervision on the basis of community protection, governments can in one sense manage the fear that many members of the public feel, reasonably or not, in relation to particular groups. In another sense, however, this book questions whether such fear is justified and whether societal reactions based on fear can be managed in ways other than via preventive detention and supervision schemes.

In his book first published in 1997, sociologist Frank Furedi used the term "the culture of fear" to describe a general trend in Western countries towards the avoidance of risk in many areas of personal and social life as well as the developing focus on safety measures. After listing a host of "scare stories" circulating at the turn of the century from childhood immunization causing autism to the risk of deadly global influenza, he pointed out (Furedi 2002: xii) that:

3

[t]he world of killer asteroids and global warming appears to be a million miles away from the sex deviant lurking in the background. Yet, they are all the construction of a culture that continually inflates the danger and risks facing people.

David Denney (2008: 563) has referred to "[l]egions of intermeshing and possible future scenarios" such as catastrophic events brought about by global warming as creating fear on a daily basis. The fear of worst-case scenarios is also reflected in the treatment of certain individuals. Denney (2008: 567) points out that "[p]articular groups, whether they be al-Qaeda or paedophiles, appear to be beyond due process" and refers to the example of the *News of the World* newspaper campaign in July 2000 to name and shame paedophiles that resulted in vigilante attacks against a number of individuals (including one instance where a paediatrician had her house vandalized, presumably because the attackers were unable to tell the difference between a paediatrician and a paedophile: BBC News 2000). Denney (2008: 567) views this as but one instance of the government failing "to protect its citizens from summary punishment imposed by a collectivity."

Denney (2008: 571) argues that fear-based policies lead to "justice" being viewed as synonymous with discipline, "with due process being given less emphasis than the politics of safety" and with certain groups being viewed as beyond principles of due process.

This book extends Denney's argument by examining the pervasive fear of harm thought to be posed by particular individuals. While preventive detention regimes have long existed, it is the interlinking of such regimes with the notion of risk that leads to serious ethical and human rights implications. Mental health practitioners are becoming increasingly involved in providing expert evidence on the risk of future harm for the purposes of preventive detention and supervision regimes. Risk assessment is now pervasive in the management and treatment of many individuals, but it raises particular issues when a person's liberty is at stake.

Two questions underlie the ensuing chapters:

• Why have certain groups of individuals been singled out for legally sanctioned preventive detention and supervision?
• How should mental health practitioners view their role in providing assessments of risk for legislative schemes that involve the deprivation of liberty?

These two questions raise important human rights and ethical issues as well as legal issues dealing with procedural fairness and the limits of the law in preventing harm. While there are no definitive answers to these questions, it will be argued that certain groups have always been singled out for legal control because of the way in which intense emotion underscores the targeting of certain groups perceived as "different" to the social norm.

The political emphasis in many Western countries has been to view detention and supervision as the predominant way of managing those who are feared to be at risk to others while, in general, expenditure on mental health and other services in the community has decreased. Emphasizing preventive detention and supervision schemes as part of a tough "law and order" response to crime control is inevitably going to be popular in a climate of fear. However, as Michael Tonry (2004: 6) points out:

> Concluding that particular policies or practices are consonant with current sensibilities is . . . the beginning but cannot be the end of assessments of their legitimacy. That evaluation needs to take account of basic human rights and moral considerations, whatever the public opinion poll results or prevailing sentiments of a particular day or year.

Accepting government policies without question needs to be avoided and one of the key themes of this book is that mental health practitioners must be careful to work within ethical frameworks for the giving of expert evidence for the purpose of schemes that ultimately breach human rights.

CURRENT PREVENTIVE DETENTION AND SUPERVISION SCHEMES

The term "preventive" detention is used throughout this book to refer to detention without charge or trial. Other terms are used in the literature such as administrative detention, ministerial detention, and extra-judicial detention. These terms overlap and can refer to the mandatory detention of asylum seekers pending a determination of their legal status, detaining people with infectious diseases on public health grounds, detention prior to extradition, and the involuntary commitment to institutions of those with alcohol or drug dependency or those with intellectual disabilities.

Sometimes, detention of certain individuals is justified on the basis or preventing a crime occurring. For example, what Lucia Zedner (2007) calls "pre-crime" methods of investigation in relation to suspected terrorists enable detention for the sake of gathering intelligence and not necessarily with the aim of bringing a prosecution. At present, risk assessment is in its infancy in relation to the detention and supervision of suspected terrorists, but there appears to be a move towards encouraging mental health practitioners to develop risk assessment instruments and techniques to provide a better evidence base for the identification and/or preventive detention of this group of individuals.

The "post-crime" criminal justice system relies on carefully delineated powers of investigation and questioning. Most forensic risk assessments by mental health practitioners occur *after* a crime has occurred in relation to bail, certain defences such as the insanity defence, automatism, diminished responsibility, and sentencing options, including indefinite sentences. Mental health practitioners may also be called upon to give evidence of risk in relation to the granting of parole. Andrew Carroll, Mark Lyall, and Andrew Forrester (2004: 411) point out that where release decisions are made by tribunals or courts, those decisions are influenced by "clinical evidence, the most critical aspect of such evidence being opinion regarding likelihood of future violence."

In addition to risk assessment for these "traditional" criminal justice purposes, some countries such as Australia and the United States have enacted post-sentence preventive detention regimes for sex offenders that enable such offenders to be kept in prison or housed in special facilities after their sentence has expired on the basis that they pose a risk of future offending. Because of the reliance on forensic mental health practitioners in the criminal process, it is understandable that their expertise has been called upon by the courts in relation to these post-sentence preventive detention regimes.

It is important to note that an order for post-sentence preventive detention differs from a sentence that is for an indeterminate period of time. One of the perceived benefits of indefinite sentencing over post-sentence detention is that the offender knows *at the time of sentencing* that he or she is being placed on an indefinite sentence and a nominal term is set that triggers a system of periodic review. In comparison, preventive detention orders are made at the point when an offender has almost completed his or her original prison sentence. Many countries that have indefinite sentencing regimes have also introduced preventive detention and extended supervision schemes.

These pre-crime, post-crime, and post-sentence forms of preventive detention are linked to a crime having occurred or the fear of a crime occurring. There are also other modes of preventive detention that may bring into play the evidence of mental health practitioners such as the detention of those with severe mental illness, personality disorders, cognitive impairments, and/or drug dependency for the purpose of treatment. Many of these schemes are predicated on risk of harm to others.

As well as detention in institutions such as hospitals or prisons, certain legislative schemes allow for a system of supervision or control orders that restrict the behaviour and liberty of the individuals concerned in specified ways. In many Western countries, there has been a proliferation in legislative schemes enabling the use of civil orders that aim to provide community protection. These include:

- control orders to prevent terrorist acts;
- community treatment orders for those with severe mental illness;
- sex offender registration schemes;
- extended supervision orders;
- sexual offence prevention orders;
- risk of sexual harm orders;
- antisocial behaviour orders;
- criminal antisocial behaviour orders;
- violent offender orders;
- serious crime prevention orders; and
- orders for lifelong restriction.

While this book concentrates on the preventive detention and supervision of sex offenders, individuals with severe mental illness, and suspected terrorists as a means of exploring how notions of risk are used to justify such schemes and the role of mental health practitioners within them, this is not to say that risk does not play a part in other detention schemes. Thérèse Murphy and Noel Whitty (2009), for example, make a salient case in relation to how risk informs the fear of certain individuals in public health emergencies. The concept of community protection plays a very large part in public policy debates and many of the themes explored in this book may carry over to other groups in society such as, for example, asylum seekers who are subject to immigration detention or those incarcerated under fitness to plead legislation.

The preventive detention and supervision laws in the jurisdictions of Australia, New Zealand, Canada, the United States, and the United Kingdom are explored primarily because they share a common law tradition that enables some comparisons to be made. However, the jurisprudence of the European Court of Human Rights is also considered, where relevant, especially in relation to the system of indefinite and preventive detention in Germany. As Marijke Malsch and Marius Duker (2012: 1) point out, punitive trends including what they term "incapacitation" "are highly interwoven with developments in Western societies" in general and many of the themes discussed in this book will also be of relevance to civil law countries.

THE MAIN THEMES AND STRUCTURE OF THIS BOOK

This book is divided into four parts:

- Part I: Introduction and Theories of Risk and Precaution;
- Part II: The Laws of Preventive Detention and Supervision;

- Part III: Human Rights and Ethical Issues;
- Part IV: Conclusion.

The next two chapters are concerned with exploring why it is that certain groups are currently being singled out for preventive detention and supervision and why risk assessment is becoming central to such legislative schemes. There are a number of theories that have been put forth to explain the political shift towards the use of coercive measures that have developed in order to prevent harm. The next chapter explores three main themes that have been identified as explaining the shift towards coercive measures to prevent harm:

- the development of the "risk society";
- the growth of "actuarial justice"; and
- the "precautionary principle" which is a term used to explain the shift from managing risk towards the necessity to take "radical prevention" in curtailing liberty before harm results.

Chapter 2 also examines perspectives from social psychology dealing with theories of decision-making and social exclusion that help explain why members of society may fear harm from specific groups of individuals.

Chapter 3 explores how risk assessment is becoming central to preventive detention and supervision schemes. It explains how risk assessment techniques have been developed for the purpose of helping with the management and treatment of offenders thought to be at high risk of reoffending rather than for the primary aim of preventive detention and supervision. It highlights some of the criticisms that have been made concerning the use of risk assessment instruments in the courtroom, particularly in relation to translating group data to the individual, and contends that risk assessment is particularly problematic in relation to individuals with severe mental illness and suspected terrorists.

Part II provides an overview of the laws of preventive detention and supervision. Chapter 4 examines the laws that enable the preventive detention of sex offenders, individuals with severe mental illness, and suspected terrorists on the basis of future harm. Chapter 5 outlines the laws that enable the supervision, control, or involuntary treatment of certain individuals. Using a series of tables, these chapters examine the similarities and differences in the laws in the United Kingdom, the United States, Canada, Australia, and New Zealand.

Michael Tonry (2004) has made the point in the context of crime control policies that different countries have different "sensibilities" or ways of thinking about crime and punishment. In relation to preventive detention and supervision regimes, it is important to keep in mind that the jurisdictions outlined have emphasized different ways of managing the fear of harm posed by certain social groups and some caution is necessary in making presumptions about common themes in the laws explored. For example, laws enabling the post-sentence detention of "sexually violent predators" in the United States may be seen as a subset of policies enacting laws that have greatly increased incarceration rates in that jurisdiction (see, for example, Tonry 2004 and Simon 2012 for an outline of the differences between imprisonment policies in the United States and European countries).

While it is important to view particular laws in their respective social contexts, the laws outlined in Chapters 4 and 5 share a common aim of protecting the community from harm and the operation of many of them require the input of evidence from mental health practitioners. On that basis, it is worthwhile providing their key elements for comparison.

Chapter 6 explores the jurisprudence in common law countries concerning the standard of proof in relation to the risk of future harm. It contrasts the requirements for evidence of a belief or suspicion on "reasonable grounds" to enable the preventive detention and control of suspected terrorists with other standards such as the "balance of probabilities," a "high degree of probability," or "beyond reasonable doubt" required in relation to sex offenders. It is argued that when a person's liberty is at stake, a high standard of proof should be required in court or tribunal proceedings, but this has not always been the case in relation to preventive detention and supervision schemes. This chapter also outlines the rules of expert evidence in court and tribunal proceedings and how judges have generally ruled risk assessment evidence to be admissible, but have considerable discretion as to the weight that should be attached to such evidence.

Part III then turns to the human rights and ethical implications of preventive detention and supervision schemes. Chapter 7 explores the international human rights framework for such schemes. Jurisprudence from the United Nations Human Rights Committee and the European Court of Human Rights is considered in relation to how such schemes may breach the right to liberty and other human rights such as the right to a fair hearing, the right not to be subject to double punishment, and the right not to be subject to retrospective laws. This chapter points out that even where international human rights bodies have declared preventive detention schemes to be in breach of fundamental human rights, the effect of such decisions on domestic laws is dependent on the willingness of the State concerned to abide by such decisions.

Chapter 8 raises some of the ethical issues concerning the use of risk assessment instruments in the courtroom. It considers the advantages and disadvantages of three ethical approaches:

- it is always unethical to give testimony on risk;
- it is always ethical to give testimony on risk; and
- it is ethical to give testimony on risk in certain circumstances.

This chapter also examines relevant Codes of Ethics in relation to expert testimony.

In Part IV, the conclusion provides an overview of the themes explored and argues that while risk assessment techniques may be useful for management and treatment purposes, such techniques raise particular concerns in relation to the detention and supervision of certain groups in order to prevent future harm. It argues that there is a need for more procedural safeguards for the use of risk assessment instruments in the courtroom and greater awareness of the ethical difficulties of using risk assessment for the deprivation of liberty on the basis of future harm.

CONCLUSION

Risk assessment by mental health practitioners is becoming central to decision-making about which groups of individuals should be detained or supervised on an ongoing basis. It is hoped that this book will provide a contextual basis for why this is occurring as well as highlighting the human rights and ethical implications of preventive detention and supervision regimes.

For those interested in a legally oriented critique of and theoretical approach to preventive detention laws, Christopher Slobogin (2003, 2006, 2011a, 2011b, 2012a) has developed seven principles derived from American and international law that he argues can legitimately circumscribe the scope of such laws. His work is particularly influential in relation to laws concerning individuals with severe mental illness as well as "sexually violent predators." Other legal academics such as Eric Janus (2003, 2004a, 2004b, 2004c, 2006, 2011) and John Q. La Fond (1992a, 1992b, 1998, 2005, 2008, 2011) have also made significant contributions to the legal literature on the preventive detention of sex offenders. While this book outlines a selection of laws enabling preventive detention and supervision, and refers to some of the legal literature in this regard, it aims to cast a broad interdicisciplinary net in seeking to explore why it is that certain groups of individuals are singled out and how mental health practitioners should view their role in relation to such laws.

Marijke Malsch and Marius Duker (2012: 5) state that detaining people in prisons or other institutions "works directly and speedily, which renders it attractive to policy makers." However, keeping individuals locked away can be a costly enterprise and Jonathan Simon (2012: 32) makes the point that "[t]hose states that have reduced crime the most are not the ones that increased incarceration the most." There is thus a need to explore options beyond merely keeping people institutionalized for long periods of time and these may include supervisory sanctions or treatments adapted to individual needs. From a human rights perspective, supervision, control, and/or treatment orders may be preferable to preventive detention, but care is still needed to ensure that such schemes are not the immediate default setting for managing the fear caused by portrayals of certain groups in society.

2

THEORIES OF RISK
AND PRECAUTION

INTRODUCTION: FROM BUSHRANGERS
TO TERRORISTS

The legally sanctioned preventive detention of certain individuals is nothing new. In nineteenth-century Australia, the Robbers and House-breakers Act 1830 gave "any person whatsoever" the power to apprehend any person reasonably suspected of being "a transported felon unlawfully at large" in order for him or her to be brought before a Justice of the Peace. The burden of proof was placed on the apprehended person to prove "to the reasonable satisfaction" of the Justice that he or she was not a felon. If the Justice was not so satisfied, the person could be detained indefinitely. The 1830 Act became known as the "Bushranging Act" as the powers within it were often used to detain suspected bushrangers (the term used for outlaws living in the Australian bush) without charge.

In 1834, New South Wales police magistrates were asked whether the 1830 Act should be renewed beyond its limited period of operation. While the majority of police magistrates favoured its continuation (Boxall 1924: 13), Justice William Westbrooke Burton (1834) of the New South Wales Supreme Court condemned the Act as being repugnant to the laws of England. He was particularly concerned that the apprehended person had the burden of proving he or she was not a felon, which was contrary to the common law principle that every person is presumed to be free. Despite these concerns, the Bushranging Act proved to be politically popular and was renewed ten times over the next two decades.

The zeal with which the police used the powers under this legislation became the subject of much complaint and it was suggested that the Bushranging Act was "extensively used for purposes of extortion and blackmail" (Boxall 1924: 16). An English mechanic, with the pen name of Alexander Harris, gave an account of his being apprehended as he was walking one evening from a farm where he had conducted some business towards where he was planning to camp (Harris 1847: 79):

> The officer shouted to me to stop; which I did. He came up, and in a most offensive way asked who and what I was. I told him, a free emigrant. "Had I any pass? Anything to show?" It happened that I had, and moreover had it with me . . . I took out "the pass", and gave it to the officer. He glanced at it quite cursorily, told me he . . . was sure this was a forgery. Nothing I said in reply was of the slightest avail: indeed, both he and his men seemed to regard this proceeding as a sort of a joke.

Alexander Harris was taken to the nearest "lock-up" overnight and then transferred to another lock-up where he was confined for four days "with a man charged with murder" (p. 79), before eventually being freed. He recounts a number of tales about members of "the labouring class" (p. 81) being apprehended on a whim and criticizes the fact that "nothing is more difficult than to get from the authorities a proper protective document" (p. 227).

It was not, however, only members of the labouring class who were apprehended. As reported by *The Australian* newspaper on January 23, 1835, Sir Francis Forbes, the first Chief Justice of New South Wales, was arrested as a suspected bushranger when walking near his country residence. He apparently "gave a lame account of himself to the police" and was taken to the district constable who quickly realized the mistake. The account in *The Australian* rather drily goes on to comment that "His Honour was however well satisfied even at his own expense, to be fully acquainted with the diligence and activity of the Mounted Police" (Domestic Intelligence 1835: 2).

The fear of bushrangers in the nineteenth century led to the enactment of the Felons Apprehension Act 1865 (NSW), which enabled those who had not surrendered themselves for trial on a charge of a "capital felony" to be taken "alive or dead." It also enabled a police officer to enter premises without warrant "and therein apprehend every person whom he shall have reasonable grounds for believing to be [an] outlaw or accused person."

On May 5, 1865, five days before the commencement of the Felons Apprehension Act 1865, Ben Hall, the son of two freed convicts, was shot dead by police. Ben Hall was alleged to have committed over 600 robberies around Forbes in New South Wales between 1862 and 1865. John Gilbert, a member of Ben Hall's gang, was shot dead on May 13, 1865. An inquest into the death of Ben Hall ruled his killing to be "justifiable homicide." This conclusion has recently been challenged by relatives of Hall who have called for a new coronial enquiry (Meacham 2007).

If the term "felon" or "bushranger" is replaced by "terrorist," a pattern can be discerned in the use of the law to detain certain individuals without charge. As will be explored further in Chapter 4, suspected terrorists can now be detained without charge on suspicion of future harm (Hogg 2007; Gani and Mathew 2008; Zedner 2009). What is interesting about the suspected felon/terrorist laws is that they enable preventive detention *prior* to a crime being committed.

In a similar fashion, there have been cycles in the incarceration of those with severe mental illness. For example, Patricia Alldderidge (1979) points out that the existence of large asylums housing those considered to be "lunatics" was but one part of a cycle in England that swung between large institutions and small specialist facilities, the latter being used at the end of the fourteenth century, in 1713, and several times in the second half of the eighteenth century. In Victorian England, the era of large institutions, not only were those with severe mental illness confined to county asylums, but also those considered to be "inconvenient people" (Wise 2012).

While laws enabling preventive detention have long existed, what is new is the growing reliance upon these laws *in conjunction with* the language of risk to detain those perceived as some form of threat to members of the community. This reliance encompasses "pre-crime" measures such as the preventive detention of suspected terrorists as well as those with certain disorders or illnesses who are considered at risk of harming others. It also encompasses "post-crime" measures such as the preventive detention or supervision of serious offenders, particularly sex offenders.

This chapter provides an overview of some of the theories postulated as to why the concepts of risk and precaution have become central to current preventive detention and supervision schemes. Sociologists and criminologists have identified various themes that attempt to explain the political shift towards the use of coercive measures in order to prevent harm. Three main themes deal with the "risk society," the growth of "actuarial justice," and a shift towards the "precautionary principle." These are explored in turn.

The final section of this chapter examines social psychology theories that seek to explain why certain groups are marginalized and, in some cases, dehumanized. The effect is that serious offenders, particularly sex offenders, individuals with severe mental illness, and suspected terrorists are often depicted in such negative terms that preventive detention regimes are seen as legitimate methods of protecting society. Theories of decision-making and social exclusion are examined to explain why certain groups are targeted for preventive detention.

PERSPECTIVES FROM SOCIOLOGY
AND CRIMINOLOGY

The Risk Society

Within the sociological literature, three major theoretical approaches to risk have been distinguished. Deborah Lupton (1999) refers to these as the "cultural/symbolic," the "governmentality," and the "risk society" approaches. The latter two approaches have been influential in the field of criminology as well as sociology, but it is the notion of the "risk society" that has been the most pervasive in the literature concerning preventive detention policies. This section outlines briefly the cultural/symbolic and governmentality approaches to risk and then examines the influence of Ulrich Beck's (1986) notion of the risk society upon preventive detention regimes.

The cultural/symbolic approach to risk

The cultural/symbolic approach originated with the work of the cultural anthropologist Mary Douglas (e.g., 1982, 1985, 1992). Douglas explores notions of risk in terms of shared cultural beliefs and practices that are based on social expectations and responsibilities. Notions of risk are seen as shared within communities and as part of a historical continuum rather than the result of any distinctive social, political, or economic conditions. What a community selects as embodying risk is that which is seen to threaten the community's moral principles. This in turn helps maintain social order.

Douglas' theoretical approach has had some influence on sociological theory, but less influence on criminologists writing in the field of risk. It may, however, be relevant in explaining why certain groups have been singled out for preventive detention. As explored in the introduction to this chapter, a pattern can be discerned in the use of the law to detain certain individuals without charge and this pattern could be explained by a sense that these individuals or "outlaws" are viewed as threatening society's common bonds. John Tulloch and Deborah Lupton (2003: 7) summarize this approach as follows:

> Certain marginalized groups are identified as posing risks to the mainstream community, acting as the repository for fears not simply about risk but about the breakdown of social order and the need to maintain social boundaries and divisions.

This focus on the risk posed by certain marginalized groups is threaded through what David Garland (2001: 135) refers to as "a criminology that trades in images, archetypes, and anxieties, rather than in careful analyses and research findings." He points out (2001: 135) that "the political discourse relies upon an archaic criminology of the criminal type, the alien other." Why this differentiation occurs and why it appears so difficult to eradicate is explored later in this chapter through the lens of social psychology.

John Tulloch and Deborah Lupton's (2003) work follows on from Mary Douglas' cultural approach and focuses on the values and attitudes of 134 people in New South Wales, England, and Wales towards risk in everyday life. Tulloch and Lupton (2003: 29) identify the influence of local conditions "including those related to the economy, politics, infrastructure" and geographical location as being integral to what people regard as risks.

Hence, this approach emphasizes that what individuals perceive to be risks will vary according to their backgrounds and location. While it has not been highly influential in relation to research on preventive detention regimes, it does help explain why certain groups may be targeted in some societies but not in others.

The governmentality approach

The "governmentality" approach to risk draws on the work of Michel Foucault (e.g., 1991). It examines the exercise of power in society and views risk "as a complex category made up of many ways of governing problems, rather than as a unitary or monolithic technology" (O'Malley 2004: 7). Nikolas Rose (2000: 324), for example, has referred to risk strategies as being divided into two kinds: "those that seek to regulate conduct by enmeshing individuals within circuits of inclusion and those that seek to act upon pathologies through . . . circuits of exclusion." For Rose (2000: 325), "circuits of inclusion" encompass all the pieces of information concerning "our credentials, activities, qualifications for entry into this or that network." Exclusionary practises, on the other hand, not only exclude certain individuals from citizenship, but also seek to control their behaviour because of a fear of what they might do. Rose (1998) views psychiatry as one profession that has been given the task of governing "the incorrigibly risky and potentially monstrous person" through risk management processes.

Pat O'Malley (2001b, 2004), while avoiding single-factor explanations for the rise of risk control strategies, emphasizes the rise of new right politics in Western democracies as integral to the emphasis on risk in criminal justice policies. He suggests that new right politics in the 1980s and 1990s were "neo-liberal" with regard to public spending, but authoritarian in relation to regulating certain groups such as the poor and criminal offenders. For example, O'Malley (2004: 68–69) refers to "welfare dependency" being diagnosed as a social ill to be remedied by "'allowances', provided on condition that the recipient performs various activities." He writes (2004: 69) that "[s]o much has the economic subsumed the social that poverty and unemployment came to be re-coded 'exclusion', and programmes to reclaim lost souls back into the market were bestowed with the sobriquet of 'social justice.'"

Governmentality theories have contributed to explanations for the development of new modes of mass surveillance and technological forms of security (see, for example, O'Malley 1991). In England in particular, there has been a proliferation of widespread monitoring techniques of public spaces, albeit with limited success. The Head of the London Metropolitan Police Unit, Detective Chief Inspector Mick Neville, has been quoted as saying that while billions of pounds have been spent on closed-circuit television cameras, not much thought has gone into how the police are going to use the images and how they will be used in court (Bowcott 2008). As a method of control, the monitoring of public spaces can be viewed as having been inefficient and imperfectly administered.

George Rigakos and Richard Hadden (2001) have criticized governmentality theories for ignoring class as an object of analysis. George Rigakos (2001: 95) argues that, from a historical perspective, class is "by far the most cogent way to understand the purpose and function of risk governance." O'Malley (2001a: 86–87) responds by pointing to a divide in the literature between those who follow the sociologist Ulrich Beck's work (discussed in the next section) where risk may be associated with class rule and other governmentality theorists who are "agnostic" about "real" risks in the form of global threats, "being concerned only with political mentalities and techniques of governing through risk."

Pat O'Malley (2001a: 87) refers to the "conceptualization of risk and theories of the risk society" as "discontinuous and variable." As a result, the stress on "the importance of fragmentation" has meant that the governmentality approach in terms of an overall theory of risk has "gained less attention" than other theories concerning risk (Denney 2005: 36). Exploring discrete areas of inclusion and exclusion can assist in understanding certain forms of governmental control, but the main drawback of this approach is that it lacks coherency.

Beck's risk society

It is the grand theory of the risk society, however, that has the most sway in the criminological literature. The term the "risk society" was coined by the influential German sociologist, Ulrich Beck (1986), to explain a shift from industrial society to one which is concerned with finding ways of controlling the unintended side effects of scientific and technological progress. Both Beck (e.g., 1992a, 1992b, 1999, 2009) and Anthony Giddens (e.g., 1990, 1991) argue that risks in current society

17

are characterized by their global reach and their indeterminate and uncertain nature. Beck (1992a: 21) defines risk as "a systematic way of dealing with hazards and insecurities induced and introduced by modernization itself." Beck (2009: 8–9) writes that "[f]ear determines the attitude towards life. Security is displacing freedom and equality from the highest position on the scale of values. The result is a tightening of laws, a seemingly rational "totalitarianism of defence against threats."

Giddens (1998) divides risks into two types. First, there are "external" risks that can strike individuals unexpectedly, but which happen regularly enough. Then there are risks that are "manufactured" by the development of science and technology. Examples of manufactured risks include the threat of nuclear contamination, nuclear war, global warming, and holes in the ozone layer. These risks threaten the very survival of the human race. In the face of such catastrophic, but uncertain risks, fear and the desire for security increases.

The approach of Beck and Giddens has been widely criticized (see Kemshall 2003: 10ff; Denney 2005: 32–33 and Arnoldi 2009 for overviews). Nevertheless, this expansive theory of risk has infused many areas of research from economic theory to environmental science to criminal justice. Deborah Lupton (1999: 59) points out that "[d]ebates and conflicts over risk have begun to dominate public, political and private arenas." Rose (1998: 180), while critical of the risk society approach for implying homogeneity where he sees risk thinking as heterogeneous, nevertheless concedes that an important common characteristic of risk thinking is the desire to bring uncertainty under control.

Beck is not directly concerned with crime and punishment and the risks posed by individuals, although he does touch on "private terrorism" in the sense of individuals accessing weapons of mass destruction (Beck 1999: 36). His notion (Beck 1992a: 49), however, that the risk society is "no longer concerned with obtaining something 'good,' but rather with preventing the worst" has been used by Richard Ericson and Kevin Haggerty (1997) in their analysis of contemporary policing. Ericson and Haggerty (1997: 18) offer extensive empirical evidence to argue that the risk society approach has infused contemporary policing so that there has been a shift away from "deterrence-based law enforcement" to a focus on "risk, surveillance, and security." For example, they point to the development of computer technology to enable the "efficient production and distribution of knowledge useful for the management of suspect populations" (1997: 439).

Bill Hebenton and Terry Thomas (1996a, 1996b) extend the notion of surveillance for risk management to the "tracking" of sex offenders in the community through the development of sex offender notification procedures and practices. The pervasiveness of surveillance techniques also encompasses control orders that permit the ongoing tracking of suspected terrorists in the community. These orders are examined in Chapter 5.

Barbara Hudson (2003: xiii) draws on the risk society approach to argue that the demand for security undermines key concepts of "justice" such as the rights of offenders to proportionate punishment in the sense of "blaming commensurate with the wrongness of the crime as well as recompense for the harm suffered by individual victims." She argues (2003: 46) that risk management in criminal justice involves a balancing act between "the risk to the public of being victimised" and "the risk to offenders (actual and potential) of undeserved restriction of liberty or other form of deprivation."

In Hudson's view, the traditional balance of criminal justice has favoured protecting offenders from undeserved punishment, but recent government policies and ensuing laws are now shifting the balance towards protecting the community from potential rather than actual offenders. Hudson (2003) also argues that there has been a move from risk management techniques that recognize the inevitability of error to that of risk control, focused on containment. This has led to government policies that are focused on the control of risk rather than enhancing social justice and Hudson calls for a rethinking of traditional theories of liberalism to counteract this focus.

Beck's notion of the risk society can thus be viewed as influencing the criminological literature dealing with the pervasiveness of surveillance techniques as well as the development of governmental policies aimed at controlling the risk of harm from specific individuals.

Together, the three major sociological approaches to risk, the "cultural/symbolic," the "governmentality" approaches, and the grand theory of the "risk society" help explain the societal context that shapes governmental reliance on current preventive detention and supervision schemes. O'Malley (2010: 16) makes the point that

> there is no necessary hiatus between governmentality and cultural approaches to risk, for the latter provide insight into the value bases out of which the governmental rationalities and technologies of risk are produced, or that create an environment in which they receive political support.

The three approaches can in fact be seen as complementary rather than oppositional. Alongside these approaches, some criminologists have examined the focus on "actuarial" techniques to support criminal justice policies. The theory of "actuarial justice" is explored in the next section.

Actuarial Justice

"Actuarial justice" is the term used by Malcolm Feeley and Jonathan Simon (1994: 173) to explain a growing reliance by governments on "techniques for identifying, classifying and managing groups assorted by levels of dangerousness." Their thesis is that the prevalence of concerns about risk and the impact of actuarialism on the construction and delivery of criminal justice amounts to a "new penality." This is seen as a key shift not just in terms of crime management, but also in terms of how the individual is viewed within the system.

According to Feeley and Simon (1992, 1994) there has been a shift away from a focus on individual offenders and the prospect of rehabilitating them. Now, the focus is on large groups of offenders who are sought to be managed by reference to actuarial inferences from statistical data sets. As a result, risk assessment is now based on classifying the individual within a large group, the profile of which is derived from large-scale data sets rather than direct clinical knowledge of the individual.

The purpose of risk assessment is viewed as the proper allocation of resources for managing offenders rather than for the best treatment that may bring about rehabilitation. According to Simon (1993) this is exemplified in parts of the United States by probation and parole officers who cease to be social workers and become risk managers. They monitor offenders via electronic checks and urine tests, all the while measuring offenders against actuarial data sets to ensure they can be classified as high, medium, or low risk.

In traditional penality, individuals were viewed as moral agents who were capable of choosing between right and wrong and were able to be transformed through the methods of social welfare (Garland 1985). Jonathan Simon (1988: 774) points out that these methods were expensive and that "[i]n our present social circumstances, it is cheaper to know and plan around people's failings than to normalize them."

According to Feeley and Simon (1994), actuarial justice arises from the rapid expansion of commercial insurance and the extension of such practices across all aspects of social life. But some dispute this and argue that the emphasis on risk calculations and social out-groups in fact predates the twentieth century. George Rigakos and Richard Hadden (2001: 64), for example, identify seventeenth-century systems of record-keeping, prudentialism, and the "econometric constructions" of "populations" under capitalism as important factors in the rise of actuarial risk management.

David Garland (2003: 65) is also sceptical about whether the development of an actuarial style of analysis is "as novel or as extensive" as Feeley and Simon suggest. He writes (2003: 65):

> A focus upon the differential risks posed by classes and categories, a notion of criminality as an aggregate phenomenon, and a concern to manage populations were all characteristic of the eugenics movement at the turn of the century, a movement

that influences both criminological discourse and penal policy at that time.

However, John Pratt (1995, 2000b) points out that even if actuarial risk management existed at the turn of the twentieth century, its revival could be explained by the rise of sophisticated statistical techniques alongside computer technology.

There has also been some debate about the extent to which actuarial justice has in fact displaced traditional penal practice (Pratt 2000a, 2000b; Garland 2003). John Pratt (2000b: 141) points out that there may not have been a completed historical change, but that "the old may well have a significant coexistence with the new."

Responding to these criticisms, Simon and Feeley (2003: 77) state "we did not claim, or mean to claim, that [the new penology] was wholly new or that it had become the dominant or even a major paradigm in contemporary criminology." They wanted simply to suggest that "there were enough instances of discourse, policies, and programmes that reflected these concerns that these developments should be treated as something more than idiosyncratic anomalies in an otherwise unchanging process." They propose (2003: 77–78) that the new penology should not be viewed as a change in the social and political order, "but rather a shift in the way crime is governed (known about and acted on)."

Certainly, in relation to preventive detention regimes, the reliance on actuarial methods of risk assessment is clearly manifest. There is now a growth industry in risk assessment instruments and techniques in relation to the management of those perceived to be high-risk offenders. The concept of potential harm to others is central to the detention of those with severe mental illness and suspected terrorists. An analysis of risk assessment instruments and techniques is the subject of the next chapter.

It may indeed have been the case, as John Pratt (2000b) suggests, that Feeley and Simon's work was written at a time when actuarial justice was just beginning to take shape. It is now far more embedded at least in relation to certain serious offenders than a decade ago. The very creation of a Risk Management Authority in Scotland in 2005 indicates that risk management by the mid-2000s was becoming a central part of governmental criminal justice policy.

The Precautionary Principle

While theories of risk still dominate the sociological and criminological literature, there has been a shift in recent years towards exploring the concept of "uncertainty" and why governments find it necessary to respond to threats that are unknown and unknowable (Ashworth 2009: 87).

What has been termed the "precautionary principle" stems from environmental science. It posits that where the risk of harm is both unpredictable and uncertain and where the damage wrought will be irreversible, any lack of scientific certainty in relation to the nature of the harm or its consequences should not prevent action being taken (Sunstein 2005). The precautionary principle ousts risk-based or evidence-based approaches to public policy and is best summed up by Australia's former Prime Minister, John Howard (2007), who said, when asked about the preventive detention without charge of suspected terrorists: "it's better to be safe than sorry."

French academic, François Ewald (1993, 2002), uses the term "precautionary logic" to explain the type of reasoning that ensures people take into account the unseen threats that lie in wait. Science should be used to master perceived threats and to uncover those that are as yet unknown. Criminologist, Richard Ericson (2007), adapted this idea to explain recent trends in criminal law and security policies. He refers to precautionary logic as the logic of uncertainty that fuels suspicion.

In relation to the law, Ericson (2007: 24) views precautionary logic as leading to criminalization through two types of "counter-law." The first type of counter-law involves the enactment of laws that erode or eliminate traditional principles that are viewed as barriers to pre-emptive measures aimed at preventing harm. This is exemplified by the suspension of normal legal principles and procedures "because of a state of emergency, extreme uncertainty, or threat to security with catastrophic potential" (2007: 26). The second type of counter-law refers to new surveillance infrastructures that extend existing surveillance networks in ways that again erode or eliminate traditional legal principles. He argues (2007: 31) that "in the context of the uncertainty and insecurity that characterize neo-liberal politics at the beginning of the 21st century, criminalization through both forms of counter-law is a dominant political strategy."

Bill Hebenton and Toby Seddon (2009) refer to the work of François Ewald and Richard Ericson in exploring how the precautionary principle has been used to justify preventive detention regimes for sexual and violent offenders. They argue that the precautionary principle is behind forms of "counter-law" such as:

- the identification of existing laws as impediments to the prevention of future harms and thus the enactment of broad powers to detain certain groups on the basis of what they might do;
- the development of surveillance infrastructure such as "electronic databases, electronic monitoring and tracking and residential restrictions" (2009: 349); and
- the transformation of "science" to support regimes based on predictions of future behaviour; decision-making based on fear, anxiety and "cultural wellsprings" (2009: 354).

22

They argue (2009: 358) that there is a need to confront the issue that "many lay people are in fact not much interested in assessing or controlling 'risk' in its probabilistic sense. They actually want certainty." Thus those called upon to provide expert assessments as to risk, even when they couch their evidence in language of probability, may simply be viewed as bolstering "selective incapacitation" regimes that aim to provide security for the community through the subversion of justice.

In a similar vein, Lucia Zedner (2007: 262) has argued that neo-liberal societies are now "on the cusp of a shift from a post- to a pre-crime society." That is, criminal justice policy has traditionally been focused on events post-crime such as the apprehension of offenders, investigation, the trial process, and sentencing. Zedner (2007) argues that there has been a *temporal* shift towards anticipating and stopping what might occur in the name of security.

Certainly, there has been a rise in surveillance techniques, private security companies, offender registers, and increasing powers given to police in relation to the investigation, detention, and charging of suspected terrorists *prior* to any crime being committed. There has also been a rise in methods of monitoring certain individuals such as through control orders and, in the United Kingdom, antisocial behavioural orders (ASBOs). (The laws enabling these orders are explored in Chapter 5.)

Zedner (2009: 84) points out that although the precautionary principle might have originally been premised on "grave and irreversible harms," it has broadened "to provide a warrant for decision making in situations of uncertainty even where the anticipated harms are of a lesser gravity." As a consequence, Zedner writes (2009: 85), incarceration becomes "increasingly central to the security complex" and it becomes the norm for those who pose potential threats to public safety.

Overlapping Theories

The above theoretical approaches that deal with the "risk society," the growth of "actuarial justice," and the shift from managing risk towards the necessity to take "radical prevention" in curtailing liberty before harm results, all offer explanations of the current emphasis on preventive detention and supervision schemes. While they have been outlined under three different headings, they do overlap and coalesce. Barbara Hudson (2003: 60) points out that "[r]isk society theory, cultural studies of risk and blame, new right politics and the rationalities of governance all contribute to an understanding of the way in which risk matters in contemporary western democracies."

These approaches to current trends in protecting the community from the fear of harm derive from sociological and criminological studies. The next section turns to an exploration of why certain groups are singled out for preventive detention, relying on some recent studies in social psychology to provide a framework for that analysis.

PERSPECTIVES FROM SOCIAL PSYCHOLOGY

The common theme running through current preventive detention regimes is the fear that certain individuals could cause harm to members of the community if the right to liberty prevailed. Cass Sunstein (2005) makes the point that in responding to the risk of future harm, governments often impose selective rather than broad restrictions on liberty. He writes (2005: 204–5):

> Selectivity creates certain risks. If the restrictions are selective, most of the public will not face them, and hence the ordinary political checks on unjustified restrictions are not activated. In these circumstances, public fear of national security risks might well lead to precautions that amount to excessive restrictions on civil liberties.

For example, selecting "terrorists" as a group to be singled out for deportation or preventive detention can appeal to the public because of a general belief that only a small minority of people would be affected. In a poll conducted by the Australian non-tabloid newspaper, *The Age* (Grattan 2005), 78 per cent of respondents supported the deportation of suspected terrorists and 56 per cent supported the detention of such suspects without charge for up to three months. In a commentary in the newspaper the following day, Andrew Lynch (2005) stated that these particular findings "will concern sections of the community for whom those methods are a reduction of what defines our society. In losing that part of ourselves, we give the terrorists a victory."

Frank Furedi (2008: 648) has observed that anti-terrorism policies are often couched in terms of "cultivating the resilience of the public" as though vulnerability is the normal public response to an act of terrorism bringing with it the prospect of mass panic and the breakdown of civil behaviour. He writes (2008: 651) that "[a] mature, complex, technologically sophisticated society is often represented as powerless against the actions of small groups of determined individuals." This fosters a "vulnerability-led approach" to public policy which, ironically, may encourage feelings of helplessness and a focus on worst-case scenarios.

But what of the fear of harm caused by specific groups of individuals? There are two strands of social psychology theory that help explain why legally sanctioned preventive detention regimes have existed for such a long time and why they are now so closely linked to the concept of risk. These two strands deal with theories of decision-making and social exclusion.

Theories of Decision-Making

Drawing from social psychology, Sunstein (2005: 36) argues that in assessing risks, people draw on heuristics or rules of thumb. He refers to the "availability heuristic" as meaning that individuals tend to refer to examples that are readily available. Thus, when thinking about the risk of terrorism, images of the planes crashing into the World Trade Center in New York, or the fires caused by the Bali bombings, or the mangled remains of a bus in the London bombings come immediately to mind. This also carries over to the stereotypical image of the sex offender being that of a paedophile stranger, an image often used in the media accompanied by a sensationalist news report (Ducat et al. 2009), or the continuing association portrayed in the media between mental illness and danger to others or criminality (Thornicroft 2006: 108ff).

Sunstein (2005: 39) also refers to the concept of "probability neglect." That is, people tend to focus on worst-case scenarios rather than the probability of such scenarios occurring. The notion of probability neglect stems largely from the work of psychologists Daniel Kahneman and Amos Tversky (e.g., Tversky and Kahneman 1973; Kahneman and Tversky 1979). During the 1970s and early 1980s, these researchers explored the ways in which people make decisions in conditions of uncertainty. They argued that decision-making can be distorted by irrelevant criteria. In their paper entitled "Prospect Theory" (1979), they posited that individuals are risk-averse when making a decision that offers the prospect of a gain, but risk-seeking when making a decision that will lead to the prospect of a loss. While this helps explain why people who play the lottery also take out insurance, it has also been taken to mean in broader studies of risk that people tend to place excessive weight on outcomes that have little prospect of occurring when the stakes are high.

Kahneman and Tversky's "prospect theory" study was primarily concerned with cognitive processes rather than emotive responses. The role of emotion in both individual and governmental decision-making has now become an important subject of enquiry. Arie Freiberg and W.G. Carson (2010: 156) point out that "the role of emotion or affect in the shaping of governmental decision must be taken into account" and that it is difficult to influence government policy in the face of strong public support "unless the underlying causes of the public's emotional discomfort are addressed" (2010: 158).

Sunstein (2005: 66ff) has explored the role of emotion in individual decision-making and argues that when strong emotions such as fear are involved in decision-making, calculations about the likelihood of certain events occurring are even less likely to occur than when strong emotions are not involved. Gerd Gigerenzer (2006: 347) refers to low probability events that cause the death of many people as "dread risks." He argues that people tend to react to dread risks through avoidance behaviour. To this end, he conducted a study that indicated many Americans shifted from plane to car travel following the terrorist attacks on September 11, 2001, presumably on the basis that they believed the probability of being killed in a car crash was much lower than if flying by plane. Ironically, this shift in travel patterns caused a spike in road accidents that fell as traffic patterns began to get back to normal. Gigerenzer (2006: 350) argues that the psychological effects of dread risks are such that they can be viewed as the indirect consequences of terrorism and that any counter-terrorism efforts should aim to "defeat the effects of terrorism acting through our minds."

Part of the explanation as to why fear elicits probability neglect is based on the notion explored in Daniel Kahneman's later work (e.g., 2011), that mental processes can be metaphorically viewed as two systems: System 1 that involves fast, intuitive thought and System 2 that involves slow deliberation. His idea is that System 1 is more influential than System 2 and it cannot be switched off. Decision-making is usually based on partially reliable information that is only occasionally thoroughly evaluated. The emotive, intuitive responses to uncertainty under System 1 help explain behaviour such as that studied by Gigerenzer and why many government policies are reactions to strong emotive responses to events, rather than the result of reflective and informed debate.

Theories of Social Exclusion

The introduction to this chapter pointed out that legally sanctioned preventive detention regimes are not new, but that they have been used to detain certain "out-groups" in society from suspected bushrangers to suspected terrorists. Another strand of social psychology that can assist in understanding why certain groups have tended to be singled out for detention is that of social exclusion theory. While researchers working in this field have looked broadly at the lack of participation of certain groups in societal activities and the psychological effects that this has, a subset of inquiry within this field focuses on the processes by which some groups become marginalized in society.

There are many interpretations of the term "social exclusion" (Millar 2007). Some criminologists, particularly those writing under the umbrella of governmentality theories, are sceptical about recent trends of highlighting social exclusion. David Gordon (2007) points out that the political idea of social exclusion was derived from French social and economic policy. The term was first used by René Lenoir in his 1974 book *Les Exclus Un Français Sur Dix* to refer, in David Gordon's words (2007: 194), to those "who had been failed by existing state and social networks – such as the poor, disabled people, suicidal people, abused children, drug addicts and so on."

As pointed out earlier in this chapter, Pat O'Malley (2004: 69) has referred to the governmental recasting of poverty and unemployment as "exclusion" which, it is presumed, can be relieved by dismantling previous welfare policies, thereby bypassing the causes of poverty and unemployment. In this vein, Chris Hale and Marian Fitzgerald (2007) argue that the emphasis placed on employment as being the solution to social exclusion is misconceived as it ignores the problems caused by "tough on crime" political agendas that often serve to exacerbate social problems.

However, social exclusion in the political context differs from the concept of exclusion in social psychology. In the latter field, the concepts of "prejudice," "stigma," and "discrimination" are central to explanations as to why certain groups are marginalized. Prejudice means prejudgment (from the Latin "prae" and "judicium") and while it is generally linked to derogatory social attitudes or beliefs, there are many studies indicating that most individuals are prejudiced in the sense of making assumptions about certain groups (Vaughan and Hogg 2011: 376ff). Susan Fiske (1998) refers to "gut level" prejudices that stem from anticipated threats, thus affecting the ways in which a certain group is seen to threaten the goals or interests of the person concerned. Such prejudices may provoke emotions such as anger, fear, anxiety, or sadness. Most research on prejudice has focused on sexism and racism rather than disability or sexual orientation (Vaughan and Hogg 2011: 378–79). Instead the concept of "stigma" has been used primarily in studies focusing on exclusion and mental illness (Thornicroft 2006).

The term "stigma" derives from the Greek for "mark" or "tattoo" and in Ancient Greece the term referred to the mark placed on those worthy of contempt by burning with a hot iron. The plural form "stigmata" in the Christian tradition referred to the marks that appeared on the devout that resembled the wounds of the crucified Christ. Erving Goffman (1963: 3) used the term to refer to an attribute that discredited an individual, reducing him or her "from a whole and usual person, to a tainted, discounted one." He distinguished three categories of stigmatizing conditions: "blemishes of individual character" that are assumed to reflect immoral or deviant behaviour; "abominations of the body" arising from physical disfigurements or deviations from what is considered "normal"; and "tribal stigmas" that are based on the membership of despised racial, ethnic, or religious group. Goffman (1963: 5) states that there is a belief that "the person with a stigma is not quite human."

27

Social exclusion is closely related to stigmatization. Carol Miller and Cheryl Kaiser (2001) observe that stigma is so interconnected with rejection and exclusion that prejudice towards members of stigmatized groups is often measured by asking people to indicate the social distance they want to keep between themselves and the stigmatized group. Brenda Major and Collette Eccleston (2005: 66) point out that there are three essential elements of stigma-based exclusion. First, it is consensual in that "[t]here is general agreement within a culture that certain types of people should be excluded." Second, exclusion is shared with others who have the same attribute so that it can be seen as based on social rather than individual identity. Third, the exclusion of stigmatized groups is viewed by members of the group doing the excluding as justified or legitimate.

Stigmatization and social exclusion are so pervasive that some researchers have posited that these processes serve to enhance personal or group self-esteem for those doing the excluding (Wills 1981; Tajfel and Turner 1986) as well as serving to alleviate discomfort and anxiety. For example, Robert Brooks (2000: 11–12) has pointed out that "almost all cultures have viewed mental illness as a deviant form, subject to negative social sanctions." In Michel Foucault's (1965) terminology, those with mental illness are seen as "the other." There is some research suggesting that those with mental illness have thus been subjected to social exclusion because people tend to feel uncomfortable around those who they know or believe to be mentally ill in part because they are perceived to be unpredictable and dangerous (Farina and Ring 1965; Farina 1998). This then serves to alleviate the feelings of anxiety within the excluding group. In relation to those with disabilities, there is some research suggesting that they are subject to social exclusion because they remind those carrying out the exclusion of their own vulnerability and mortality (Major and Eccleston 2005). There may thus be self-protective motives at play both at an individual and also a group level when certain groups are excluded and denigrated (Reed and Aquino 2003).

There are also "system justification" theories that view stigma as a method of justifying existing social inequalities and maintaining the status quo (Sidanius and Pratto 1993; Jost and Banaji 1994) and evolutionary theories that view stigma as a method of excluding individuals who are perceived to be poor partners in order to preserve reproductive fitness (Neuberg et al. 2000; Kurzban and Leary 2001).

In recent years, there has been a move away from the concept of stigma towards that of discrimination to explain the experiences of those who are excluded. This is because the term "stigma" is seen as locating the problem within the individual who is excluded rather than focusing on the negative attitudes of those carrying out exclusory practices. Graham Thornicroft (2006: 191) argues that much of the work on stigma "has been beside the point" because it has concentrated on the attitudes of "normal" people to certain groups of individuals and has focused on hypothetical situations, rather than examining the actual experiences of those who have been "shunned." He states that shifting the focus from stigma to discrimination has the advantage of focusing on actual behaviour rather than just attitudes and can lead to much needed research on interventions to change discriminatory behaviour.

Judi Chamberlin in the foreword to Graham Thornicroft's book (2006: xii) defines discrimination as "the societal codification of [negative] attitudes, as expressed in laws and customs that result in [certain individuals] having a lower social status and fewer rights than non-labelled people." Chamberlin makes the point (2006: xiii, emphasis in original) that "[w]hile 'changing attitudes' may have a warm, fuzzy appeal, changing discriminatory *behaviour* is, I believe far more important."

Explaining Preventive Detention and Supervision Schemes through Social Psychology

Social psychological theories of decision-making and social exclusion assist in explaining why it is that certain groups have been singled out for preventive detention and supervision. In relation to suspected terrorists, the "availability heuristic" and "probability neglect" highlight community fears of catastrophic events, thereby justifying measures for anticipatory containment. Intense emotion also has a role to play in the way the community reacts to certain offenders and those with severe mental illness. Hazel Kemshall and Jason Wood (2008) point out that it is the "extraordinary cases" such as brutal sexual assaults and murders that invoke the strongest punitive responses in the name of public protection.

Theories of social exclusion and related work on stigmatization and, more recently, discrimination, also shed light on why certain groups have been singled out for community approbation.

Preventive detention and supervision laws should thus be seen in the context of a long tradition of emotional responses to certain groups targeted because of "difference."

CONCLUSION

There are a number of theories that have been put forth by socio-logists and criminologists to explain the political shift towards the use of coercive measures in order to prevent harm. However, legally sanctioned preventive detention regimes have long existed. Preventive detention laws are nothing new as exemplified by the powers given to police under the Bushranging Act in 1830. What *is* new is the growing reliance upon preventive detention and supervision regimes at both the pre-crime and

29

post-sentence ends of the spectrum *in conjunction with* a growing emphasis on risk and precaution. As Barbara Hudson (2003: 53) has pointed out, an emergent theme in criminology "is the joining together of the actuarial, probabilistic nature of risk and the moral language of blame."

The first section of this chapter examined three main themes that have been identified by criminologists as explaining the shift towards coercive measures to prevent harm:

1   the development of the "risk society";
2   the growth of "actuarial justice"; and
3   the shift from managing risk towards the necessity to take "radical prevention" in curtailing liberty before harm results.

The reliance on preventive detention and supervision in conjunction with the growing emphasis on risk and precaution may thus be viewed as the product of different, but coalescing trends.

While the focus of this book is on preventive detention and supervision schemes in relation to serious offenders, particularly sex offenders, those with severe mental illness, and suspected terrorists, John Pratt (1998) has observed that there are constant shifts as to which societal groups are subjected to legal control. Similarly, Mark Finnane and Susan Donkin (2013) have referred to several instances of history repeating itself in attempts to control those perceived to be dangerous. David Garland (1996) has explained this historical trend of controlling certain societal groups by referring to the concept of the "alien other" whose dangerousness can only be addressed by removing such individuals from circulation in order to protect the public. Garland writes (1996: 461) that certain individuals are targeted as "dangerous members of distinct . . . social groups which bear little resemblance to 'us'" and that the rhetoric of the "alien other" leads to the perspective that "[t]he only practical and rational response to such types is to have them 'taken out of circulation' for the protection of the public." He refers (1996: 461) to the "criminology of the self" that characterizes offenders as "rational consumers" like "us" who may be rehabilitated through welfare programmes and the "criminology of the other" that focuses on "the threatening outcast, the fearsome stranger, the excluded and the embittered."

Government policies supporting preventive detention regimes certainly reflect this concept of the "alien other" and the second main section of this chapter has focused on why such rhetoric taps in to societal concerns about certain groups.

Theories of decision-making and social exclusion drawn from social psychology help explain why preventive detention and supervision schemes have proved to be such a popular response to certain out-groups in society.

The social exclusion of certain stigmatized groups may serve a variety of psychological functions (Major and Eccleston 2005), thereby making it difficult to change negative attitudes. The focus has, therefore, shifted somewhat from stigma to discrimination.

The next chapter examines the increased use of risk assessment instruments in forensic practice. It will highlight some of the criticisms that have been made in relation to the use of risk assessment instruments in the courtroom, particularly in relation to translating group data to the individual and makes the point that while risk assessment is now a growth industry when it comes to managing offenders, the concept of risk is treated very differently when it comes to those with severe mental illness and suspected terrorists.

3

RISK ASSESSMENT
INSTRUMENTS AND
TECHNIQUES

INTRODUCTION: JACOB RANGAITA PETA

Jacob Rangaita Peta was born in 1984 in the Manawatu Wanganui region of the North Island of New Zealand. At the age of 14, he was convicted of aggravated burglary and in the ensuing eight years, he was convicted of numerous other offences including theft, assault, unlawfully possessing a pistol, unlawful interference with a motor vehicle, escaping from custody, and possessing cannabis.

In September 2005, Peta and another man, James Lahina, broke into a house in Palmerston North on two consecutive days and assaulted two men. Peta and Lahina were convicted on November 6, 2007 of burglary, aggravated robbery, injuring with intent, and wounding with intent in relation to these "home invasions." The jury was told at their trial there was a suggestion these incidents were about "taxing" occupants of the house over drug debts. A subsequent appeal against conviction was successful and a retrial was ordered (*R v Lahina and Peta* 2008).

While on bail for the charges relating to the home invasion, Peta visited a friend's house where the friend's two young daughters were sleeping. Peta was apparently under the influence of drugs and alcohol when he went into the girls' bedrooms over a period of ten minutes. He approached the first child as she lay in bed, pulled down his pants, exposed his penis, and told her to kiss it. The girl pretended to be asleep. He then went into the sister's bedroom, kissed her on the cheek, exposed himself, and asked her to kiss his penis. When the girl began to cry, he left the room. He later told both girls not to tell their mother and, according to one of the girls, threatened to kill them. Peta admitted being at the house but initially claimed not to have done anything at all. However, he later pleaded guilty to two counts of committing an indecent act with a girl under 12 and was sentenced to nine months' imprisonment.

The Chief Executive of the Department of Corrections made an application to the sentencing judge under section 107I of the Parole Act 2002 (NZ) for Peta to be placed on an extended supervision order. On

January 5, 2006, after considering a report by a senior psychologist from the Department of Corrections, Judge Nevin Dawson of the Palmerston North District Court granted this application. Under the Parole Act 2002, an extended supervision order may be made for up to ten years where an offender has committed a sexual offence against a person under the age of 16 and the court considers that the offender is likely to commit similar offences in the future. In assessing such a likelihood, the court can rely on the report of a "health assessor" that must take into account the factors set out in section 107F(2) of the Parole Act 2002:

(a) the nature of any likely future sexual offending by the offender, including the age and sex of likely victims;
(b) the offender's ability to control his or her sexual impulses;
(c) the offender's predilection and proclivity for sexual offending;
(d) the offender's acceptance of responsibility and remorse for past offending;
(e) any other relevant factors.

Peta appealed against the imposition of the extended supervision order. The New Zealand Court of Appeal unanimously upheld the appeal, finding that the reasons given by the Judge for the imposition of the supervision order were so inadequate that the Court needed to consider the matter afresh on the basis of additional evidence (*R v Peta* 2007). Justice Glazebrook delivered the decision of the Court quashing the extended supervision order.

The decision in *R v Peta* raised some serious issues with the way in which the assessment of Peta's risk of sexual reoffending was carried out. Justice Glazebrook was particularly scathing of the way in which the original health assessor had administered two actuarial risk assessment instruments, the "Automated Sexual Recidivism Scale" (Skelton *et al.* 2006) and the "Sex Offender Needs Assessment Rating" (Hanson and Harris 2000), to reach his conclusion that Peta was in the medium to high risk of reoffending (*R v Peta* 2007: paras [62]–[75]). The health assessor had apparently scored the risk assessment instruments incorrectly, misinterpreted the results, and not fully explained to the Court how he had reached his conclusion. Justice Glazebrook (2007: para. [62]) considered it "disturbing" that the Director of Psychological Service at the Department of Corrections, who gave evidence at the appeal hearing, agreed that the original health assessor's application of the risk assessment instruments "was not expert." Justice Glazebrook (2007: para. [62]) stated that "[j]udges should be able to rely on evidence from the Corrections Department meeting best practice standards. In this case the problems with the original health assessor's report mean that no reliance can be placed on that report."

The Court of Appeal decision in *Peta*'s case raises the issue of the involvement of mental health practitioners in providing expert evidence on the risk of future harm in preventive detention and supervision cases. Since the nineteenth century, medical experts have been called upon to give their expert opinions in courtrooms in relation to the mental state of certain individuals (Eigen 1995; Gutheil 2005). However, requiring evidence as to whether a particular individual is at risk of reoffending has its origins alongside the rise of the politics of risk explored in the previous chapter. As Simon (1998: 453) points out, the role of risk assessment has "become more formal and associated with statistical forms of inference."

This chapter focuses on some of the problems associated with endeavouring to assess the risk of future harm by serious offenders, individuals with severe mental illness, and suspected terrorists. Certainly in terms of the harm posed by offenders, a whole industry has emerged in relation to the use of actuarial risk prediction and prevention instruments, some of which is outlined in this chapter.

In relation to those with severe mental illness, however, administrative tribunals, in reviewing detention and supervision decisions, tend to rely solely on the clinical judgment of the treating psychiatrist in relation to the potential for future harm to self or others, rather than weighing up evidence based on risk assessment instruments. This raises issues concerning the sufficiency of evidence for a finding that an individual is at risk of harm to self or others.

Mental health practitioners have rarely been involved in the assessment of risk in relation to suspected terrorists for the purposes of detention and supervision. Generally, these regimes are based on the "reasonable" suspicions or beliefs of police officers or intelligence operatives that the individuals concerned pose a risk of harm to others. There are, however, moves towards using risk assessment instruments to identify the risks posed by suspected terrorists and this needs to be examined in the light of criticisms of such instruments in general.

Much of this chapter examines the criticisms around predicting risk of future harm as it relates to serious offenders. The next section outlines the context of the development of actuarial risk assessment instruments, and examines some of the main criticisms that have been made of them. The chapter then outlines some of the issues raised in relation to the prediction of risk of harm posed by persons with severe mental illness and suspected terrorists.

THE GROWTH OF ACTUARIAL RISK ASSESSMENT INSTRUMENTS TO PREDICT FUTURE HARM

The previous chapter outlined the theory posited by Malcolm Feeley and Jonathan Simon (1992, 1994) that there has been a shift in penal practice away from a focus on individual offenders with the prospect of rehabilitating them towards managing large groups of offenders. Individuals are classified within a large group, the profile of which is derived from large-scale data sets rather than the direct clinical knowledge of each person.

Certainly in relation to violent and/or sex offenders, there has been a massive growth in the use of risk assessment instruments and techniques to classify the risk of future harm for both management and prediction purposes. Yet, assessing the risk of future violence is a notoriously difficult task (Mullen 2001; Johnson 2005). Paul Mullen (2001) outlines how assessments of risk deal in general with the following issues:

- *past violence* (on the assumption that the best predictor of future violence is past violence);
- *pre-existing vulnerabilities* (such as being male, antisocial traits, suspiciousness, childhood marred by disorganization and/or abuse, youth, impulsivity, and irritability);
- *social and interpersonal factors* (such as poor social networks, lack of education and work skills, itinerant lifestyle, poverty, and homelessness);
- *symptoms of mental illness* (such as active symptoms, poor compliance with medication and treatment, poor engagement with treatment services, treatment resistance, and a lack of understanding of the nature of the illness);
- *substance abuse* (particularly alcohol abuse);
- *state of mind* (such as the presence of anger or fear, delusions that evoke fear or provoke indignation or produce jealousy, clouding of consciousness or confusion, ideas of influence, and command hallucinations);
- *situational triggers* (such as loss, demands and expectations, confrontations, ready availability of weapons, and physical illness);
- *personality construc*ts (such as "psychopathy" which is discussed below).

The challenge has been to work out ways to avoid too much assessor subjectivity in weighing up these factors. This section provides an overview of how risk assessment instruments and techniques have developed in light of the move towards managing large groups of offenders. The next section examines some of the criticisms made of such instruments and techniques. While the state of knowledge on risk assessment has improved in recent years and assessment instruments may assist in *managing* risk within hospital settings, nevertheless, there is no current assessment procedure that can *predict* risk with certainty and this may have serious repercussions when a person's liberty is at stake.

Clinical Assessments of "Dangerousness"

During the 1970s and early 1980s, the emphasis was placed on making clinical assessments of "dangerousness," which did not provide a medical diagnosis, but involved "issues of legal judgment and definition, as well as issues of social policy" (Steadman 2000: 266). Under this approach, there were no restrictions as to the ways in which information could be used to reach a decision.

Research indicates that during this time, mental health practitioners tended to be especially cautious in their assessments of possible future offending and to over-predict violence (McAuley 1993: 7). John Monahan, in his seminal work, *The Clinical Prediction of Violent Behavior* (1981), conducted a review of cases involving risk assessment and concluded that predictions of risk were accurate in only about one-third of cases. He stated (1981: 47, 49):

> psychiatrists and psychologists are accurate in no more than one out of three predictions of violent behavior over a several-year period among institutionalized populations that had both committed violence in the past (and thus had high base rates for it) and who were diagnosed as mentally ill.

The over-prediction of future violence can result in large numbers of "false positives," where individuals have been identified as likely to commit further offences but who, upon release, have not actually reoffended (Steadman 2000). An example of this is provided by what occurred following the United States Supreme Court case of *Baxstrom v Herold* (1966).

In 1961, Johnnie K. Baxstrom was serving a prison sentence for assault when he was certified as insane by a prison physician. Baxstrom had a long history of convictions for property and alcohol offences and had been diagnosed with epilepsy. He was transferred from prison to Dannemora State Hospital, an institution run by the New York Department of Correction and used for the purpose of confining and caring for male prisoners declared mentally ill while serving a criminal sentence. When his sentence was about to finish, the Director of Dannemora filed a petition in the Surrogate's Court of Clinton County requesting that Baxstrom be civilly committed. This meant that he would fall under the jurisdiction of the Department of Mental Hygiene. The Surrogate's Court held that it did not have the power to order the Department of Mental Hygiene to commit Baxstrom under civil laws, the Department having already determined that it did not believe Baxstrom was suitable for care in a civil hospital. Baxstrom, therefore, remained at Dannemora after his sentence had expired.

A writ of "habeus corpus" was pursued on Baxstrom's behalf. The United States Supreme Court held that Baxstrom had been wrongfully detained. Chief Justice Earl Warren delivered the decision of the Court which held that Baxstrom had not been afforded equal protection of the laws by his civil commitment to an institution maintained by the Department of Correction beyond the expiration of his prison term. The upshot of this decision was that 967 individuals were released from State correctional department maximum security units, most being initially transferred into civil hospitals and then into the community. Prior to their release, each of these individuals had been assessed by two psychiatrists as mentally ill and "dangerous" (Steadman 2000: 266). Harry Steadman and Joseph Cocozza (1974) carried out a four-year follow-up study of a cohort of 176 of these individuals and found that only a small percentage had been reconvicted, the majority for non-violent offences. They concluded that "there was substantial over-prediction of dangerousness in the range of four to one not dangerous (i.e. not assaultive) to dangerous (assaultive)" (Steadman 2000: 266).

For Johnnie Baxstrom, the consequences of the Supreme Court decision proved to be tragic. Baxstrom did not wait for transfer to a civil hospital pending release into the community, but petitioned for a jury trial to determine whether he should be detained on the basis of mental illness. The jury found in his favour. Baxstrom was released into the community, but unfortunately when he attempted to obtain medication for his epilepsy, he was told to wait until he had received his records from Dannemora Hospital. He died within two weeks of his release from uncontrolled epileptic fits.

The research conducted on those released following the Supreme Court decision challenged the way in which evidence of risk was led in the courtroom. Harry Steadman (2000: 267) points out that the legal context during the 1970s required a "Yes–No" dichotomy:

> When dangerousness was the lynchpin of mental health law and the organizing concept for empirical research, it was often characterized by questions from the bench such as, "Doctor, can you assure me that this man will not be dangerous if I release him?"
>
> That question was usually accompanied by the answer, "No, your Honor." "Should this person be committed? Yes or no?" "Should this person be released? Yes or no?" "Is this person dangerous? Yes or no?" "What is your conclusion?" "Tell me, is he dangerous or not?"

Steadman (2000: 267) observed that this dichotomy gradually transformed into a more nuanced approach where "dangerousness" had three components: "risk factors" that are used to predict violence; "harm" that refers to the amount and type of violence being predicted; and "risk level" that refers to the probability of the harm (rather than any trait of the person).

Why clinicians make erroneous decisions concerning the risk of future harm also became the object of study. Ken McMaster and Leon Wells (2006: 12) point out that some of the factors that may adversely influence the reliability of clinical assessments include the rapid formation of judgments by assessments, the limited ability of individuals to process information adequately, and difficulties in articulating the decision-making process. McMaster and Wells (2006: 12) point out that the information given to clinicians on which to base risk assessments is often via self-reports that are unreliable given that offenders may minimize or deny their offences. Gary Melton and colleagues (2007: 301) also refer to cultural differences between the assessor and the individual being assessed as leading to errors in judgment.

The intuitive and subjective nature of the unstructured clinical assessment of risk led an American Psychiatric Association task force (1974: 30) to comment that "the state of the art regarding predictions of violence is very unsatisfactory. The ability of psychiatrists or any other professionals to reliably predict future violence is unproved." Similarly, an American Psychological Association task force (1978: 1110) stated that "psychologists are not professionally competent to make such judgments."

John Monahan (1981: 63) argued that in order to avoid errors in clinical judgment, there should be "an increased emphasis on using statistical concepts in clinical prediction, and a heightened sensitivity to environmental and contextual variables." This call was heeded by a number of researchers and led to the development of a range of actuarial risk assessment instruments that involved a "formal, algorithmic, objective procedure (e.g., equation) to reach a decision" (Grove and Meehl 1996: 293–94).

The Rise of Actuarial Prediction

Between the mid-1980s and the mid- to late-1990s, the focus shifted from assessing dangerousness to a focus on assessment scales based on statistical or actuarial risk prediction. These scales assess the particular offender against a range of factors that are thought to be associated with future offending (Rose 1998; Berlin *et al.* 2003). The shift to risk assessment and risk management has seen the rise of "scientific" literature examining a range of risk factors that have a statistical association to a future event. Table 3.1 on p. 40 sets out some of the main actuarial risk assessment instruments that are now commonly used to measure the risk of reoffending.

Davis and Ogloff (2008: 143) describe the development of actuarial risk assessment instruments as follows:

> researchers coded a wealth of possible risk factors (e.g., demographic factors, criminal and violence history, psychiatric history, substance abuse history) from correctional and psychiatric files. They subsequently contained the criminal records of those released and identified who had recidivated violently. Statistical analyses were used to identify those factors that, when combined, most reliably related to violence.

The majority of the actuarial risk assessment instruments set out in Table 3.1 originated in Canada, perhaps partly because in the mid-1990s the Correctional Service of Canada and the Canadian National Parole Board saw offender risk assessment as being integral to their work and the Department of the Solicitor General Canada was given the task of developing risk assessment instruments to aid the assessment process. Instruments such as the Psychopathy Checklist-Revised (PCL-R) (Hare 1991) and the Violence Risk Appraisal Guide (VRAG) (Quinsey et al. 1998) focus on variables that have been ascertained by actuarial studies (Norko and Baranoski 2005; Freckelton and Selby 2009). In the United States, the Macarthur Study of Mental Disorder and Violence, a major programme of research first funded in 1988 by a grant from the John D. and Catherine T. MacArthur Foundation to the University of Virginia, has also led to the development of a classification tree model referred to as an "iterative" classification tree (ICT) (Monahan et al. 2001; Monahan 2002).

In relation to sex offenders, the Static-99 (Hanson and Thornton 1999) is sometimes used to predict future offending. Like the more general actuarial-based scales, this instrument includes questions dealing with a number of variables. The Static-99 is intended to be used on adult sex offenders and consists of ten items dealing with "static" variables such as age, persistence of sexual offending, "deviant" sexual interests, relationship to victims, and general criminality. The Static-2002 (Hanson and Thornton 2003) is an updated version that retains the Static-99 risk factors except for "never lived with a lover for two years" (which was found to be hard to confirm in practice) and adds several new items.

In developing the VRAG, Vernon Quinsey and colleagues (1998: 171) made it clear that there was no role for clinical judgment in assessing risk:

> What we are advising is not the addition of actuarial methods to existing practice, but rather the complete replacement of existing practice with actuarial methods . . . actuarial methods are too

Table 3.1 Actuarial risk assessment instruments

Name	Year developed	Developer/COUNTRY	Type of risk assessed
Psychopathy Checklist-Revised (PCL-R)	1991	Robert Hare/CANADA	Psychopathic personality traits
Violence Risk Appraisal Guide (VRAG)	1993	Grant Harris, Marnie Rice and Vernon Quinsey/CANADA	Violence recidivism among offenders with mental disorders. Uses only static factors
Historical, Clinical, Risk-20 Item (HCR-20)	1995 Version 1 1997 Version 2	Christopher Webster, Derek Eaves, Kevin Douglas and Anne Wintrup/CANADA Christopher Webster, Kevin Douglas, Derek Eaves and Stephen Hart/CANADA	Violence recidivism
Level of Service Inventory-Revised (LSI-R)	1995	Donald Andrews and James Bonta/CANADA	Violence recidivism in correctional settings
The Rapid Risk Assessment for Sexual Offence Recidivism (RRASOR)	1997	R. Karl Hanson/CANADA	Sexual recidivism
Sexual Offender Risk Appraisal Guide (SORAG)	1998	Vernon Quinsey, Grant Harris, Marnie Rice and Catherine Cormier/CANADA	Violence recidivism
Static-99 and Static-2002	1999 2003	R. Karl Hanson and David Thornton/CANADA	Sexual and violent recidivism. Uses only static factors
Sex Offender Need Assessment Rating (SONAR)	2000	R. Karl Hanson and Andrew Harris/CANADA	Aims to evaluate changes in risk of sexual recidivism. Uses only dynamic factors

Instrument	Year	Authors / Country	Description
Risk Matrix 2000 (RM2000)	2000–2003	First developed by David Thornton in 2000 and tested in 2003 by David Thornton, Ruth Mann, Steve Webster, Linda Blud, Rosie Travers, Caroline Friendship and Matt Erikson/UNITED STATES and ENGLAND	Two versions: one measuring risk of non-sexual violent recidivism in sex offenders and one for measuring the risk of sexual recidivism. Uses only static factors
Iterative Classification Tree (ICT)	2000	John Monahan, Henry Steadman, Pamela Robbins, Eric Silver, Paul Appelbaum, Thomas Grisso, Edward Mulvey and Loren Roth/UNITED STATES	Violence risk assessment
Risk of Sexual Violence Protocol (RSVP)	2003	Stephen Hart, P. Randall Kropp and D. Richard Laws with Jessica Klaver, Caroline Logan and Kelly Watt/CANADA	Risk of sexual violence
Short-Term Assessment of Risk and Treatability (START)	2004	Christopher Webster, Mary-Lou Martin, Johann Brink, Tonia Nicholls and Connie Middleton/CANADA	Risk of violence in the short term
Classification of Violence Risk (COVR)	2005	John Monahan, Henry Steadman, Pamela Clark Robbins, Paul Appelbaum, Steven Banks, Thomas Grisso, Kirk Heilbrun, Edward Mulvey, Loren Roth and Eric Silver/UNITED STATES	Assessment of violence
Automated Sexual Recidivism Scale (ASRS)	2006	Alexander Skelton, David Riley, David Wales and James Vess/NEW ZEALAND	Sexual recidivism
Structured Assessment of Protective Factors for Violence Risk (SAPROF)	2011	Vivienne de Vogel, Corine de Ruiter, Yvonne Bouman and Michiel de Vries Robbé/THE NETHERLANDS	Assesses protective factors for violence risk

good and clinical judgment too poor to risk contaminating the former with the latter.

The sole reliance on actuarial methods to predict risk became the subject of debate during the 1990s and there have been a number of criticisms of actuarial risk assessment scales, some of which are outlined later in this chapter. To foreshadow one of the criticisms of second-generation risk assessment instruments, Hanson (2003) has argued that the reliance on "static" or historical variables is insufficient. Rather, there is a need to include "dynamic" variables as well – ones that can change over time, such as coping strategies – to ensure risk assessments become more accurate and in order to identify useful treatment (Hanson 2003; see also Hanson *et al.* 2007).

Accordingly, instruments such as the Sexual Violence Risk-20 (SVR-20) (Boer *et al.* 1997) and the Risk of Sexual Violence Protocol (RSVP) (Hart *et al.* 2003) include dynamic as well as static factors, while the Sex Offender Need Assessment Rating, generally referred to as SONAR (Hanson and Harris 2000) is based on dynamic factors alone.

SONAR aims to measure changes in risk factors by measuring dynamic factors such as non-cooperation with supervision, access to victim(s), sexual preoccupations, anger and acute changes in mood. The SVR-20 consists of 20 items dealing with the offender's "psychosocial adjustment", history of sexual offending, and future plans. In 2003, the RSVP was developed to build on the SVR-20 while revising some items and adding more.

Much of the literature relating to risk assessment instruments deals with validation and reliability issues and why certain instruments are better than others. For example, the Scottish Risk Management Authority (2007) has produced a directory of risk assessment instruments, categorized into relevant areas of work, known as the Risk Assessment Tools Evaluation Directory or RATED. This Directory includes evaluations of 34 instruments under the headings, "Tools for General Application," "Tools for Assessing Violence Risk," "Tools for Assessing Sexual Violence Risk," and "Tools for Assessing Children and Young Offenders." Interestingly, however, Jennifer Skeem and John Monahan (2011) point to studies that have indicated that the predictive qualities of well-validated risk assessment instruments are "interchangeable," perhaps because they tap into common dimensions of long standing patterns of dysfunctional and aggressive lifestyles (see, for example, Campbell *et al.* 2009; Yang *et al.* 2010).

In the past decade, mental health practitioners have called for a combination of actuarial and clinical methods of assessment in order to produce better results tailored to the individual (Hanson 2003: 67). The process of combining clinical and actuarial approaches has been termed "structural clinical judgment" (Heilbrun *et al.* 1999) or "structured professional judgment" (Davis and Ogloff 2008). This process is explored in the next section.

Structured Professional Judgment and Risk Management

While risk assessment instruments such as the VRAG and the Static-99 are concerned with the *prediction* of risk, more recent instruments are designed to be used in risk *prevention* in the sense that they are meant to serve the development of a management or risk prevention plan. "Structured professional judgment" attempts to incorporate the strengths of both actuarial and clinical methods into a single decision-making approach. The structured professional judgment approach uses instruments that are designed to act as guidelines for clinical assessment. Michael Davis and James Ogloff (2008: 146) describe the process:

> These instruments include a number of risk factors, both static and dynamic, that are derived rationally from consideration of the literature. The evaluator must carefully score each of these risk factors from an administration manual. While a total 'score' can be calculated, it has no substantive meaning in terms of a probability estimate, other than the fact that a higher score means that more risk factors are present. Thus, assessing clinicians are advised not to sum the items in an actuarial fashion. Rather, after carefully coding each risk factor they make what is considered to be a structured clinical opinion of low, moderate or high risk.

Perhaps the most prominent instrument designed to be used in the structured professional judgment approach is the Historical, Clinical, Risk-20 (HCR-20) (Webster *et al.* 1997).

The HCR-20 has been described as the leading structured professional judgment instrument (Davis and Ogloff 2008: 148). It consists of 20 items on three scales – ten on the historical scale, five on the clinical scale, and five on the risk management scale. The items on the clinical and the risk management scales are dynamic or changeable and they can serve as the focus for risk management. The HCR-20 does not structure the process of combining risk factors to reach an overall estimate of risk, but allows the assessor to combine the 20 items in "an intuitive manner" to provide an overall estimate of risk (Monahan 2008: 22).

Other instruments attempt to assess protective factors for future offending risk such as the Short-Term Assessment of Risk and Treatability (START) (Webster *et al.* 2004) and the Structured Assessment of Protective Factors for Violence Risk (SAPROF) (De Vogel *et al.* 2007, 2011). These instruments attempt to go beyond the exclusive focus on risk factors of the current generation of risk assessment instruments.

While the risk assessment instruments for structured professional judgment are designed to produce information for risk management, some mental health practitioners have also used them in the same way as earlier instruments for risk *prediction* purposes. Davis and Ogloff (2008: 148) have referred to a number of studies indicating that the HCR-20 is reliable and able validly to predict violence regarding those in forensic psychiatric, correctional, and civil psychiatric settings.

The emphasis on dynamic factors in recent instruments has importance for risk management and treatment planning because changes in these factors may reduce the risk of future reoffending. Nevertheless, research into the effect of dynamic factors on the risk of reoffending is in its infancy. There is little to guide assessors in relation to determining whether offenders have benefited or changed as a result of treatment (Mercado and Ogloff 2007: 55) and "[p]rospective research is needed with multiple follow-up periods to track the fluctuation in dynamic factors and risk over time" (Davis and Ogloff 2008: 150).

The number and variety of risk assessment instruments are on the increase and it can be difficult to work out the reliability and validity of newer instruments. If these instruments are to be used correctly, it is imperative that assessors are properly trained in their use and know the limitations of each. The next section provides an overview of some of these limitations.

CRITICISMS OF ACTUARIAL RISK ASSESSMENT INSTRUMENTS

There is a growing awareness of the limitations of using risk assessment instruments to identify those individuals who are at a high risk of harming others, particularly with regard to preventive detention regimes.

In addition to criticisms of the reliability of individual actuarial scales (see, for example, Ward and Eccleston 2000; Cooke and Michie 2010), a number of problems have been identified with using actuarial-based scales for individual offenders. This section explores some of the key problems with using actuarial risk assessment instruments in court settings. There have been criticisms of:

- the specific variables used in actuarial instruments;
- the variable-based approach itself;
- applying group data to the individual;
- translating the use of instruments to particular groups; and
- the use of risk assessment techniques in the courtroom.

Criticisms of Specific Variables and the Variable-Based Approach

The empirical research on the prediction of risk is "variable-oriented" (Lussier and Davies 2011: 534). Researchers have focused on identifying the main risk variables or factors associated with the risk of reoffending. From this perspective, risk factors tend to focus on stable individual differences that can be aggregated using a single risk score (or empirical value). The accumulation of risk factors is seen as the basis for a linear increase in risk scores. Lussier and Davies (2011: 534–35) point out that there are four assumptions that underlie the variable-oriented approach:

(a) the risk of reoffending is heterogenous across offenders; (b) that heterogeneity can be captured by the accumulation (or not) of risk factors statistically related to recidivism; (c) the accumulation of risk factors is linearly related to the risk of reoffending; and (d) between-individual differences in offending are relatively stable over time.

These assumptions have been challenged. Some risk assessment scales focus exclusively on variables that are historical in nature (Sullivan *et al.* 2005: 319). The main focus is on "static" risk factors that cannot change over time and that cannot be changed through treatment and intervention, such as the age of first offending, the offender's prior criminal history, and victimology. Many risk assessment scales do not consider current clinical variables (such as response to treatment or motivation), protective factors (such as stable employment), or variables that reduce the risk of reoffending (such as physical illness or frailty).

There is some evidence of awareness of the limitations of the use of "static" tests in the case law, particularly in relation to the use of the Static-99 in preventive detention cases in Western Australia. In *Director of Public Prosecutions (WA) v Moolarvie* (2008: paras [41]–[43]), Justice Blaxell remarked:

The evidence before me shows that various instruments or tools have been developed over the past 10 years in response to concerns that subjective clinical assessments as to the risk of sexual reoffending might be unreliable. It is also clear from a number of published articles in reputable international journals . . . that these tools are at an early stage of development and involve an area of behavioural science which is the subject of some controversy . . . The 'Static 99' is one such actuarial risk assessment instrument. . . . It's great shortcoming is that it does not take account of dynamic or changing factors which might increase or reduce the risk, and which would differentiate an individual offender from the group. A further drawback of the 'Static 99' (in the context of the present application) is that it purports to assess the risk of recidivism for sexual offending generally rather than for 'serious sexual offending' as defined by the Act.

In a subsequent case, Justice McKechnie in *Director of Public Prosecutions (WA) v Free* (2011) refused to order a hearing under the Dangerous Sexual Offenders Act (WA) 2006 where the expert evidence relied solely on the Static-99. He found that the emphasis on static factors did not amount to sufficient evidence to establish reasonable grounds for the belief that a court might find that the respondent in that case, Leslie Free, was a serious danger to the community.

There are other examples of individual judges questioning the use of certain actuarial instruments (McSherry 2012), but more often than not, the use of static tests passes without judicial comment on their potential unreliability (see, for example, *Attorney-General (Qld) v Carpenter* 2008: para. [28]; *RJE v Secretary to the Department of Justice & Ors* 2008: para. [93] per Weinberg JA).

In *Peta*'s case, two expert witnesses were called to give evidence at the New Zealand Court of Appeal hearing: the Director of Psychological Services for the Department of Corrections, David Riley and Dr James Vess, a senior lecturer in abnormal psychology. Both men had been involved in developing the Automated Sexual Recidivism Scale (ASRS) that had been used to assess Jacob Peta's risk of sexual reoffending in the original trial. The ASRS (Skelton *et al.* 2006) is largely based on the Static-99 in assessing static risk factors, but has adapted some of the factors for use on a New Zealand population. Not surprisingly, Justice Glazebrook noted (*R v Peta* 2007: para. [40]) that both experts "were in general agreement that empirically validated actuarial measures for ascertaining risk based on static factors should form the foundation of risk assessments in relation to sex offenders." Despite a comment about the emphasis on static factors in the ASRS being a "limitation" (2007: para. [30]), the Court of Appeal was prepared to accept evidence of risk based on such instruments.

There has also been criticism of the actual variables chosen as predictors of violence. The category of personality constructs is perhaps the most controversial of violence predictor variables. Robert Hare (2002: 27) states that psychopathy is:

a personality disorder defined by a cluster of interpersonal, affective, and lifestyle characteristics that results in serious, negative consequences for society. Among the most devastating features of the disorder are a callous disregard for the rights of others and a propensity for predatory behaviour and violence.

Robert Hare's Psychopathy Checklist-Revised (PCL-R) has been hailed as the unparalleled single predictor of violence (Salekin *et al.* 1996). However, its use as a predictive tool has been questioned (Skeem and Cooke 2010a, 2010b) and the terms "psychopath" and "antisocial personality disorder" have been criticized as being social constructs (Cavadino 1998; McCallum 2001). John Ellard (1996: 62) points out:

> If you are a rather disagreeable small-time thief with a bad temper you are likely to be described as suffering from Antisocial Personality Disorder. If without any contrition you waste millions of dollars of other people's money and achieve nothing but notoriety you will be called an entrepreneur.

The debate as to the limitations of personality constructs as a predictor of future violence led to an interesting set of circumstances that raised issues concerning editorial obligations and peer review processes in academic journals. Jennifer Skeem and David Cooke (2010a) wrote an article that passed through a peer review process and was accepted for publication on February 27, 2007. In this article, they argued that the PCL-R is heavily dependent on information about criminal behaviour and does not take into account other key characteristics of psychopathy such as low anxiety. Robert Hare, the developer of the PCL-R, believed the original manuscript misrepresented his work. Prior to publication, Hare's counsel sent a letter to the authors and to the editor of the journal stating that publication of the paper amounted to defamation and that financial damages would be sought if the paper was published. After a lengthy period of time and after some revisions to the paper, the matter was resolved with Skeem and Cooke's paper being published in 2010 with a reply by Robert Hare and Craig Neumann (2010) published in the same edition. Hare's conduct drew criticism from other academics such as Norman Poythress and John Petrila (2010) and sparked a debate about academic freedom (Minkel 2010).

As well as criticism of the variables used in different scales, other authors have noted that "there are different types of offenders and risk profiles which may not be accounted for by a single instrument based on a variable-oriented approach" (Lussier and Davies 2011: 535). There have thus been attempts by developmental psychologists to shift the focus away from variables to individuals through a "person-oriented" approach (Bergman and Magnusson 1997). Developmental criminologists have also begun focusing on longitudinal studies examining individual-level trajectories of offending (e.g., Thornberry and Krohn 2003; Farrington 2005). Such trajectories are characterized by certain phases such as an activation phase, a plateau, and a desistance phase that vary at different levels (Lussier and Davies 2011).

In relation to adult sex offenders, Patrick Lussier and his colleagues (2010) have identified four offending trajectories that apply to high-rate offenders, low-rate desistors, late bloomers, and very low-rate offenders. In this study, they found significant between-individual and within-individual changes in offending in these categories. For example, they found the late bloomers offending at the same rate as the high-rate offenders in their early thirties. Patrick Lussier and Garth Davies (2011: 537) make the point that "[a]ctuarial tools are not designed to capture such dynamic shifts in between-individual differences in offending" and "actuarial tools for sex offenders do not adjust for the aging factor of offenders or for the fact that the aging factors might function differently to different offenders."

Applying Group Data to the Individual

Actuarial scales are based on determining whether an individual offender has the same characteristics or risk factors as a "typical" kind of offender (Campbell 2000, 2003). Risk assessments can classify an individual within a group – as "high risk," "medium risk," or "low risk" – but they cannot say where in this group a given person lies and, therefore, cannot identify the *precise* risk an individual poses. Kris Gledhill (2011: 86) explains this:

> [A] conclusion that a defendant presents a 30 per cent risk of committing a further offence within the next 10 years means that 30 per cent of people sharing the defendant's characteristics will commit a further offence if they act in the same way as the group on whom the study was based. The tool cannot say whether an individual will be one of the group who will [offend] or one of the group who will not.

Stephen Hart, Christine Michie, and David Cooke (2007; Cooke and Michie 2010; Cooke and Michie 2011; Hart and Cooke 2013) have been at the forefront of criticizing the precision of the probability estimates provided by certain actuarial risk assessments. Cooke and Michie (2010: 259) argue that because actuarial risk assessment instruments are based on variables that apply *across* individuals, they give rise to the "statistical truism that the mean of a distribution tells us about everyone, yet no one."

In 2007, Hart *et al.* examined the Violence Risk Appraisal Guide and the Static-99 and found a considerable overlap in the confidence intervals for the various risk categories of each instrument. This led them to conclude that the various risk categories were not distinct. They also calculated confidence intervals for individuals and found that these "were so high as to render risk estimates virtually meaningless"

(Hart *et al.* 2007: s 60). This latter conclusion has been criticized on the basis that on conceptual and mathematical grounds, an individual confidence level cannot exist (Davis and Ogloff 2008). That is, an individual "cannot have a confidence interval around their own subsequent recidivism – they are either violent or not" (Davis and Ogloff 2008: 144).

R. Karl Hanson and Philip Howard (2010) have also criticized Hart, Michie, and Cooke's finding that confidence intervals for individuals were so high as to render risk estimates "virtually meaningless." Hanson and Howard argue that finding a wide margin of error for individual risk assessments results from having only two possible outcomes – violent or not violent – and thus does not actually assess the predictive utility of risk assessment instruments.

However, while the Hart, Michie, and Cooke (2007) study proved to be controversial (Mossman and Selke 2007; Davis and Ogloff 2008; Craig and Beech 2009; Hanson and Howard 2010), it is clear that assigning risk to an individual offender based on the characteristics of a group may lead to inaccurate assessments (Janus and Prentky 2003).

Edward Mulvey and Charles Lidz (1985: 212) point out, "even a highly predictive scheme (in the range of 90%) would produce a large proportion of false positives . . . as long as the base rate of the predicted behavior is low." This base rate issue is an important one (Szmukler and Rose 2013). Certain behaviour such as serious self-harm has a much lower frequency than say reoffending in general following a prison sentence. Sexual reoffending in particular is not a high frequency occurrence (Doyle and Ogloff 2009; McSherry and Keyzer 2010). The relatively low base rate for sexual recidivism means that attempting to predict who will commit further serious sexual offences will be less accurate than predicting other offences that occur at a higher rate (Doyle *et al.* 2011). Mental health practitioners thus need to know the relevant base rate for specific populations and be able to frame their assessment according to the average risk posed by a member of that population.

Differences in Particular Groups

Actuarial risk assessment scales may also pose difficulties when used with particular groups of offenders. As Christopher Slobogin (2012b: 207) points out, "the population on which the actuarial device is validated may be quite different from the population to which it is applied." For example, Australian indigenous offenders as a group have higher rates of childhood abuse victimization and early substance abuse, both of which are included as factors associated with high-risk status in many risk assessment instruments. Indigenous offenders are, therefore, more likely to be classified as high risk than are non-indigenous offenders (Sullivan *et al.* 2005: 319).

Some judges are aware of this problem. In *Director of Public Prosecutions (WA) v Moolarvie* (2008: para. [44]), Justice Blaxell remarked in relation to the Static-99:

> Yet another problem with the 'Static 99' is that it was developed for use with Canadian and English offenders of European origin. The literature suggests that risk factors for indigenous violence may well differ from those for non-indigenous Australians and people of other cultures.

Expert witnesses in Australian cases have also questioned whether instruments that have not been validated through studies involving Australian indigenous offenders should be relied on in Australian courts (*Attorney-General (Qld) v McLean* 2006: para. [26]; *Attorney-General (Qld) v George* 2009: para. [33]). As mentioned above, in *Peta's* case, the expert witnesses used their own actuarial tool, the Automated Sexual Recidivism Scale (ASRS), which drew upon the static factors used in the Static-99, but adapted some of the factors for a New Zealand population. Similarly in Western Australia, Alfred Allan and Deborah Dawson (2002) attempted to develop an actuarial tool, the "3-Predictor Model" that captured the predictors of violence in Australian indigenous communities, but they were not able to construct a single instrument for violent and sexual reoffending. Rather their model was to some extent able to assess the risk of sexual reoffending alone, but Allan and Dawson cautioned that more research was needed to test the viability of this model.

Adapting or developing risk assessment instruments for indigenous populations may be problematic because of small samples and issues concerning cultural differences between the developers of such instruments and those being assessed. There are also obvious problems with using actuarial instruments developed from male populations for female offenders.

Applying Risk Assessment Techniques in the Courtroom

The use of risk assessment scales may be justifiable for the purpose of treatment in a clinical environment, but problems with such scales are amplified by their use in legal forums, where they can be "prone to manipulation and misinterpretation" (Sullivan *et al.* 2005: 319). Risk assessment scales can lead to unnecessary detention due to "false positives" – that is a "positive" finding that the individual concerned is at risk of harming others when this is not really the case.

On the basis of such criticisms, Frank Farnham and David James (2001: 1926) have questioned the whole premise that such scales are scientific in nature stating that "would-be clairvoyants engaged in this form of assessment exercise will make use of 'tools' in the form of actuarially-based checklists, which give spurious scientific value to estimations that perform less well than chance."

In *Director of Public Prosecutions (WA) v Mangolamara* (2007), Justice Hasluck rejected psychiatric evidence based on the Static-99, the Sexual Violence Risk-20 (Boer *et al.* 1997) and the Risk of Sexual Violence Protocol (Hart *et al.* 2003). He stated (2007: para. [165]):

> I am of the view . . . that little weight should be given to those parts of the reports concerning the assessment tools. In my view, the evidence in question does not conform to long-established rules concerning expert evidence. The research data and methods underlying the assessment tools are assumed to be correct but this has not been established by the evidence. It has not been made clear to me whether the context for which the categories of assessment reflected in the relevant texts or manuals were devised is that of treatment and intervention or that of sentencing.

There have been issues raised with the way in which evidence of risk has been presented in court. In the words of John Petrila (2004: 10):

> In some circumstances [in legal proceedings], clinicians have not acknowledged the limitations of the instruments, leading to situations in which courts have characterized the instruments as able to "predict" future sexual offending in individual cases; this has the practical effect of inappropriately transforming a tool for assessing probabilities for future offending into something perceived as predictive for the defendant before the court.

In *Peta*'s case, the Court of Appeal was highly critical of the way in which the testimony on risk had been initially presented to Judge Dawson. The original assessor made a number of mistakes in administering and scoring the risk assessment instruments. The ASRS is "automated" in the sense that it is meant to be scored electronically, but the assessor scored the test manually and included convictions in the Youth Court that is against the coding rules. He also failed to properly score the SONAR, using the risk factors set out in it simply as a guide for making a clinical assessment. This was not questioned by counsel or the sentencing judge and no contrary evidence was presented. The presentation of risk assessment evidence is one area that needs more attention. Ian Coyle (2011: 271) makes the point that "demonstrable limitations of risk assessments and the instruments or techniques on which they are based are all too often simply ignored by forensic practitioners of various persuasions, if they are comprehended in the first place."

When *Peta's* case was decided, the Court of Appeal did not have the power to remit the matter back to the original court for resentencing. It, therefore, heard the matter afresh and on the basis of the evidence of risk presented by the expert witnesses, the Court held that Jacob Peta's risk of sexual recidivism against children was not such as to justify the making of an extended supervision order.

Justice Glazebrook ([2007] 2 NZLR 627 at paras [51]–[53]) set out a number of requirements for "best practise" in providing an "individualized assessment" in the courtroom. These include:

- the proper administration and scoring of risk assessment instruments;
- the integration of the results from such instruments with "other relevant information known to relate to the risk of reoffending" (para. [51]);
- the explicit identification of factors other than those in the actuarial instruments that have been used to formulate the individual assessment;
- the identification of any "recognisable contingencies that will influence the degree of risk present" (para. [51]);
- reference to "the likely victims and the likely severity of harm of subsequent offences" (para. [51]);
- adequate training in the effective communication of properly conducted risk assessment; and
- the use of categories of risk such as "high, moderate or low risk should be qualified by probability statements that give corresponding re-offence rates for groups of similar offenders and the numbers of offenders in each category should be specified" (para. [53]).

Justice Glazebrook (2010: 101) expanded on these requirements in a subsequent article which stressed that the "limitations of the risk assessment instruments and the health professional's expertise must be conveyed to the court." The ethics relating to such testimony will be considered in Chapter 8.

RISK ASSESSMENT AND INDIVIDUALS WITH SEVERE MENTAL ILLNESS

Terry Carney and colleagues (2011: 51–52) have pointed out that traditionally, the criteria for enabling the involuntary detention and treatment of those with severe mental illness "have been categorised according to whether they are based on dangerousness (invoking the so-called 'police power') or need for treatment (invoking the protective parens patriae jurisdiction of the courts)." In some countries such as Australia, the relevant mental health laws combine both the need for treatment and dangerousness criteria. This is explored further in Chapter 4.

The "dangerousness" criterion in mental health laws generally refers to evidence of risk of harm to self *or* others. While this book is focusing on preventive detention and supervision on the basis of the potential harm to others, it should be noted that it is difficult to predict when a person is likely to self-harm. Alex Pokorny (1983) conducted a large-scale prospective trial of the prediction of suicide made at the point of admission of 4,800 individuals to the inpatient psychiatric services of a Veterans Administration Medical Center in Houston. He was unable to find any combination of clinical or other factors that could be used in practice. He concluded (1983: 257) that "[a]lthough we may reconstruct causal chains and motives after the fact, we do not possess the instruments to predict particular suicides before the fact." There have been few subsequent studies of predictors of suicide and there is some evidence to suggest that suicides often occur during periods when the risk of self-harm appears to be low (Dong *et al.* 2005).

The criterion of harm to self thus has the potential to be interpreted broadly and some have argued that this criterion should be removed because of the difficulties associated with predicting future harm (Large *et al.* 2008).

In relation to the risk of harm to others, Jennifer Skeem, Jillian Peterson, and Eric Silver (2011) point out that there is a widely held belief among the public and thus policy makers that mental illness *causes* criminal behaviour. They point out (2011: 113) that "there is little compelling evidence that (a) mental illness directly causes criminal behaviour for this population, or (b) that effective mental health services meaningfully reduce new crimes and new victims." Yet involuntary detention and treatment legislation may be based on the premise that severe mental illness is directly linked to harm to others.

Christopher Ryan (2011: 248) argues that it is inappropriate to base mental health laws on the risk of harm to others given that those with mental impairments are "by and large, no more dangerous" than other members of society and because of the low base rate of violence among those with mental impairments, it is impossible to predict who will become violent in the future. Similarly, Matthew Large, Christopher Ryan, Olav Nielssen, and Robert Hayes (2008: 879) argue that because there are problems associated with predicting the risk of harm to others and there is a tendency of psychiatrists to err on the side of safety, "[t]he dangerousness criterion effectively condones the detention of many mentally ill people who will never become dangerous, so that it might capture the few who will."

The dangerousness criterion has also been criticized for being discriminatory in singling out those with mental impairments for preventive detention when other groups (such as those with a history of being violent under the influence of alcohol or drugs) are not (Hewitt 2008; Large *et al.* 2008; Ryan 2011; Szmukler and Rose 2013).

Certainly risk assessment research in relation to those with severe mental illness has not produced a clear and accurate picture of who may be likely to harm others. Michael Norko and Madelon Baranoski (2005: 24) reviewed a number of studies on correlates of violence, focusing particularly on mental illness as a key correlate, and concluded that the "research on violence has not produced a clearly uniform picture of the most important mental health variables associated with risk of violent behaviour." They also reviewed the accuracy of predictions of future harm in relation primarily to those studied in psychiatric emergency departments and concluded that "[c]linical assessments of risk achieve better-than-chance accuracy, although clinicians may not be particularly good at identifying specific conditions under which violence will occur (2005: 23)."

Most of the risk assessment actuarial instruments outlined in the previous sections were developed after compiling data from offender populations rather than those detained in psychiatric institutions on the basis of severe mental illness. In the United States, the research arising from the MacArthur Violence Risk Assessment Study provides one example of an actuarial instrument, the Classification of Violence Risk (COVR), which was developed after gathering data from a population of those civilly detained on the basis of mental disorder (Monahan *et al.* 2001; Monahan *et al.* 2005). In the original study (Monahan *et al.* 2001), 1,136 male and female civil mental health patients between 18 and 40 years old were monitored for violence to others during the first year after discharge. This cohort was compared to a group of 519 people living in the neighbourhoods in which the individuals resided after hospital discharge. This study used a multiple iterative classification tree (ICT) model. A subsequent study (Monahan *et al.* 2005) carried out a prospective test of this model by focusing on 700 individuals in the cohort, of which a random sample of 177 who were classified as having a higher or lower risk of violence were followed in the community for four months after discharge from the hospital. Follow-up data consisting of interviews with the individuals and their families as well as police and hospital records were obtained for 89 per cent of the sample. The results of this study were that during the follow-up process, one in ten of the individuals classified as "low" risk of violence committed a violent act and one in two of the patients classified by the instrument as "high" risk of violence committed a violent act. This validation process resulted in software incorporating the multiple ICT model that was named COVR.

Interestingly, the MacArthur Violence Risk Assessment research suggests that a diagnosis of severe mental illness, in particular a diagnosis of schizophrenia, was associated with a *lower* rate of violence than a diagnosis of a personality or "adjustment" disorder (Monahan 2002). However, a coexisting diagnosis of substance abuse was found to be strongly predictive of violence. The presence of delusions was not associated with violence, but a generally "suspicious" attitude towards others was related to it occurring (Monahan 2002). Obviously the results of this study may be limited because the population was emerging from acute facilities in Pittsburgh, Pennsylvania, Kansas City, Missouri, and Worcester, Massachusetts and the study did not examine those emerging from less acute settings.

More recently, American studies suggest that a small subgroup or those with severe mental illness may be arrested because their hallucinations or delusions lead to violence or because they are causing a public disturbance (Junginger *et al.* 2006; Petersen *et al.* 2012). However, the vast majority of those arrested appear to have lifetime patterns of crime that are very similar to those of offenders without mental illness (Petersen *et al.* 2012). The one factor that does seem to be universally associated with a significantly increased risk of violence is substance abuse (Norko and Baranoski 2005). In a series of studies conducted on a sample of individuals with severe mental illness in Victoria, Australia, Paul Mullen and his colleagues found that the highest rates of violence occurred for those diagnosed with schizophrenia in conjunction with a substance abuse problem (Mullen *et al.* 2000; Wallace *et al.* 1998; Wallace *et al.* 2004).

Usually the decision to detain an individual with severe mental illness for treatment without his or her consent will be reviewed by a tribunal within a certain period of time. Tribunal hearings are generally informal in nature and are not bound by the rules of evidence that apply in courtrooms (Carney *et al.* 2011). Any evidence relating to the potential harm to others is generally presented to the tribunal by treating clinicians and their opinions are often based upon their own "observations and experiences . . . which have not been scientifically tested and validated" (Winick 2003: 28). Such evidence may not be rigorously examined, but accepted by the tribunal without question. Any evidence based on actuarial risk assessment instruments is exceedingly rare in this jurisdiction.

The problems with assessing the risk of harm to others alongside recent trends in international human rights law (explored in Chapter 7) have provided the impetus for involuntary treatment criteria to be based on decision-making capacity rather than notions of dangerousness. There have also been calls to abolish separate mental health legislation in favour of generic mental capacity legislation that would enable the involuntary treatment of those with mental and intellectual impairments regard-less of the cause and regardless of notions of "dangerousness" (Dawson and Szmukler 2006; Szmukler *et al.* 2010). Whether or not this will eventuate, the current state of play is that risk to others remains a key criterion in most mental health legislation and the evidence of risk that is presented to mental health tribunals is often cursory and not adequately tested.

PREVENTIVE DETENTION OF SUSPECTED TERRORISTS AND THE LACK OF RISK ASSESSMENT

As will be explored in Chapter 4, the key legal terms justifying the preventive detention and supervision of suspected terrorists are generally that of "reasonable suspicion" or a belief on "reasonable grounds" that the individual concerned is a terrorist or will engage in a terrorist act. What this means is open to debate and the case law on proving a reasonable suspicion or belief is explored in Chapter 6.

What is significant is that there is no mention of "risk" in the laws related to the preventive detention of suspected terrorists. Precautionary measures such as detention based on reasonable suspicion completely bypass the need for risk assessments by mental health practitioners. Mental health practitioners are now publishing some material about how the risks of terrorism may be reduced (e.g., Stout 2004). However, what is striking about preventive detention of suspected terrorists is the relative lack of attention to "risk" terminology that is so common in preventive detention regimes for convicted offenders and in civil commitment laws for those with severe mental illness. Charlie Savage and colleagues (2011) claim that at a practical level, detainees at Guantanamo Bay, Cuba, were at one stage rated in terms of having a high, medium, or low risk of terrorism if released, but that this had been dropped in favour of a more nuanced approach. Little, however, is known as to how such assessments are carried out.

The concept of reasonable suspicion and belief is common to laws relating to arrest; thus criminal justice procedure may be reflected in the laws governing the preventive detention of suspected terrorists. However, it may also be the case that it has been difficult for risk assessment to get a foothold in relation to terrorism because, in the words of Martha Crenshaw (1981: 390), "the outstanding common characteristic of terrorists is their normality."

Jeff Victoroff (2005) in an extensive review of psychological explanations for terrorism has concluded that the majority of studies in this area have lacked a sound empirical basis, with many approaches being based on the subjective interpretation of anecdotal evidence. There now seems to be a move towards encouraging mental health practitioners to develop instruments and techniques that provide a better evidence base for the identification and/or preventive detention of suspected terrorists. Gisli Gudjonsson (2009: 519) posits that "psychology has a great deal to offer in providing meaningful conceptual and theoretical frameworks for the risk assessment of terrorist offenders, which can guide research and individual assessments."

D. Elaine Pressman (2009) has argued that current risk assessment instruments are of questionable relevance for identifying the risk posed by suspected terrorists because the factors used do not include the background and motivations of such individuals. She has proposed that a specific structured professional judgment tool entitled the Violent Extremism Risk Assessment (VERA) be introduced to assess the risk of violence from certain individuals. The factors to be assessed include attitude items (such as attachment to an ideology justifying violence), contextual items (such as the use of extremist websites), historical items (such as state-sponsored military or paramilitary training), protective items (such as the rejection of violence to achieve goals), and demographic items (Pressman 2009: 34). Pressman (2009: i) points out that the VERA is still a "conceptual 'research' tool intended to generate debate and discussion." How such a tool could be tested for reliability and validity is left open.

John Monahan (2012) points to a number of problems with adapting existing actuarial risk assessment instruments to predicting terrorist acts because current research suggests that the four key factors predicting violence, criminal history, an irresponsible lifestyle, psychopathy and criminal attitudes, and substance abuse (Kroner et al. 2005) do not characterize those who commit terrorist acts.

Models for prediction have typically been developed for use with specific populations such as serious sexual offenders. It is debatable whether a group that can be labelled as "terrorists" even exists, given the considerable controversy about what the term "terrorism" actually means (McSherry 2004: 358). John Monahan (2012) points to a number of barriers in formulating an actuarial risk assessment instrument in regard to suspected terrorists. These include difficulties in identifying appropriate risk factors and finding an appropriate population on which to validate such an instrument. Monahan (2012: 193) compares the validation process for COVR outlined above with a similar process for validating a terrorism risk assessment instrument and poses the following questions:

- Where does one find 700 people [the number that COVR was tested on] who have committed an act of terrorism to whom the terrorism risk assessment instrument could be administered?
- When does it happen that virtually all (99.6 per cent) of the people adjudicated as terrorists are released into the community in a short period of time?

- How does one locate, interview, and obtain official data concerning the great majority (89 per cent) of those terrorists who have been released into the community, in order to determine whether or not they have, in fact, committed a new act of terrorism?

Even if a risk assessment tool such as the VERA proves to be of some benefit, there is a question as to who would be best placed to use it. Mats Dernevik, Alison Beck, and colleagues (2009: 512) point out that "mental health practitioners are not likely to have training in certain areas which are crucial to terrorist violence, such as political and cultural science or social and political psychology." They suggest that collaboration is needed between mental health practitioners and individuals with expertise in "areas of political science, anthropology, cultural diversity, and so on" (2009: 512).

Lazar Stankove, Derrick Higgins, Gerard Saucier, and Goran Kneževié (2010) provide an example of one interdisciplinary research team working on constructing scales based on linguistic and traditional psychometric approaches to measure the mindset of militant extremism. There may also be some promise in collaborative teams exploring behavioural rather than psychological traits to construct a picture of those likely to be involved in terrorist activity (Victoroff 2005; Wilson 2008).

It remains the case, however, that risk assessment is not (yet) a central focus of regimes enabling the preventive detention and supervision of suspected terrorists.

CONCLUSION

The New Zealand Court of Appeal decision in *R v Peta* (2007) raises a number of issues relating to risk assessment for the purposes of preventive detention and supervision of those considered at high risk of reoffending. Ultimately, that case resulted in Jacob Rangaita Peta not being indefinitely supervised because the Court found that he was unlikely to commit sexual offences in the future. This was an unusual outcome. Generally, when evidence is given that an offender is at risk of reoffending, this is accepted without sufficient and detailed analysis by either defence counsel or judges. This may in part be explained by lawyers' faith in the expertise of mental health practitioners to make predictions of future harm. In *Peta's* case (2007: para. [13]), Justice Glazebrook expressed surprise that it was unusual for counter-evidence to be called by the defence as to the factors relevant to the imposition of extended supervision orders.

It is disturbing that expert testimony in court regarding preventive detention and supervision is generally accepted by judges without challenge. This is especially so given that actuarial risk assessment instruments and their use in courts have been widely criticized on numerous grounds, including the use of specific variables and the variable-based approach itself, problems associated with applying group data to the individual, differences in particular groups, and the prospect of unnecessary deprivation of liberty due to "false positives." Eric Silver and Lisa Miller (2002: 155) go so far as to observe that actuarial risk assessment techniques "may inadvertently contribute to the generalization of stigma from the targeted (negative) behavior to the characteristics of the groups designated at high risk, thereby placing a scientific stamp on the public's prejudice and fear."

In the context of decisions relating to the detention and supervision of individuals with severe mental illness, risk assessment is generally based on the treating clinicians' views, without recourse to any actuarial instruments or thorough analysis. In comparison, risk assessment is currently not a focal point of the preventive detention of suspected terrorists, although this may be changing.

The development of actuarial risk assessment instruments and the dependence on risk assessment in a number of areas of the law outside of preventive detention and supervision has in many ways been a boon for the development of forensic psychology as a profession. Cynthia Mercado and James Ogloff (2007: 58), two forensic psychologists, have pointed out that the majority of research published on risk assessment has been conducted by psychologists.

Perhaps because of a tension between the professions of psychology and psychiatry, some psychiatrists have been at the forefront of criticisms of the overreliance on actuarial scales, emphasizing the importance of clinical judgment and diagnostic abilities based on medical training. The Royal College of Psychiatrists for the United Kingdom and the Republic of Ireland (2005: 75) has pointed out:

> There appears to be a consensus view among British forensic psychiatrists that clinical assessment has an ethically justifiable edge over other risk measures because they are individually sensitive and dynamic. Actuarial risk measures should therefore be presented in the context of clinical assessment.

The developing field of structured professional judgment certainly seems to be an improvement on clinical judgment alone, but its purpose is to help with the management and treatment of offenders. It has not developed with the primary aim of preventive detention and supervision. The use of risk assessment instruments and clinical judgment may have a role in clinical environments, but another level of criticism demands caution and restraint in the use of assessments in the legal system. Issues relating to legal requirements for proving risk are explored in Chapter 6, and the ethics of providing evidence of risk for preventive detention and supervision schemes are explored in Chapter 8.

Overall, while risk assessment techniques have advanced over the past decades, Herschel Prins' (1996) view that there is no ideal, or even sophisticated approach available to the assessment of risk remains of concern. In the words of Andrew Carroll, Mark Lyall, and Andrew Forrester (2004: 413), "[n]o method, clinical, actuarial or combined, achieves anywhere near 100% predictive power, whether short or long term risk is considered."

Part II

PREVENTIVE DETENTION
AND SUPERVISION

4

LAWS OF PREVENTIVE
DETENTION

INTRODUCTION

Kenneth Donaldson was born on May 22, 1908 in Erie, Pennsylvania. He attended Syracuse University for 18 months, but left University to work in various jobs in different towns. He and his wife Olive had three children, David, Beverly, and Peter. In 1943, at the age of 34, Kenneth was working as an operator of a milling machine at General Electric's defence plant in Syracuse, New York, while taking Adult Education classes at night. After what he thought at the time was a "nervous breakdown" (Donaldson 1976: 16), he was committed to the State Hospital in Marcy, New York, for four months.

The events leading up to his admission were that Donaldson thought that the other men at the plant were watching him and making derogatory comments about him behind his back. He described (1976: 15) himself as being "physically run down" at the time, not only due to his work and study, but also because of financial and emotional difficulties. He said that: "In a span of twelve months, my wife had been operated on; one of our three children had been in an oxygen tent for weeks; and I had had two herniotomies. We were saddled with doctor bills . . ."

At Marcy State Hospital, Donaldson was given electroshock therapy twice a week for nearly three months. After his discharge, his relationship with his wife deteriorated, partly it appears because she had given authorization for the electroshock therapy which he saw as punishment (Donaldson 1976: 24, 34). They subsequently divorced.

Donaldson continued to move from town to town in search of work, occasionally being employed as a carpenter, a salesman, and a shipping clerk. During this time, he became interested in Christian Science.

In late 1956, Donaldson went to visit his parents in Florida. In December of that year, his father signed a document known as an "inquisition of incompetence" authorizing the police to arrest him and bring him before a judge. Donaldson was found by a county judge to be "incompetent." He was taken to the Florida State Hospital in

Chattahoochee in January 1957 where he was diagnosed as having paranoid schizophrenia.

Donaldson (1976: 320–21) wrote about this committal:

> What had my parents done and why had they done it? They had loved me and had taken the signs of turbulence in my life to heart. I was a grown man and yet I seemed to them rootless and problematical. Twenty years before, they had accepted a psychiatric diagnosis which forever rent the fabric of my life. Thereafter, not only society at large but members of my family would see not Ken the son and father and friend, but Ken the mental patient. From this would flow unimagined misery, a fog which would envelop all our lives. And our situation would be, of course, representative of millions. The fog would seep into my employment, my relations with doctors, my access to lawyers and the courts. Every enterprise in which I would engage would be poisoned by the label. It haunted me and frightened others.

Donaldson remained in the Florida State Hospital for fourteen and a half years despite repeated attempts to obtain his release through filing a series of petitions in a Florida district court for a writ of habeas corpus, claiming illegal imprisonment. Because of Donaldson's beliefs concerning Christian Science (which emphasizes healing through faith rather than medicine) and that he needed no treatment, he refused any medication. After the New York Civil Liberties Union agreed to represent him in court, in February 1971 Donaldson filed a claim in the United States District Court for the Northern District of Florida, alleging that Dr. James O'Connor, the Hospital's Superintendent and other members of the hospital staff, had intentionally and maliciously deprived him of his constitutional right to liberty. The Florida State Hospital had discharged Donaldson prior to this case being concluded.

After a four-day trial, the jury found in Donaldson's favour and ordered both compensatory and punitive damages amounting to $20,000 be paid to Donaldson by Dr. O'Connor and a co-defendant. The Court of Appeals for the Fifth Circuit affirmed this judgment. Dr. O'Connor then petitioned the United States Supreme Court (*O'Connor v Donaldson* 1975) for a review of the matter. The Supreme Court unanimously decided in favour of Donaldson, ruling that the hospital had violated his right to liberty by keeping him hospitalized without providing treatment and upheld the lower court's order for damages.

The Supreme Court's decision had important repercussions for the criteria for civil commitment of those with severe mental illness in the United States, which is discussed in the next section. The Court observed (1975: 575) that involuntary commitment was a "massive curtailment of liberty" and held that it was unconstitutional to confine, without more, "a non-dangerous individual who is capable of surviving safely in freedom by himself [or herself] or with the help of willing and responsible family members or friends." This set the focus on evidence of mental illness *and* dangerousness as the cornerstone for mental health laws in the United States.

Donaldson wrote of his experiences in a book entitled *Insanity Inside Out* (1976). During the late 1970s, he went on tour, championing the rights of those detained in mental hospitals and promoting his book. He died on January 5, 1995 in Sierra Vista, Arizona.

This chapter explores the laws that enable individuals such as Kenneth Donaldson to be detained indefinitely on the basis of community protection. In particular, it focuses on notions of risk and dangerousness as defined in mental health laws, sex offender legislation, and preventive detention laws for suspected terrorists. Using a series of tables for ease of reference, it examines the similarities and differences in the laws in England, Wales and Scotland, the United States, Canada, Australia, and New Zealand.

LAWS ENABLING THE PREVENTIVE DETENTION OF INDIVIDUALS WITH SEVERE MENTAL ILLNESS

The legal criteria for the detention of those with severe mental illness in England, Wales and Scotland, North America, and Australasia include all or some of the following five criteria. The individual concerned must:

- have a mental illness or mental disorder as defined in the legislation;
- be likely to self-harm or cause harm to others because of the illness;
- be at risk of mental or physical deterioration;
- need psychiatric treatment;
- be incapable of making an admission or treatment decision.

In many mental health acts, involuntary inpatient admission must also be the least restrictive alternative to the person's right to liberty.

All jurisdictions require the individual to have a mental illness or mental disorder as defined in the relevant legislation. Differences can occur in the name, specificity, severity and consequences of symptoms, and exclusions.

In addition to the existence of a mental illness or disorder, there must be evidence that the person is likely to self-harm or cause harm to others *or* be in need of treatment to prevent deterioration in health. In some countries such as Australia, the relevant mental health laws combine both the need for treatment *and* some form of risk of harm criteria. Evidence of the risk of harm to others is, therefore, not a *requirement* for commitment in some jurisdictions, but it certainly remains an important option for involuntary detention in the majority of mental health laws. As set out in Chapter 7, the coming into force of the Convention on the Rights of Persons with Disabilities has inspired a rethinking of the criteria for mental health laws and whether "stand alone" laws are in fact necessary.

In *O'Connor v Donaldson* (1975: 574), the US Supreme Court stated:

> A finding of 'mental illness' alone cannot justify a State's locking a person up against his [or her] will and keeping him [or her] indefinitely in simple custodial confinement. Assuming that that term can be given a reasonably precise content and that the 'mentally ill' can be identified with reasonable accuracy, there is still no constitutional basis for confining such persons involuntarily if they are dangerous to no one and can live safely in freedom . . . May the State fence in the harmless mentally ill solely to save its citizens from exposure to those whose ways are different? One might as well ask if the State, to avoid public unease, could incarcerate all who are physically unattractive or socially eccentric.

This case thus propelled mental health laws across the United States to include a criterion of dangerousness along with a criterion of mental illness. Interestingly, the Supreme Court (1975: 573) was careful to point out that it did not have to decide whether those considered a danger to others had a right to treatment upon committal, or whether it was permissible to detain involuntarily a non-dangerous individual with a severe mental illness for the purpose of treatment.

Joaquin Zuckerberg (2010: 301) points out that in Canada, the enactment of the Canadian Charter of Rights led to "challenges to a number of mental health laws on the basis of constitutional incompatibility." As a result, Canadian provincial legislation moved towards including some form of "dangerousness" criterion.

In *Thwaites v Health Sciences Centre Psychiatric Facility* (1988), the Manitoba Court of Appeal struck down the compulsory admission provisions of the then current Mental Health Act on the basis that it did not contain "objective" criteria and thus breached section 9 of the Canadian Charter of Rights and Freedoms which states that "[e]veryone has the right not to be arbitrarily detained or imprisoned." Associate Justice Philp, in delivering the judgment of the Court, stated (1988: para. [41]):

> In the absence of objective standards, the possibility of compulsory examination and detention hangs over the heads of all persons suffering from a mental disorder, regardless of the nature of the

66

disorder, and the availability and suitability of alternative and less restrictive forms of treatment.

In the Court's view (1988: para. [41]), a "'dangerousness' or like standard" would amount to a sufficient objective criterion that would comply with the Charter. Nevertheless, as mentioned in Chapter 3, the dangerousness criterion in mental health laws has been criticized as inappropriate because it is impossible to predict who will be violent due to the low base rate of violence among those with mental impairment and for being discriminatory in singling out those with mental impairments for preventive detention when other groups are not (Hewitt 2008; Large *et al.* 2008; Ryan 2011; Szmukler and Rose 2013).

In England and Wales, while there is a Mental Capacity Act 2005, which governs medical treatment for those who lack capacity to make treatment, financial, and lifestyle decisions, Genevra Richardson (2010: 184) points out that the Mental Health Act 1983 differs in its focus because it "is primarily concerned with the reduction of the risks flowing from mental disorder both to the patient and to others." Similarly, the Adults with Incapacity (Scotland) Act 2000 puts in place a decision-making regime for those who lack capacity to make some or all decisions about treatment, financial, and lifestyle matters for themselves. However, the Mental Health (Care and Treatment) (Scotland) Act 2003 sets out a separate scheme that enables the involuntary commitment of those with a "mental disorder" where there is a "significant risk to the safety" of others.

As it is impossible to set out in detail all the laws in countries that have multiple pieces of legislation, Table 4.1 sets out a sample of the key criteria for involuntary detention in selected jurisdictions, with the criteria relating to harm to others highlighted.

The Law on Danger to Others

As Table 4.1 shows, there are different ways of setting out a "dangerousness" criterion in mental health laws from a very broad concept of "the protection of others from harm" to more circumscribed requirements of "likely to cause serious bodily harm" or an "imminent risk" of causing harm.

There is little case law on what is meant by such terms perhaps partly because there is a great deal of discretion given to clinicians as to what is meant by the likelihood of harm to others. Generally, a tribunal reviews the clinician's decision, but there is no legal requirement that there be evidence of any overt act for harm to be considered "likely" to eventuate in the future.

In *Re H* (2005: para. [6]), the Ontario Consent and Capacity Board observed in relation to the likelihood of harm to self that "the feared

Table 4.1 Detention of individuals under mental health legislation

Jurisdiction, act and section	Criteria for involuntary detention
Australian Capital Territory Mental Health (Care and Treatment) Act 1994 ss 28, 30, 36, 36B	• the person has a mental illness; and • The ACT Civil and Administrative Tribunal (ACAT) has reasonable grounds for believing that because of the illness, **the person is likely to:** 　• **do serious harm to himself, herself, or someone else;** or 　• **suffer serious mental or physical deterioration** • unless subject to involuntary psychiatric treatment; and • ACAT is satisfied that psychiatric treatment is likely to reduce the harm or deterioration (or likelihood of harm or deterioration) and result in an improvement in the person's psychiatric condition; and • the treatment cannot be adequately provided in a way that would involve less restriction of the freedom of choice and movement of the person • (in which case ACAT may make a psychiatric treatment order) OR • the person is mentally dysfunctional; and • ACAT has reasonable grounds for believing that, because of the mental dysfunction, **the person is likely to:** 　• **do serious harm to himself, herself, or someone else;** or 　• **suffer serious mental or physical deterioration** • unless subject to involuntary treatment, care, or support; and • ACAT is satisfied that treatment, care, or support is likely to reduce the harm, or the likelihood of harm, mentioned [above]; and • ACAT is satisfied that a psychiatric treatment order should not be made; and • the treatment, care, or support cannot be adequately provided in a way that would involve less restriction of the freedom of choice and movement of the person than would result if the person is an involuntary patient • (in which case ACAT may make a community care order) Having made a psychiatric treatment order or a community care order ACAT or the chief psychiatrist may make a restriction order to detain the person if satisfied that it is in the interests of the person's health or safety or public safety to do so.

| New South Wales Mental Health Act 2007 ss 12–15, 18, 27, 35 | For a mentally ill person:

 • the person is suffering from mental illness; and
 • owing to that illness, there are reasonable grounds for believing that **care, treatment, or control of the person is necessary for the person's own protection from serious harm, or the protection of others from serious harm.**

 In considering whether a person is a mentally ill person, the continuing condition of the person, including any likely deterioration in the person's condition and the likely effects of any such deterioration, are to be taken into account.

 OR

 For a mentally disordered person:

 • a person (whether or not the person is suffering from mental illness) is a mentally disordered person if the person's behaviour for the time being is so irrational as to justify a conclusion on reasonable grounds that temporary care, **treatment, or control of the person is necessary:**
    • for the person's own protection from serious physical harm; or
    • **for the protection of others from serious physical harm.**

 For a person to be detained involuntarily in a mental health facility an authorized medical officer must be of the opinion that the person is a mentally ill person or a mentally disordered person, and no other care of a less restrictive kind, that is consistent with safe and effective care, is appropriate and reasonably available to the person.
 Ongoing involuntary detention for a specified period of up to three months may be ordered by the Mental Health Review Tribunal if satisfied, on the balance of probabilities, that the person is mentally ill and is of the opinion that no other care of a less restrictive kind, that is consistent with safe and effective care, is appropriate and reasonably available. |

(continued)

Table 4.1 (continued)

Jurisdiction, act and section	Criteria for involuntary detention

Northern Territory Mental Health and Related Services Act ss 14–15	The criteria for the involuntary admission of a person on the grounds of mental illness are that:
	
	• the person has a mental illness;
	• as a result of the mental illness:
	  • the person requires treatment that is available at an approved treatment facility; and **without the treatment, the person is likely to:**
	    - **cause serious harm to himself or herself or to someone else; or**
	    - suffer serious mental or physical deterioration; and
	  • the person is not capable of giving informed consent to the treatment or has unreasonably refused to consent to the treatment; and
	• there is no less restrictive means of ensuring that the person receives the treatment.
	
	The criteria for the involuntary admission of a person on the grounds of mental disturbance are that:
	
	• the person does not fulfil [the above] criteria;
	• the person's behaviour is, or within the immediately preceding 48 hours has been, so irrational as to lead to the conclusion that:
	  • the person is experiencing or exhibiting a severe impairment of or deviation from his or her customary or everyday ability to reason and function in a socially acceptable and culturally appropriate manner; and
	  • **the person is behaving in an abnormally aggressive manner** or is engaging in seriously irresponsible conduct that justifies a determination that the person requires psychiatric assessment, treatment, or therapeutic care that is available at an approved treatment facility;
	• unless the person receives treatment or care at an approved treatment facility, **he or she:**
	  • **is likely to cause serious harm to himself or herself or to someone else; or**
	  • **will represent a substantial danger to the general community; or**
	  • is likely to suffer serious mental or physical deterioration;
	• the person is not capable of giving informed consent to the treatment or care or has unreasonably refused to consent to the treatment or care; and
	• there is no less restrictive means of ensuring that the person receives the treatment or care.

Queensland
Mental
Health Act
2000
ss 14, 109

The treatment criteria for a person, are all of the following:

- the person has a mental illness; and
- the person's illness requires immediate treatment; and
- the proposed treatment is available at an authorised mental health service; and
- because of the person's illness:
  - **there is an imminent risk that the person may cause harm to himself or herself or someone else; or**
  - the person is likely to suffer serious mental or physical deterioration; and
- there is no less restrictive way of ensuring the person receives appropriate treatment for the illness; and
- the person:
  - lacks the capacity to consent to be treated for the illness; or
  - has unreasonably refused proposed treatment for the illness.

In making the involuntary treatment order, the authorized doctor must decide the category of the order. The category of the order must be – if the patient needs to be treated as an inpatient of an authorized mental health service or the patient is a classified patient – inpatient.

**South
Australia**
Mental
Health Act
2009
ss 21, 25, 29

A medical practitioner or authorized health professional may make an order that a person be detained and receive treatment in a treatment centre (a level 1 detention and treatment order) if it appears to the medical practitioner or authorized health professional, after examining the person, that:

- the person has a mental illness; and
- because of the mental illness, **the person requires treatment for:**
  - the person's own protection from harm (including harm involved in the continuation or deterioration of the person's condition); or
  - **the protection of others from harm;** and
- there is no less restrictive means than a detention and treatment order of ensuring appropriate treatment of the person's illness.

Tasmania
Mental
Health Act
1996
s. 24

A person may be detained as an involuntary patient in an approved hospital if:

- the person appears to have a mental illness; and
- **there is, in consequence, a significant risk of harm to the person or others;** and
- the detention of the person as an involuntary patient is necessary to protect the person or others; and
- the approved hospital is properly equipped and staffed for the care or treatment of the person.

(continued)

Table 4.1 (continued)

Jurisdiction, act and section	Criteria for involuntary detention
Victoria Mental Health Act 1986 s 8	The criteria for the involuntary treatment of a person under this Act are that: • the person appears to be mentally ill; and • the person's mental illness requires immediate treatment and that treatment can be obtained by the person being subject to an involuntary treatment order; and • because of the person's mental illness, **involuntary treatment of the person is necessary** for his or her health or safety (whether to prevent a deterioration in the person's physical or mental condition or otherwise) or **for protection of members of the public**; and • the person has refused or is unable to consent to the necessary treatment for the mental illness; and • the person cannot receive adequate treatment for the mental illness in a manner less restrictive of his or her freedom of decision and action.

Western Australia Mental Health Act 1996 s. 26	A person should be an involuntary patient only if:
	• the person has a mental illness requiring treatment; and
	• the treatment can be provided through detention in an authorized hospital or through a community treatment order and **is required to be so provided in order:**
	• **to protect the health or safety of that person or any other person;** or
	• to protect the person from self-inflicted harm, including:
	  – serious financial harm;
	  – lasting or irreparable harm to any important personal relationship resulting from damage to the reputation of the person among those with whom the person has such relationships; and
	  – serious damage to the reputation of the person; or
	• to prevent the person doing serious damage to any property; and
	• the person has refused or, due to the nature of the mental illness, is unable to consent to the treatment; and
	• the treatment cannot be adequately provided in a way that would involve less restriction of the freedom of choice and movement of the person than would result from the person being an involuntary patient.

New Zealand Mental Health (Compulsory Assessment and Treatment) Act 1992 ss 2, 27, 28(2)	On an application for a compulsory treatment order, the court shall determine whether or not the patient is mentally disordered. A person is mentally disordered if the person:
	
	• has an abnormal state of mind (whether of a continuous or intermittent nature), characterized by delusions or by disorders of mood or perception or volition or cognition, of such a degree that it:
	  • **poses a serious danger to the health or safety of that person or of others;** or
	  • seriously diminishes the capacity of that person to take care of himself or herself.
	
	If the court considers that the patient is mentally disordered, it shall determine whether or not, having regard to all the circumstances of the case, it is necessary to make a compulsory treatment order.
	
	Every compulsory treatment order shall be either a community treatment order; or an inpatient order. On making a compulsory treatment order the court shall make a community treatment order unless the court considers that the patient cannot be treated adequately as an outpatient, in which case the court shall make an inpatient order.

England and Wales Mental Health Act 1983 ss 2–3	A patient may be admitted to a hospital and detained there for the period allowed by [the Act] in pursuance of an application for admission for assessment on the grounds that: • [the patient] is suffering from mental disorder of a nature or degree which warrants the detention of the patient in a hospital for assessment (or for assessment followed by medical treatment) for at least a limited period; and • [the patient] ought to be so detained in the interests of his [or her] own health or safety or **with a view to the protection of other persons.** OR A patient may be admitted to a hospital and detained there for the period allowed by [the Act] in pursuance of an application for admission for treatment on the grounds that: • [the patient] is suffering from mental disorder of a nature or degree which makes it appropriate for him or her to receive medical treatment in a hospital; and • it is necessary for the health or safety of the patient **or for the protection of other persons** that he or she should receive such treatment and it cannot be provided unless he [or she] is detained under this section; and • appropriate medical treatment is available for him or her.

(continued)

Table 4.1 (continued)

Jurisdiction, act and section	Criteria for involuntary detention

Scotland Mental Health (Care and Treatment) (Scotland) Act 2003 s. 64	The tribunal may make a compulsory treatment order if satisfied that:
	• the patient has a mental disorder;
	• medical treatment is available for the patient which would be likely to:
	  • prevent the mental disorder worsening; or
	  • alleviate any of the symptoms, or effects, of the disorder;
	• if the patient were not provided with such medical treatment there would **be a significant risk**:
	  • to the health, safety, or welfare of the patient; or
	  • **to the safety of any other person;**
	• because of the mental disorder the patient's ability to make decisions about the provision of such medical treatment is significantly impaired; and
	• the making of a compulsory treatment order in respect of the patient is necessary.

Ontario, Canada Mental Health Act, RSO 1990 s. 20	The attending physician shall complete a certificate of involuntary admission or a certificate of renewal if, after examining the patient, he or she is of the opinion that the patient: • has previously received treatment for mental disorder of an ongoing or recurring nature that, when not treated, is of a nature or quality that likely **will result in serious bodily harm to the person** or to another person or substantial mental or physical deterioration of the person or serious physical impairment of the person; • has shown clinical improvement as a result of the treatment; • is suffering from the same mental disorder as the one for which he or she previously received treatment or from a mental disorder that is similar to the previous one; • given the person's history of mental disorder and current mental or physical condition, **is likely to cause serious bodily harm to himself or herself or to another person** or is likely to suffer substantial mental or physical deterioration or serious physical impairment; • has been found incapable, within the meaning of relevant legislation, of consenting to his or her treatment in a psychiatric facility and the consent of his or her substitute decision-maker has been obtained; and • is not suitable for admission or continuation as an informal or voluntary patient.

OR

- is suffering from mental disorder of a nature or quality that likely will result in:
  - serious bodily harm to the patient;
  - **serious bodily harm to another person**; or
  - serious physical impairment of the patient;
- unless the patient remains in the custody of a psychiatric facility; and
- the patient is not suitable for admission or continuation as an informal or voluntary patient.

California, USA*
California Welfare and Institutions Code s. 5250

The professional staff of the agency or facility providing evaluation services has analyzed the person's condition and has found the person is, as a result of mental disorder or impairment by chronic alcoholism:

- **a danger to others, or to himself or herself;** or
- "gravely disabled" (cannot survive safely without involuntary detention with the help of responsible family, friends, or others who are both willing and able to help provide for the person's basic personal needs for food, clothing, or shelter).

The facility providing intensive treatment is designated by the county to provide intensive treatment, and agrees to admit the person.

The person has been advised of the need for, but has not been willing or able to accept, treatment on a voluntary basis.

Note
*A table of inpatient and outpatient criteria in every State of the United States can be found at: http://treatmentadvocacycenter.org/storage/documents/State_Standards_-_The_Chart-_June_28_2011.pdf (accessed January 31, 2013).

harm must be likely to occur within some reasonable period after discharge" and noted that "there is a temporal element but it is ill defined and flexible." The Queensland legislation refers to an "imminent risk," thereby introducing some notion of proximity into the assessment of risk.

In *Foucha v Louisiana* (1992), the United States Supreme Court held that States must maintain the same standard for involuntarily committed insanity acquittees as they do for those individuals who have been civilly committed. This meant (1992: 80) that the State must show by "clear and convincing" evidence that the individual concerned is both mentally ill and dangerous. However, the Court did not go on to say what such clear and convincing evidence would be.

The notion of "harm" is also vague. Some laws refer to "serious" harm and in Canada, this has been held to include harms that relate to the social, family, vocational, or financial matters (*Bobbie v Health Services Centre, Director of Psychiatric Services and Mental Health Review Board* 1989; *McCorkell v Director of Riverview Hospital* 1993).

In Canada, there is some difference in the provinces as to whether harm to others must be "bodily" harm rather than "psychological" harm. In *Re LA* (2007) the Ontario Consent and Capacity Board interpreted bodily harm in the legislative criteria as meaning harm to the "brain" rather than the "mind," thereby excluding psychological harm. In comparison, section 8(1)(c)(ii) of New Brunswick's Mental Health Act 1973 specifically refers to a "substantial risk of imminent physical or psychological harm to the person or to others," thereby broadening the scope of the harm criterion.

Ian Freckelton (2010) states that in practice, if there is evidence of past violence to others, a decision will generally be made in favour of involuntary detention. However, he also points out (2010: 219) that:

> [t]he recycling of accounts of patients' acts of violence (especially in hospital records) and the drawing of an inference because of one instance of aggressive conduct or instances of such conduct in a particular context that a person is 'violent' can be unfairly prejudicial and counter-therapeutic to patients.

The difficulty in determining the risk of harm to self or others has led Christopher Ryan, Sascha Callaghan, and Matthew Large (2012: 3) to observe that:

> clinicians will deem a person "at risk" if they report wanting to harm someone, or if they have harmed someone in the past, or they cause the examiners themselves to feel threatened. The use of common sense in such situations is understandable, but over

time it will mean even higher rates of false positives and negatives will occur than would be achieved with evidence-based tools.

Overall, as Joaquin Zuckerberg (2010: 306) points out, "[t]he question as to whether 'harm' to others should be broadly or narrowly defined still remains unanswered by the courts." It is simply left to individual clinicians to use their "common sense" in this regard. The ethical implications of this are taken up in Chapter 8.

LAWS ENABLING THE PREVENTIVE DETENTION OF SEX OFFENDERS

Four states in Australia and 20 states in the United States (Petrila 2010) enable the post-sentence preventive detention of sex offenders. This is to be contrasted with laws that enable indefinite detention in prison *at the time* of sentence, which exist in many common law countries.

In the United States, "sexual psychopath" laws were enacted between the 1930s and 1980s. These laws enabled the incarceration of such individuals for treatment, generally in lieu of sentence (La Fond 2011). The laws were often cast very broadly to encompass those "who have committed almost all common sexual offences from rape to incest, from indecent exposure to obscene telephoning, from homosexual behavior to indecent liberties with children, from transvestism to voyeurism" (Di Furia and Mees 1963: 532–33). Because treatment programmes for "sexual psychopaths" were subject to increasing criticism, these laws were gradually repealed (Gleb 1991).

It was in the 1990s that new laws were enacted in many United States jurisdictions following the lead of Washington State's Community Protection Act, which came into effect on July 1, 1990 (Act of January 24, 1990, Wash Laws ch. 3, 101–1406 1990). These laws have become known as "sexually violent predator" laws and enable the incapacitation of such offenders through civil detention in special facilities. The Australian laws that enable post-sentence detention in prison were enacted in the past decade, with Queensland the first state to introduce such legislation in 2003.

Table 4.2 sets out some of the key elements of these laws. It outlines the Australian laws and uses the United States federal law as an example of sexually violent predator laws in that country.

A major difference between these schemes is that the Australian model of civil detention is not tied to any diagnostic criteria, whereas the United States model requires evidence that the offender has a "mental abnormality or personality disorder." Whether this makes much of a difference in practice is debatable, as the term "mental abnormality" is very broad and

Table 4.2 Preventive detention under sex offender legislation

Key elements	Jurisdiction, act and section	Legislative requirements
Who may order detention	**New South Wales** Crimes (Serious Sex Offenders) Act 2006 s. 17	Supreme Court
	Queensland Dangerous Prisoners (Sexual Offenders) Act 2003 s. 13	
	Victoria Serious Sex Offenders (Detention and Supervision) Act 2009 s. 35(1)	
	Western Australia Dangerous Sexual Offenders Act 2006 (WA) s. 8	
	United States Adam Walsh Child Protection and Safety Act 2006 s. 4248	District Court

| Grounds for ordering detention | New South Wales Crimes (Serious Sex Offenders) Act 2006 s. 17 | • The prisoner is currently serving a custodial sentence for a serious sex offence.
• The Supreme Court is satisfied to a high degree of probability that the offender poses an unacceptable risk of committing a serious sex offence if he or she is not kept under supervision and that adequate supervision will not be provided by an extended supervision order. The Supreme Court is not required to determine that the risk of a person committing a serious sex offence is more likely than not in order to determine that the person poses an unacceptable risk of committing a serious sex offence.
• The Court must have regard to the following matters in addition to any other matter it considers relevant:
  • the safety of the community;
  • the reports received from [psychiatrists and psychologists] appointed under statute to conduct examinations of the offender, and the level of the offender's participation in any such examination;
  • the results of any other assessment prepared by a qualified psychiatrist, registered psychologist, or registered medical practitioner as to the likelihood of the offender committing a further serious sex offence, the willingness of the offender to participate in any such assessment, and the level of the offender's participation in any such assessment;
  • the results of any statistical or other assessment as to the likelihood of persons with histories and characteristics similar to those of the offender committing a further serious sex offence;
  • any treatment or rehabilitation programs in which the offender has had an opportunity to participate, the willingness of the offender to participate in any such programs, and the level of the offender's participation in any such programs;
  • the offender's criminal history (including prior convictions and findings of guilt in respect of offences committed in New South Wales or elsewhere), and any pattern of offending behaviour disclosed by that history;
  • any other information that is available as to the likelihood that the offender will in future commit offences of a sexual nature;
  • any report by Corrective Services NSW as to the extent to which the offender can reasonably and practicably be managed in the community;
  • the level of the offender's compliance with any obligations to which he or she is or has been subject while on release on parole, etc., or while subject to an interim supervision order or an extended supervision order;
  • the views of the original sentencing court at the time the sentence of imprisonment was imposed on the offender. |

(continued)

Table 4.2 (continued)

Key elements	Jurisdiction, act and section	Legislative requirements

	Queensland
	Dangerous Prisoners (Sexual Offenders) Act 2003
	s. 13
		• The prisoner is currently serving a custodial sentence for a serious sex offence.
		• The court is satisfied the prisoner is "a serious danger to the community".
		• A prisoner is a serious danger to the community if there is an unacceptable risk that the prisoner will commit a serious sexual offence if the prisoner is released from custody; or if the prisoner is released from custody without a supervision order being made.
		• The court may make the order only if it is satisfied by acceptable, cogent evidence, and to a high degree of probability that the evidence is of sufficient weight to justify the decision.
		• In deciding whether a prisoner is a serious danger to the community the court must have regard to the following:
		  • any report produced under section 8A;
		  • the reports prepared by the psychiatrists under section 11 and the extent to which the prisoner cooperated in the examinations by the psychiatrists;
		  • any other medical, psychiatric, psychological, or other assessment relating to the prisoner;
		  • information indicating whether or not there is a propensity on the part of the prisoner to commit serious sexual offences in the future;
		  • whether or not there is any pattern of offending behaviour on the part of the prisoner;
		  • efforts by the prisoner to address the cause or causes of the prisoner's offending behaviour, including whether the prisoner participated in rehabilitation programs;
		  • whether or not the prisoner's participation in rehabilitation programs has had a positive effect on the prisoner;
		  • the prisoner's antecedents and criminal history;
		  • the risk that the prisoner will commit another serious sexual offence if released into the community;
		  • the need to protect members of the community from that risk;
		  • any other relevant matter.
		• In deciding whether to make the order the paramount consideration is to be the need to ensure adequate protection of the community. The Attorney-General has the onus of proving that a prisoner is a serious danger to the community.

Victoria
Serious Sex Offenders
(Detention and
Supervision) Act 2009
ss 35, 37

- Act applies to "eligible offender" (a person serving a custodial sentence for a "relevant offence" – [an offence listed Schedule 1]).
- The Supreme Court may make an order in respect of an eligible offender only if the Court is satisfied that the offender poses an unacceptable risk of committing a relevant offence if a detention order or supervision order is not made and the offender is in the community. The Supreme Court may decide that it is satisfied as required by the Act only if it is satisfied by acceptable, cogent evidence and to a high degree of probability that the evidence is of sufficient weight to justify the decision. In determining whether the offender is likely to commit a relevant offence, the Supreme Court must have regard to:
  - any assessment report or progress report filed in the Court, whether by or on behalf of the Director of Public Prosecutions or the offender;
  - any other report made, or evidence given, in relation to the application; and
  - anything else the Court considers appropriate.
- In determining whether or not the offender poses an unacceptable risk, the Supreme Court must not consider the means of managing the risk or the likely impact of a detention order on the offender.
- For the avoidance of doubt the Supreme Court may determine that an offender poses an unacceptable risk of committing a relevant offence even if the likelihood that the offender will commit a relevant offence is less than a likelihood of more likely than not.
- The Director of Public Prosecutions has the burden of proving that the offender poses an unacceptable risk.

(continued)

Table 4.2 (continued)

Key elements	Jurisdiction, act and section	Legislative requirements

	Western Australia
	Dangerous Sexual
	Offenders Act 2006
	ss 7, 17
		• The person is under sentence of imprisonment wholly or in part for a serious sexual offence.
		• If the court finds that the offender is a serious danger to the community, the court may order that the offender be detained in custody for an indefinite term for control, care, or treatment.
		• Before the court finds that a person is a serious danger to the community, the court has to be satisfied that there is an unacceptable risk that, if the person were not subject to a continuing detention order or a supervision order, the person would commit a serious sexual offence.
		• The court has to be satisfied by acceptable and cogent evidence; and to a high degree of probability.
		• In deciding whether to find that a person is a serious danger to the community, the court must have regard to:
		  • any report that a psychiatrist prepares as required by section 37 for the hearing of the application and the extent to which the person cooperated when the psychiatrist examined the person;
		  • any other medical, psychiatric, psychological, or other assessment relating to the person;
		  • information indicating whether or not the person has a propensity to commit serious sexual offences in the future;
		  • whether or not there is any pattern of offending behaviour on the part of the person;
		  • any efforts by the person to address the cause or causes of the person's offending behaviour, including whether the person has participated in any rehabilitation program;
		  • whether or not the person's participation in any rehabilitation program has had a positive effect on the person;
		  • the person's antecedents and criminal record;
		  • the risk that, if the person were not subject to a continuing detention order or a supervision order, the person would commit a serious sexual offence;
		  • the need to protect members of the community from that risk; and
		  • any other relevant matter.

	Duration: initial/interim
United States Adam Walsh Child Protection and Safety Act 2006 ss 4247, 4248	• The individual is in prison custody, has been found incompetent to stand trial, or has been found not guilty due to mental impairment. • Clear and convincing evidence that the individual is a "sexually dangerous person" – a person who has engaged or attempted to engage in sexually violent conduct or child molestation and who suffers from a serious mental illness, abnormality, or disorder as a result of which he would have serious difficulty in refraining from sexually violent conduct or child molestation if released (is "sexually dangerous to others").
New South Wales Crimes (Serious Sex Offenders) Act 2006 s. 16	For a period not exceeding 28 days; may be renewed from time to time, but not so as to provide for the detention of the offender under such an order for periods totalling more than three months. (Indefinite until final hearing).
Queensland Dangerous Prisoners (Sexual Offenders) Act 2003 s. 14	An interim detention order has effect in accordance with its terms on the order being made or at the end of the prisoner's period of imprisonment, whichever is the later; and for the period stated in the order, unless earlier rescinded.
Victoria Serious Sex Offenders (Detention and Supervision) Act 2009 s. 57	The total period for which the offender may be made subject to an interim order pending the determination of the application cannot exceed four months, unless the court making or extending the order considers that exceptional circumstances exist. (Indefinite until final hearing).
Western Australia Dangerous Sexual Offenders Act 2006 (WA) s. 14(2)(b)	The court may order that the offender be detained in custody for the period stated in the order if the offender: • is in custody and might otherwise be released from custody before the application is finally decided; or • is not in custody.

(continued)

Table 4.2 (continued)

Key elements	Jurisdiction, act and section	Legislative requirements
	United States Adam Walsh Child Protection and Safety Act 2006 s. 4248(a)	(Indefinite until final hearing). In relation to a person who is in the custody of the Bureau of Prisons, or who has been committed to the custody of the Attorney-General pursuant to section 4241(d), or against whom all criminal charges have been dismissed solely for reasons relating to the mental condition of the person, the Attorney-General or any individual authorized by the Attorney-General or the Director of the Bureau of Prisons may certify that the person is a sexually dangerous person, and transmit the certificate to the clerk of the court for the district in which the person is confined. The clerk shall send a copy of the certificate to the person, and to the attorney for the government, and, if the person was committed pursuant to section 4241(d), to the clerk of the court that ordered the commitment. The court shall order a hearing to determine whether the person is a sexually dangerous person. A certificate filed under this subsection shall stay the release of the person pending completion of procedures contained in this section.
Maximum duration: final	**New South Wales** Crimes (Serious Sex Offenders) Act 2006 s. 18	Not exceeding five years from the day on which it commences.
	Queensland Dangerous Prisoners (Sexual Offenders) Act 2003 s. 13(5)	The court may order that the prisoner be detained in custody for an indefinite term for control, care, or treatment.
	Victoria Serious Sex Offenders (Detention and Supervision) Act 2009 s. 40	Not exceeding three years.

Western Australia Dangerous Sexual Offenders Act 2006 (WA) ss 17, 25	The court may order that the offender be detained in custody for an indefinite term for control, care, or treatment subject to annual review. A continuing detention order has effect in accordance with its terms from the time the order is made until rescinded by a further order of the Supreme Court.
United States Adam Walsh Child Protection and Safety Act 2006 s. 4248	Until the person's condition is such that he (or she) is no longer sexually dangerous to others, or will not be sexually dangerous to others if released under a prescribed regimen of medical, psychiatric, or psychological care or treatment.

has been criticized as going beyond recognized diagnostic categories of mental disorder (Winick and La Fond 2003).

Robert John Fardon was the first person in Australia to be subjected to post-sentence preventive detention in prison. The circumstances that led to his detention are set out in Chapter 7. Whether such detention was constitutional was considered by the High Court of Australia which, by a majority of six judges to one, held that the Queensland Act was valid (*Fardon v Attorney-General (Qld)* 2004). This decision opened the door for similar schemes to be introduced in Australia (McSherry 2005), with New South Wales and Western Australia quickly following suit and Victoria introducing a similar scheme in 2009. The Northern Territory Parliament is currently debating its Serious Sex Offenders Bill 2013.

Fardon challenged the constitutional validity of the Queensland scheme on the basis that it authorized the Supreme Court to order the civil commitment of a person to prison without a fresh crime, or a trial or conviction for that crime, meaning that the law authorized double punishment. He argued that for these reasons, the law was inconsistent with the essential character of a court and, consequently, the separation of judicial power under the Australian Constitution (Keyzer *et al.* 2004).

The constitutional argument was based on a previous decision of the High Court of Australia in *Kable v Director of Public Prosecutions (NSW)* (1996). In that case, a majority of the High Court struck down New South Wales legislation that empowered the Supreme Court of New South Wales to order the preventive detention of Gregory Wayne Kable who had been convicted of the manslaughter of his estranged wife and who had allegedly made threats against her family. In that case, one of the majority, Justice Gummow observed (1996: 132):

> Whilst imprisonment pursuant to Supreme Court order is punitive in nature, it [was] not [made] consequent upon any adjudgment by the Court of criminal guilt. Plainly . . . such an authority could not be conferred by a law of the Commonwealth upon this Court, any other federal court, or a State court exercising federal jurisdiction . . . [N]ot only is such an authority non-judicial in nature, it is repugnant to the judicial process in a fundamental degree.

The majority of the High Court in *Kable*'s case struck down the New South Wales legislation on the basis that it had imposed functions that were incompatible with the exercise of federal judicial power (Hanks *et al.* 2004).

In *Fardon v Attorney-General (Qld)* (2004) the majority of the High Court distinguished *Kable*'s case on the basis that the legislation in that matter was aimed at one person whereas the Queensland scheme refers to a class of prisoners, namely serious sex offenders. The majority also dismissed the double punishment argument on the basis that detention in prison is not correctly characterized as punishment if it is ordered for non-punitive reasons (2004: 592, 597, 610, 647, 654). Justices Callinan and Heydon stated (2004: 654) that "[t]he [Act] . . . is intended to protect the community from predatory sexual offenders. It is a protective law authorising involuntary detention in the interests of public safety. Its proper characterisation is as a protective rather than a punitive enactment."

The majority of the High Court also held that there were sufficient safeguards in place to ensure that the Supreme Court was exercising its judicial discretion in making preventive detention and supervision orders.

Gleeson CJ (2004: 586) was careful to point out that the High Court had no jurisdiction to consider policy issues concerning the legislation:

> There are important issues that could be raised about the legislative policy of continuing detention of offenders who have served their terms of imprisonment, and who are regarded as a danger to the community when released. Substantial questions of civil liberty arise. This case, however, is not concerned with those wider issues. The outcome turns upon a relatively narrow point, concerning the nature of the function which the Act confers upon the Supreme Court.

Justice Kirby, the sole dissentient in *Fardon*'s case, held that continued detention in prison *did* amount to double punishment (2004: 643–44) and he was also concerned (2004: 639) with the "free hand given to the psychiatric witnesses upon whose evidence the Act requires the State court to perform its function." He stated (2004: 647):

> In Australia . . . punishment is reserved to courts in respect of the crimes that prisoners are proved to have committed. It is not available for crimes that are feared, anticipated or predicted to occur in the future on evidence that is notoriously unreliable and otherwise would be inadmissible and by people who do not have the gift of prophesy.

Justice Kirby's approach was later echoed by the decisions of the United Nations Human Rights Committee in the *Fardon* and *Tillman* communications (2010) that are explored in Chapter 7. However, in terms of whether or not post-sentence preventive detention is constitutional, the majority decision in Fardon's case remains the law in Australia.

In the United States, the constitutional parameters of post-sentence detention of sexually violent predators have also been tested. In *Kansas v Hendricks* (1997), the Supreme Court, by a majority of five justices to four, upheld the constitutionality of the Kansas Sexually Violent Predator Act (1994). Leroy Hendricks, who had an extensive criminal history of sexual offending, challenged the constitutionality of the Kansas statute on the basis that it failed to require a finding of mental illness that might justify civil commitment.

Justice Thomas, in delivering the judgment of the majority, held that the "mental abnormality" underlying a post-sentence commitment need not be severe mental illness such as a psychotic disorder. Rather, it could consist of a less severe disorder, providing it made the person "dangerous beyond [his or her] control" (*Kansas v Hendricks* 1997: 357). That is (1997: 358), the state must prove that the individual suffered from a condition that makes it "difficult, if not impossible, for the person to control their dangerous behaviour." Justice Thomas noted (1997: 360–61) that Hendricks had been diagnosed as a paedophile and this fell within the ambit of a "mental abnormality." The Supreme Court of the United States subsequently limited the application of the Kansas scheme to those having "serious difficulty controlling behaviour" (*Kansas v Crane* 2002).

As with the majority in Fardon's case, the majority in *Hendrick*'s case (1997: 365–68) held that the Kansas scheme was not punitive in intent or effect. Further (1997: 366), treatment needed only to be provided where a condition was treatable. State legislatures have since been careful to draft legislation that is not expressed in punitive terms, but rather focuses on preventive measures to reduce the risk of harm to others.

The Supreme Court has, therefore, clarified that "mental illness" sufficient for commitment under mental health laws is not required for the detention of sexually violent predators, but there must be some evidence of dangerousness stemming from a "mental abnormality" that leads to serious difficulty in controlling behaviour.

The Australian and United States schemes for the preventive detention of sex offenders have thus been upheld as constitutional by the highest courts in these countries. This is not to say, however, that they do not breach international human rights law. This issue is discussed in Chapter 7.

LAWS ENABLING THE PREVENTIVE DETENTION OF SUSPECTED TERRORISTS

There are far-reaching legislative powers in relation to the pre-charge preventive detention of suspected terrorists that were introduced in certain countries following the terrorist attacks in the United States on September 11, 2001. These powers enable an individual to be detained for community protection purposes rather than for the traditional processes of investigation and questioning.

These are controversial laws and the preventive detention regime that was introduced in the United Kingdom two months after the terrorist attacks in the United States via the Anti-Terrorism, Crime and Security

Act 2001 (UK) has been repealed after it was found to breach the right to liberty. Part 4 of the Anti-Terrorism, Crime and Security Act 2001 (UK) allowed the Home Secretary to detain indefinitely any non-British citizen who was suspected of being a terrorist, pending deportation, even if such a deportation would be prohibited. A challenge to the legality of these provisions was brought by nine foreign nationals who had been detained without charge in Belmarsh prison as suspected international terrorists. This challenge was upheld by the House of Lords in *A and others v Secretary of State for the Home Department* (2004). The reasons for this decision concern human rights law and are discussed in Chapter 7.

After the House of Lords decision, the preventive detention provisions were repealed and replaced by control orders under the Prevention of Terrorism Act 2005. These were in turn abolished by the Terrorism Prevention and Investigation Measures Act 2011 and replaced by "measures" that can still serve to restrict a person's liberty. These are outlined in the next chapter. Under section 41 of the Terrorism Act 2000 (UK) a person may be arrested and detained for up to 48 hours without a warrant on the basis of a reasonable suspicion that the person is a terrorist. Detention beyond that time can be extended by a judge for periods that can last up to 28 days from arrest, as laid down in Schedule 8 of the Act.

Interestingly, Canada and New Zealand did not introduce laws enabling the preventive detention of suspected terrorists. This may have been because of concerns that they would breach the rights of the Canadian Charter of Rights and Freedoms and New Zealand's Bill of Rights Act 1990. For example, section 23(2) of New Zealand's Bill of Rights Act 1990 states that "[e]veryone who is arrested for an offence has the right to be charged promptly or to be released" which provides a human rights framework antithetical to detention without charge.

In lieu of preventive detention, Canada's Anti-Terrorism Act 2001 amended its Criminal Code to include section 83.28 that allows a judge to require a person to attend a judicial hearing on the investigation of the commission of or potential future terrorist acts (the latter being based on the belief on reasonable grounds that "a terrorism act will be committed": section 83.28(4)). Constitutional challenges to these powers were dismissed by the Supreme Court of Canada in *Re Application under section 83.28 of the Criminal Code* [2004] 2 SCR 248 and *Re Vancouver Sun* [2004] 2 SCR 332 (see Alex Conte (2010): 512ff for an overview of these cases). The recently passed Combating Terrorism Act 2013 includes provisions relating to investigative conditions and "recognizance-with-conditions" measures.

Table 4.3 outlines some of the specific schemes that allow for the pre-charge detention of terrorist suspects for the purposes of community protection in Australia, the United States, and the United Kingdom.

Each jurisdiction has laws regarding permissible periods of detention pending charges being laid for all criminal suspects that are not explored here. Australia also enables detention without charge for renewable periods of seven days with the maximum time allowable being 28 days

Table 4.3 Preventive detention under terrorism legislation

Key elements	Jurisdiction, act and section	Legislative requirements
Who may order detention?	**Australian Capital Territory** Terrorism (Extraordinary Temporary Powers) Act 2006 s. 18(1)	Supreme Court
	New South Wales Terrorism (Police Powers) Act 2002 ss 26H, 26I	
	Tasmania Terrorism (Preventive Detention) Act 2005 s. 7(1)	
	Victoria Terrorism (Community Protection) Act 2003 s. 13E	
	Australia (Federal) Criminal Code ss 105.2, 100.1(1), 105.8	The Minister may, by writing, appoint as an issuing authority for continued preventative detention orders: • a person who is a judge of a State or Territory Supreme Court; • a person who is a judge; • a person who is a Federal Magistrate; • a person who has served as a judge in one or more superior courts for a period of five years and no longer holds a commission as a judge of a superior court; or • a person who holds an appointment to the Administrative Appeals Tribunal as President or Deputy President and is a legal practitioner for at least five years.

Key elements	Jurisdiction, act and section	Legislative requirements
		The Minister must not appoint a person unless the person has, by writing, consented to being appointed. Issuing authority for initial preventative detention orders means a senior Australian Federal Police member.
	Northern Territory Terrorism (Emergency Powers) Act s. 21C	The Administrator may, in writing, declare a judge to be an eligible judge for this Part. A declaration cannot be made for a judge unless the judge has consented in writing to the declaration.
	Queensland Terrorism (Preventative Detention) Act 2005 s. 7(1), (2)	The issuing authority for an initial order is a senior police officer. The issuing authority for a final order is a judge or a retired judge (in either case appointed by the Minister).
	South Australia Terrorism (Preventative Detention) Act 2005 s. 4(1)(2)(3)	The Minister may, by writing, appoint a judge as an issuing authority for preventative detention orders. The Minister must not appoint a judge as an issuing authority unless the judge has, by writing, consented to the appointment. A senior police officer is an issuing authority for a preventative detention order if there is an urgent need for the order and it is not reasonably practicable in the circumstances to have the application for a preventative detention order dealt with by a judge.
	Western Australia Terrorism (Preventative Detention) Act 2006 s. 7	The Governor may, in writing, appoint a judge or retired judge as an issuing authority for preventative detention orders.

(continued)

Table 4.3 (continued)

Key elements	Jurisdiction, act and section	Legislative requirements
		A judge or retired judge cannot be appointed as an issuing authority unless the judge or retired judge has consented in writing to the appointment.
	United Kingdom Terrorism Act 2000 s. 41(1) Sch 8 s. 29(4)	A constable may arrest without a warrant a person whom he or she reasonably suspects to be a terrorist.
	United States Detention, Treatment and Trial of Certain Non-Citizens in the War Against Terrorism Executive Order §. 2	The President
	Immigration and Nationality Act 1952 § 1226a	The Attorney-General
Grounds for ordering detention	**Australia** (Federal) Criminal Code s. 105.4(4)(5)	There are reasonable grounds to suspect that the subject: • will engage in a terrorist act; • possesses a thing that is connected with the preparation for, or the engagement of a person in, a terrorist act; or • has done an act in preparation for, or planning, a terrorist act; and making the order would substantially assist in preventing a terrorist act occurring and detaining the subject for the period for which the person is to be detained under the order is reasonably necessary for the purpose of preventing a terrorist act occurring. • A terrorist act must be one that is imminent and must be one that is expected to occur, in any event, at some time within the next 14 days. OR • A terrorist act has occurred within the last 28 days; and

Key elements	Jurisdiction, act and section	Legislative requirements
		• it is necessary to detain the subject to preserve evidence of, or relating to, the terrorist act; and • detaining the subject for the period for which the person is to be detained under the order is reasonably necessary to preserve evidence of, or relating to, the terrorist act.
		An issuing authority may refuse to make a preventative detention order unless the AFP member applying for the order gives the issuing authority any further information that the issuing authority requests concerning the grounds on which the order is sought.
		A preventative detention order cannot be applied for, or made, in relation to a person who is under 16 years of age.
	Australian Capital Territory Terrorism (Extraordinary Temporary Powers) Act 2006 ss 18(4)(5)(6)(7)	The Supreme Court is satisfied, on reasonable grounds, that the person: • intends, and has the capacity, to carry out a terrorist act; • possesses something connected with the preparation for, or carrying out of, a terrorist act; or • has done an act in preparation for, or planning, a terrorist act; and the Supreme Court is satisfied, on reasonable grounds, that it is reasonably necessary to detain the person to prevent a terrorist act and that detaining the person under the order is the least restrictive way of preventing the terrorist act and that detaining the person for the period for which the person is to be detained under the order is reasonably necessary to prevent the terrorist act.

(continued)

93

Table 4.3 (continued)

Key elements	Jurisdiction, act and section	Legislative requirements
		The terrorist act must be imminent and, in any event, be expected to happen some time within the next 14 days.
		OR
		The Supreme Court is satisfied, on reasonable grounds, that
		• a terrorist act has happened within the last 28 days;
		• it is reasonably necessary to detain the person to preserve evidence in the ACT or elsewhere of, or relating to, the terrorist act;
		• detaining the person under the order is the only effective way of preserving the evidence of or relating to a terrorist act; and
		• detaining the person for the period for which the person is to be detained under the order is reasonably necessary to preserve the evidence.
		If the person has impaired decision-making ability, the court must also consider the following in deciding whether to make a preventative detention order for the person: the nature and extent of the person's impairment; and any other way it may be appropriate to deal with the person under a territory law.
	New South Wales Terrorism (Police Powers) Act 2002 s. 26D(1)	A preventative detention order may be made against a person if there are reasonable grounds to suspect that the person:
		• will engage in a terrorist act;
		• possesses a thing that is connected with the preparation for, or the engagement of a person in, a terrorist act; or
		• has done an act in preparation for, or planning, a terrorist act; and

94

Key elements	Jurisdiction, act and section	Legislative requirements
		making the order would substantially assist in preventing a terrorist act occurring and detaining the person for the period for which the person is to be detained under the order is reasonably necessary for the purpose of substantially assisting in preventing a terrorist act occurring. Any such terrorist act must be imminent and, in any event, be expected to occur at some time in the next 14 days. OR A preventative detention order may also be made against a person if: • a terrorist act has occurred within the last 28 days; • it is necessary to detain the person to preserve evidence in New South Wales or elsewhere of, or relating to, the terrorist act; and • detaining the person for the period for which the person is to be detained under the order is reasonably necessary for the purpose of preserving any such evidence.
	Northern Territory Terrorism (Emergency Powers) Act s. 21G(1)(a)	The eligible judge is satisfied, on reasonable grounds, that the person: • will engage in a terrorist act; • possesses or has under the person's control (whether solely or jointly with anyone else) a thing that is connected with the preparation for, or the engagement of a person in, a terrorist act; or • has done an act in preparation for, or planning, a terrorist act; and

(continued)

Table 4.3 (continued)

Key elements	Jurisdiction, act and section	Legislative requirements
		making the order would substantially assist in preventing a terrorist act occurring and detaining the person for the period for which the person is to be detained under the order is reasonably necessary for the purpose of substantially assisting in preventing a terrorist act occurring.
		OR
		The eligible judge is satisfied, on reasonable grounds, that:
		• a terrorist act has occurred within the last 28 days;
		• it is necessary to detain the person to preserve evidence in the Territory or elsewhere of, or relating to, the terrorist act; and
		• detaining the person for the period for which the person is to be detained under the order is reasonably necessary for the purpose of preserving any such evidence.
		A terrorist act must be imminent and, in any event, be expected to occur at some time in the next 14 days.
	Queensland Terrorism (Preventative Detention) Act 2005 s. 8(3)(4)	The police officer or issuing authority is satisfied there are reasonable grounds to suspect that the person:
		• will engage in a terrorist act;
		• possesses a thing that is connected with the preparation for, or the engagement of a person in, a terrorist act; or
		• has done an act in preparation for, or in planning, a terrorist act; and

Key elements	Jurisdiction, act and section	Legislative requirements
		making the order would substantially assist in preventing a terrorist act occurring and detaining the person for the period for which the person is to be detained under the order is reasonably necessary for the purpose of substantially assisting in preventing a terrorist act occurring.
		A terrorist act must be imminent and, in any event, be expected to occur at some time in the next 14 days.
		OR
		The police officer or issuing authority is satisfied, on reasonable grounds, that:
		• a terrorist act has occurred within the last 28 days;
		• it is necessary to detain the person to preserve evidence in Queensland or elsewhere of, or relating to, the terrorist act; and
		• detaining the person for the period for which the person is to be detained under the order is reasonably necessary for the purpose of preserving the evidence.
	South Australia Terrorism (Preventative Detention) Act 2005 s. 6(3)(4)	The police officer or issuing authority suspects, on reasonable grounds, that the person:
		• will engage in a terrorist act;
		• possesses a thing that is connected with the preparation for, or the engagement of a person in, a terrorist act; or
		• has done an act in preparation for, or in planning, a terrorist act; and

(continued)

Table 4.3 (continued)

Key elements	Jurisdiction, act and section	Legislative requirements
		the police officer or issuing authority is satisfied on reasonable grounds that making the order would substantially assist in preventing a terrorist act occurring and detaining the subject for the period for which the subject is to be detained under the order is reasonably necessary for the purposes of preventing a terrorist act.
		The terrorist act must be one that is imminent and must be one that is expected to occur, in any event, at some time in the next 14 days.
		OR
		A terrorist act has occurred within the last 28 days and the police officer or issuing authority is satisfied on reasonable grounds that:
		• it is necessary to detain the subject to preserve evidence of, or relating to, the terrorist act; and
		• detaining the subject for the period for which the person is to be detained under the order is reasonably necessary for the purpose of preserving evidence of, or relating to, the terrorist act.
	Tasmania Terrorism (Preventative Detention) Act 2005 s. 7(1)(2)	The Supreme Court or the senior police officer is satisfied, on reasonable grounds, that the person:
		• will engage in a terrorist act;
		• possesses or has under his or her control (whether solely or jointly with any other person) a thing that is connected with the preparation for, or the engagement of a person in, a terrorist act; or

Key elements	Jurisdiction, act and section	Legislative requirements
		• has done an act in preparation for, or in planning, a terrorist act; and
		the Supreme Court or the senior police officer is satisfied, on reasonable grounds, that making the order would substantially assist in preventing a terrorist act occurring and detaining the person for the period for which he or she is to be detained under the order is reasonably necessary for the purpose of preventing a terrorist act.
		OR
		The Supreme Court or the senior police officer is satisfied, on reasonable grounds, that:
		• a terrorist act has occurred within the last 28 days;
		• it is necessary to detain the person to preserve evidence of, or relating to, the terrorist act; and
		• detaining the person for the period for which he or she is to be detained under the order is reasonably necessary for the purpose of preserving evidence of, or relating to, the terrorist act.
		A terrorist act referred to must be one that is imminent and that is expected to occur, in any event, at some time in the next 14 days.
	Victoria Terrorism (Community Protection) Act 2003 s. 13E(1)(a)	The Supreme Court is satisfied, on reasonable grounds, that the person:
		• will engage in a terrorist act;
		• possesses or has under his or her control (whether solely or jointly with any other person) a thing that is connected with the preparation for, or the engagement of a person in, a terrorist act; or

(continued)

Table 4.3 (continued)

Key elements	Jurisdiction, act and section	Legislative requirements
		• has done an act in preparation for, or planning, a terrorist act; and
		the Supreme Court is satisfied, on reasonable grounds, that making the order would substantially assist in preventing a terrorist act occurring and detaining the person for the period for which he or she is to be detained under the order is reasonably necessary for the purpose of preventing a terrorist act.
		OR
		The Supreme Court is satisfied, on reasonable grounds, that:
		• a terrorist act has occurred within the last 28 days;
		• it is necessary to detain the person to preserve evidence of, or relating to, the terrorist act; and
		• detaining the person for the period for which he or she is to be detained under the order is reasonably necessary for the purpose of preserving evidence of, or relating to, the terrorist act.
		A terrorist act must be one that is imminent and that is expected to occur, in any event, at some time in the next 14 days.
	Western Australia Terrorism (Preventative Detention) Act 2006 s. 9; s. 13(1)(b)(i)	The legislative provisions apply to:
		• "a person to whom section 9 applies," meaning the person is going to engage in a terrorist act;
		• a person who possesses a thing that is connected with the preparation for, or the engagement of a person in, a terrorist act; or
		• a person who has done an act in preparation for, or planning, a terrorist act;
		and making a preventative detention order in relation to the person would substantially assist in preventing a terrorist act occurring.

100

Key elements	Jurisdiction, act and section	Legislative requirements
		The terrorist act must be one that is imminent and that is expected to occur, in any event, at some time in the next 14 days.
		The issuing authority is satisfied, on reasonable grounds, that:
		• the person is a person to whom section 9 applies; and • detaining the person for the period for which the person is to be detained under the order is reasonably necessary for the purpose of substantially assisting in preventing a terrorist act occurring, or preserving any evidence referred to.
	United Kingdom Terrorism Act 2000 s. 41(1) Sch 8 s. 32	Initially, a constable may arrest without a warrant a person whom he reasonably suspects to be a terrorist.
		A warrant of further detention may be issued by a judicial authority only if satisfied that:
		• there are reasonable grounds for believing that the further detention of the person to whom the application relates is necessary to obtain relevant evidence whether by questioning him or otherwise or to preserve relevant evidence; and • the investigation in connection with which the person is detained is being conducted diligently and expeditiously.
		"Relevant evidence" means, in relation to the person to whom the application relates, evidence which relates to his commission of an offence [defined as as terrorist offence], or indicates that he is a person concerned in the commission, preparation, or instigation of acts of terrorism.

(continued)

101

Table 4.3 (continued)

Key elements	Jurisdiction, act and section	Legislative requirements
	United States Detention, Treatment and Trial of Certain Non-Citizens in the War Against Terrorism Executive Order § 2(a)	The term "individual subject to this order" shall mean any individual who is not a United States citizen with respect to whom [the President] determine[s] from time to time in writing that there is reason to believe that such individual, at the relevant times, • is or was a member of the organization known as al-Qaeda; • has engaged in, aided or abetted, or conspired to commit, acts of international terrorism, or acts in preparation therefor, that have caused, threaten to cause, or have as their aim to cause, injury to or adverse effects on the United States, its citizens, national security, foreign policy, or economy; or • has knowingly harbored one or more individuals described [above]; and it is in the interest of the United States that such individual be subject to this order.

	United States
	Immigration and Nationality Act 1952 § 1226a(a)(3)
		• Individual is not a US citizen
		• Reasonable grounds to believe individual:
		
		  • entered the US to engage solely, principally, or incidentally in espionage, sabotage or violent/forceful/unlawful control or overthrow of the US government
		
		  OR
		
		  • has, is, or is likely to engage in a terrorist activity, has incited a terrorist activity, is a member or representative of a terrorist organization, has received military training by a terrorist organization, or is the spouse/child of an individual engaging in the above behaviour in the last five years
		
		  OR

Key elements	Jurisdiction, act and section	Legislative requirements
		• is engaged in any other activity that endangers US national security.
Duration: initial/interim	**Northern Territory** **South Australia** **Western Australia** **United States** Detention, Treatment and Trial of Certain Non-Citizens in the War Against Terrorism Executive Order	No initial/interim orders
	Australia (Federal) Criminal Code s. 105.10(5)	The period as extended, or further extended, must end no later than 24 hours after the person is first taken into custody under the order.
	Australian Capital Territory Terrorism (Extraordinary Temporary Powers) Act 2006 ss 20(6), 23(3)(a)	The date and time fixed must be no later than 24 hours after the interim order is made. The period as extended, or further extended, must be stated in the order and must end no later than 24 hours after the person is first detained under the order.
	New South Wales Terrorism (Police Powers) Act 2002 s. 26L	48 hours (no possible extensions). An interim preventative detention order ceases to have effect if the Supreme Court has not heard and determined the application in respect of which the interim order was made within 48 hours after the person was first taken into custody under the interim order.
	Queensland Terrorism (Preventative Detention) Act 2005 s. 17(5)	The period of time stated in the order must not be more than the prescribed 24 hour period.
	Tasmania Terrorism (Preventative Detention) Act 2005 s. 9(3)	The maximum period that may be specified in an interim preventative detention order made by the Supreme Court as the period during which a person may be detained under the order is 48 hours.

(continued)

Table 4.3 (continued)

Key elements	Jurisdiction, act and section	Legislative requirements
	Victoria Terrorism (Community Protection) Act 2003 s. 13G(2); 13E(6)	The maximum period that may be specified in an interim preventative detention order made by the Supreme Court as the period during which a person may be detained under the order is 48 hours.
	United Kingdom Terrorism Act 2000 s. 41(3)	A person detained under this section shall (unless detained under any other power) be released not later than the end of the period of 48 hours.
	United States Immigration and Nationality Act 1952 § 1226a(a)(5)	The Attorney-General shall place an alien detained under paragraph (1) in removal proceedings, or shall charge the alien with a criminal offence, not later than seven days after the commencement of such detention. If the requirement of the preceding sentence is not satisfied, the Attorney-General shall release the alien.
Maximum duration: final	**Australia** (Federal) Criminal Code s. 105.14(6)	The period as extended, or further extended, must end no later than 48 hours after the person is first taken into custody under the initial preventative detention order.
	Australian Capital Territory Terrorism (Extraordinary Temporary Powers) Act 2006 s. 21(3)(a)(b)	The end time for any other preventative detention order must be no later than seven days after the person is first detained under the order; and no later than 14 days after the person is first taken into custody and detained, or detained, under any preventative detention order, or corresponding preventative detention order, made on the same basis for the same terrorist act.

Key elements	Jurisdiction, act and section	Legislative requirements
	New South Wales Terrorism (Police Powers) Act 2002 s. 26K(2)	The maximum period for which a person may be detained under a preventative detention order (other than an interim order) is 14 days. That maximum period is reduced by any period of actual detention under a related order against the person in relation to the same terrorist act.
	Northern Territory Terrorism (Emergency Powers) Act s. 21K(1)	The object of this Part is to allow a person to be taken into custody and detained for a short period of time in order to prevent a terrorist act occurring in the near future or preserve evidence of, or relating to, a recent terrorist act.
	Queensland Terrorism (Preventative Detention) Act 2005 ss 25(6), 31(3)	The period of time stated under subsection (4)(b) must not be more than the prescribed 14 day period. The period as extended, or further extended, must end no later than the prescribed 14 day period.
	South Australia Terrorism (Preventative Detention) Act 2005 s. 10(5)(a)(b)	The period of time specified in the order must not exceed – if the issuing authority is a senior police officer – 24 hours and if the issuing authority is a judge – 14 days.
	Tasmania Terrorism (Preventative Detention) Act 2005 ss 8(3), 9(1)	The maximum period that may be specified in a preventative detention order made by a senior police officer as the period during which a person may be detained under the order is 24 hours. Subject to section 9, the period of time specified in the order must not exceed 14 days.

(continued)

Table 4.3 (continued)

Key elements	Jurisdiction, act and section	Legislative requirements
		Subject to subsection (3), the maximum period (including that period, as extended, or further extended) that may be specified in a preventative detention order made by the Supreme Court as the period during which a person may be detained under the order is 14 days less any period during which the person is actually detained under:
		(a) a preventative detention order made by a senior police officer; or
		(b) an order for the person's detention made under a corresponding preventative detention law – on the same basis.
	Western Australia Terrorism (Preventative Detention) Act 2006 s. 13(3)	The permitted detention period must not exceed 14 days.
	United Kingdom Terrorism Act 2000 s. 41(3) Sch. 8, s. 32	A warrant of further detention may be issued by a judicial authority of up to 28 days.
	United States Detention, Treatment and Trial of Certain Non-Citizens in the War Against Terrorism Executive Order	Unlimited
	United States Immigration and Nationality Act 1952 § 1226a(a)(6)	An alien detained solely under paragraph (1) who has not been removed under section 1231(a)(1)(A) of this title, and whose removal is unlikely in the reasonably foreseeable future, may be detained for additional periods of up to six months only if the release of the alien will threaten the national security of the United States or the safety of the community or any person.

106

Key elements	Jurisdiction, act and section	Legislative requirements
Disclosure offences – detainees	**Australian Capital Territory** **New South Wales** **United Kingdom** **United States**	None
	Australia (Federal) Criminal Code s. 105.41(1)	A person (the subject) commits an offence if: (a) the subject is being detained under a preventative detention order; (b) the subject discloses to another person: (i) the fact that a preventative detention order has been made in relation to the subject; (ii) the fact that the subject is being detained; or (iii) the period for which the subject is being detained; (c) the disclosure occurs while the subject is being detained under the order; and (d) the disclosure is not one that the subject is entitled to make under section 105.36, 105.37, or 105.39. Penalty: imprisonment for five years.
	Northern Territory Terrorism (Emergency Powers) Act s. 21ZO(1)	A person (the detainee) commits an offence if: (a) the detainee is being detained under a preventative detention order; (b) the detainee discloses to another person: (i) the fact that a preventative detention order has been made in relation to the detainee; (ii) the fact that the detainee is being detained; (iii) the place where the detainee is being detained; or (iv) the fact that a prohibited contact order has been made in relation to the detainee's detention;

(continued)

Table 4.3 (continued)

Key elements	Jurisdiction, act and section	Legislative requirements
		(c) the disclosure occurs while the detainee is being detained under the order; and
		(d) the disclosure is not one that the detainee is entitled to make under section 21ZI, 21ZJ, 21ZK, or 21ZL.
		Maximum penalty: imprisonment for five years.
	South Australia Terrorism (Preventative Detention) Act 2005 s. 41(1)	A person (the subject) commits an offence if:
		(a) the subject is being detained under a preventative detention order;
		(b) the subject intentionally discloses to another person:
		(i) the fact that a preventative detention order has been made in relation to the subject;
		(ii) the fact that the subject is being detained; or
		(iii) the period for which the subject is being detained under the order;
		(c) the disclosure occurs while the subject is being detained under the order; and
		(d) the disclosure is not one that the subject is entitled to make under section 36, 37, or 39.
		Maximum penalty: imprisonment for five years.
	Tasmania Terrorism (Preventative Detention) Act 2005 s. 38(1)	A person (the "subject") commits an offence if:
		(a) the subject is being detained under a preventative detention order;
		(b) the subject intentionally discloses to another person:
		(i) the fact that a preventative detention order has been made in relation to the subject;

Key elements	Jurisdiction, act and section	Legislative requirements
		(ii) the fact that the subject is being detained; or
		(iii) the fact that a prohibited contact order has been made in relation to the subject's detention;
		(c) the disclosure occurs while the subject is being detained under the order; and
		(d) the disclosure is not one that the subject is entitled to make under section 33, 34, or 36.
		Penalty: imprisonment for a term not exceeding five years.
	Victoria Terrorism (Community Protection) Act 2003 s. 13ZJ(1)	A person (the subject) commits an offence if:
		(a) the subject is being detained under a preventative detention order;
		(b) the subject intentionally discloses to another person:
		(i) the fact that a preventative detention order has been made in relation to the subject;
		(ii) the fact that the subject is being detained; or
		(iii) the fact that a prohibited contact order has been made in relation to the subject's detention;
		(c) the disclosure occurs while the subject is being detained under the order; and
		(d) the disclosure is not one that the subject is entitled to make under section 13ZD, 13ZE, 13ZF, or 13ZH.
		Level 6 imprisonment (five years maximum).

(continued)

Table 4.3 (continued)

Key elements	Jurisdiction, act and section	Legislative requirements
	Western Australia Terrorism (Preventative Detention) Act 2006 s. 46(1)	If the detainee, while in detention under the PDO, discloses to another person:
		(a) the fact that a preventative detention order has been made in relation to the detainee;
		(b) the fact that the detainee is in detention; or
		(c) the period for which the detainee is to be kept in detention,
		the detainee commits a crime unless the disclosure is one that the detainee is entitled to make under section 42, 43, or 45.
		Penalty: imprisonment for five years.
Disclosure offences – others	**Australian Capital Territory** **New South Wales** **United Kingdom** **United States**	None
	Australia (Federal) Criminal Code ss 105.41, 105.35	Offences replicated for:
		• *Lawyer* contacted by the individual.
	Northern Territory Terrorism (Emergency Powers) Act s. 21ZO(2)-(9)	• *Parent/guardian* of individual who discloses to another person who is not entitled to have contact with the individual (including another parent/guardian who has not had contact with the individual). NB parent/guardian can tell another person that the individual is safe but not contactable.
	Queensland Terrorism (Preventative Detention) Act 2005 ss 64–68	
	South Australia Terrorism (Preventative Detention) Act 2005 s. 41(2)–(7)	• *Interpreter* monitoring the individual's contact with another person.
	Tasmania Terrorism (Preventative Detention) Act 2005 s. 38(2)–(7)	• *Recipient of information* obtained improperly under this Act. • *Monitor* monitoring the individual's contact with another person.

Key elements	Jurisdiction, act and section	Legislative requirements
	Victoria Terrorism (Community Protection) Act 2003 s. 13ZJ(2)–(10)	Exceptions arise for proceedings, applications, and complaints about the PDO, treatment of the individual, or the performance of the PDO etc.
	Western Australia Terrorism (Preventative Detention) Act 2006 s. 46(2)–(9)	Generally, it is permissible to inform others that individual is safe but not contactable.
Proceedings Open/Closed	**Australia** (Federal) **Australian Capital Territory Victoria United States**	Proceedings open to the public unless specific order to the contrary
	Queensland Terrorism (Preventative Detention) Act 2005 s. 76	Despite any rule or practice to the contrary, proceedings under this Act are not to be conducted in public nor publicized in any public list of the Supreme Court's business.
	New South Wales Terrorism (Police Powers) Act 2002 s. 26P	Any such proceedings must be heard in the absence of the public.
	Northern Territory Terrorism (Emergency Powers) Act s. 21U(2)	The proceeding must be heard in the absence of the public.
	South Australia Terrorism (Preventative Detention) Act 2005 s. 47	Despite any rule or practice to the contrary, proceedings under this Act are not to be conducted in public nor publicized in any public list of the Supreme Court's business.
	Tasmania Terrorism (Preventative Detention) Act 2005 s. 50	Any such proceedings must be heard in the absence of the public.
	Western Australia Terrorism (Preventative Detention) Act 2006 s. 53	Despite any rule or practice to the contrary, proceedings under this Act are not to be conducted in public nor publicized in any public list of the Supreme Court's business.

(continued)

Table 4.3 (continued)

Key elements	Jurisdiction, act and section	Legislative requirements
	United States Detention, Treatment and Trial of Certain Non-Citizens in the War Against Terrorism Executive Order § 7(b)(2)	With respect to any individual subject to this order, military tribunals have exclusive jurisdiction with respect to offences by the individual. The individual shall not be privileged to seek any remedy or maintain any proceeding, directly or indirectly, or to have any such remedy or proceeding sought on the individual's behalf, in: (i) any court of the United States, or any State thereof; (ii) any court of any foreign nation; or (iii) any international tribunal.

relating to investigation by the Australian Security Intelligence Organisation (McSherry 2011).

At an international level, there has been difficulty finding a definition of terrorism that does not outlaw the struggle for self-determination. Terrorism was not included as an international crime within the jurisdiction of the International Criminal Court partly because parties at the Conference that adopted the Rome Statute could not agree on a definition (Kittichaisaree 2001: 227). M. Cherif Bassiouni (1999: 771) has pointed out that the "search for an internationally agreed upon definition may well be a futile and unnecessary one." He states (1999: 771) that one of the principal problems in defining terrorism "lies in the fundamental values that are at stake in the acceptance or rejection of terrorist-inspiring violence as a means of accomplishing a given goal, particularly when that goal reflects certain values."

Under section 100.1 of the Australian Criminal Code, a terrorist act can range from threatening or causing serious physical harm to a person, causing death, or endangering life, to serious interfering with an electronic system, providing it is done with the intention of "advancing a political, religious or ideological cause," or with the intention of coercing or influencing through intimidation a government or intimidating the public or section of the public.

The United States definition is similar in its broad scope. Section 802 of the Uniting and Strengthening America by Providing Appropriate Tools Required to Intercept and Obstruct Terrorism Act of 2001 (better known as the PATRIOT Act) amended the definition of "domestic terrorism" within Title 18 of the United States Code. Section 2331(5) of Title 18 now defines "domestic terrorism" as activities that "involve acts dangerous to human life" that "appear to be intended":

(i) to intimidate or coerce a civilian population;
(ii) to influence the policy of a government by intimidation or coercion; or
(iii) to affect the conduct of a government by mass destruction, assassination, or kidnapping.

The Australian legislation specifically excludes "advocacy, protest, dissent or industrial action" from the definition of terrorist act (s. 100.1(3)(a)), whereas the United States definition does not list any exceptions, leading some commentators to criticize it as too broad (Golder and Williams 2004: 294).

In Australia, the Anti-Terrorism Act (No 2) 2005 inserted a new Division 105 into the Commonwealth Criminal Code allowing for "preventative-detention orders." Under section 105.4(4) an order may be made if the following criteria are met:

(a) there are reasonable grounds to suspect that the subject:

   (i) will engage in a terrorist act;
   (ii) possesses a thing that is connected with the preparation for, or the engagement of a person in, a terrorist act; or
   (iii) has done an act in preparation for, or planning, a terrorist act;

(b) making the order would substantially assist in preventing a terrorist act occurring; and
(c) detaining the subject for the period for which the person is to be detained under the order is reasonably necessary for the purpose referred to in paragraph (b).

In addition, section 105.4(5) requires that the terrorist act be imminent and expected to occur "in any event, at some time in the next 14 days." The period that a person may be detained under such an order is 24 hours, although in limited circumstances, a continuation of the order may be made by a judicial officer for up to 48 hours (section 105.12). As set out in Table 4.3, some state laws that are based on the federal scheme enable longer periods of detention of up to 14 days.

If a terrorist act has already occurred within the last 28 days, section 105.5(6) enables the preventive detention of a person on the grounds that it is "reasonably necessary" to preserve relevant evidence. Interestingly, it is this provision rather than section 105.4 that has attracted criticism on the basis that detaining those who have not committed or are suspected of being about to commit a crime infringes the right to liberty and presumption of innocence (Conte 2010: 581).

These particular provisions have not been the subject of constitutional challenges in Australia, but given the High Court of Australia's approach to control orders, which is discussed in the next chapter, it appears likely that these provisions would be upheld "if implemented only when necessary and by proportional means" (Conte 2010: 581). The Council of Australian Governments (2013: 68) has, however, recently recommended that preventive detention laws be repealed across Australian jurisdictions.

In the United States, section 1226a of the Immigration and Nationality Act (as amended by the PATRIOT Act) enables the Attorney-General to detain a non-citizen (an "alien" in legislative terminology) who is certified as a suspected terrorist for up to six months at a time, pending a decision to remove him or her from the United States.

In addition, under executive orders, suspected terrorists who are referred to as "enemy combatants" may also be subject to preventive detention. On November 13, 2001, President Bush issued a Military Order for the Detention, Treatment and Trial of Certain Non-Citizens in the War against Terrorism, which set up military commissions. Persons subject to this Military Order were described as not privileged to "seek any remedy or maintain any proceeding, directly or indirectly" in federal or state court, the court of any foreign nation, or any international tribunal (Military Order: § 7(b)).

The powers given to these commissions were tested in *Hamdi v Rumsfeld* (2004) and *Rasul v Bush* (2004). In *Hamdi v Rumsfeld* (2004), eight of the nine justices of the Supreme Court held that the executive branch did not have the power to hold indefinitely a citizen of the United States without due process protections and that such citizens had the right to challenge their enemy combatant status before a judge.

In *Rasul v Bush* (2004), the United States Supreme Court by a majority of six to three held that the Supreme Court's power to issue a writ of habeas corpus under the United States Code (28 USC § 2241) entitled the detainees to challenge the validity of their detention.

In response to these decisions, the Deputy Secretary of Defense made an Order on July 7, 2004 setting up the Combatant Status Review Tribunal to check on the assignment of "enemy combatant" status. The Defense Department also established Administrative Review Procedures for Enemy Combatants on May 11, 2004 that enables annual reviews to check whether detainees still pose a sufficient threat to justify detention.

The Detainee Treatment Act 2005 limited judicial review to the procedures rather than the merits of decisions by the Combatant Status Review Tribunal. The United States Supreme Court in *Hamdan v Rumsfeld* (2006), by a majority of five justices to three, limited the scope of this legislation to future cases only and held that the military commissions set up under the 2001 Military Order were illegal under the Uniform Code of Military Justice (10 US Code §§ 801–941) and Article 3 of the Third Geneva Convention that sets out the minimal protections to be afforded to prisoners in relation to non-international conflicts. This case was particularly significant in ruling that enemy combatants were protected by the Geneva Conventions that consist of four treaties, and three additional protocols, which set out the standards of international law for the humanitarian treatment of the victims and prisoners of war.

Subsequently, the Military Commissions Act 2006 (PL 109–366, 10 US Code §. 948a) invested the President with broad discretion to determine whether an individual was an "unlawful enemy combatant" and reasserted military commissions to try them (§§ 948a(1), 950v(24)).

In *Boumediene v Bush* (2008), the Supreme Court held that the Detainee Treatment Act 2005 and the Military Commissions Act 2006 failed to provide adequate substitutes to the constitutionally guaranteed right of a habeus corpus review.

In 2009, President Obama temporarily halted military commissions to review their procedures as well as the detention programme at Guantanamo Bay in general. Subsequently, the Military Commissions Act 2009 (PL 111-84) amended Chapter 47A of Title 10, United States Code and set out extensive procedural rules for future hearings (Elsea 2010).

The National Defense Authorization Act for Fiscal Year 2012, which was passed on December 31, 2011, also contains provisions regarding the preventive detention of terrorist suspects. Section 1021 refers to "the authority of the President to use all necessary and appropriate force pursuant to the Authorization for Use of Military Force (Public Law 107–40; 50 U.S.C. 1541) includ[ing] the authority for the Armed Forces of the United States to detain covered persons . . . pending disposition under the law of war."

"Covered persons" include:

- a person who planned, authorized, committed, or aided the terrorist attacks that occurred on September 11, 2001, or harbored those responsible for those attacks;
- a person who was a part of or substantially supported al-Qaeda, the Taliban, or associated forces that are engaged in hostilities against the United States or its coalition partners, including any person who has committed a belligerent act or has directly supported such hostilities in aid of such enemy forces.

Section 1022 of the Act allows for "detention under the law of war without trial until the end of the hostilities authorized by the Authorization for Use of Military Force." It is unclear how the Act applies to United States citizens and lawful aliens.

President Obama issued a statement on December 31, 2011 noting that he had signed the Bill to ensure defence funding "despite having serious reservations with certain provisions that regulate the detention, interrogation, and prosecution of suspected terrorists" and that section 1022 was "ill-conceived and will do nothing to improve the security of the United States" (White House Office of the Press Secretary 2011).

The United States powers for the preventive detention of suspected terrorists are thus far-reaching and remain the most extensive in common law jurisdictions.

CONCLUSION

Kenneth Donaldson's detention in the Florida State Hospital for fourteen and a half years provided the impetus for linking mental illness with dangerousness in mental health laws in the United States. The risk of harm to others remains an important criterion for admission to mental health facilities, although in some jurisdictions, this criterion exists as an alternative to risk of harm to self or the need for treatment.

The protection of the community also underlies preventive detention and supervision schemes relating to serious sex offenders and suspected terrorists. These laws have been tested through the courts that have set out the parameters of such schemes, with the majority being upheld as constitutional.

A major exception to the general acceptance of such schemes by the courts has been the repeal of the United Kingdom scheme for the preventive detention of suspected terrorists following the House of Lords decision in *A and others v Secretary of State for the Home Department* (2004), which is discussed in Chapter 7. This can be viewed in the historical context of previous schemes of detention without trial in the United Kingdom. For example, after a campaign of violence by the Irish Republican Army, the Northern Ireland government brought into operation extrajudicial measures of detention and internment of suspected terrorists.

The Civil Authorities (Special Powers) Act (Northern Ireland) 1922 was an enabling Act under which Regulations could be made and brought into operation. It empowered the Minister of Home Affairs for Northern Ireland, and later, the Secretary of State for Northern Ireland, to take all such steps and issue all such orders as might be necessary for preserving peace and maintaining order. Under Regulation 12(1), which commenced on August 9, 1971, suspected terrorists could be interned indefinitely. Around 600 suspects were held between 1971 and 1975, many of whom were brutally treated as set out in the European Court of Human Rights decision of *Ireland v United Kingdom* (1978). These executive powers were allowed to lapse and were eventually terminated by the Northern Ireland (Emergency Provisions) Act 1998 after a report by Lord Lloyd (1996) recommended other options to combat terrorism. Attempts to revive these executive powers in 2000 were resisted (Donohue 2001; Walker 2011).

Ironically, the use of powers of internment in Northern Ireland was a factor leading to more rather than less attacks by the Irish Republican Army (Donahue 1980: 397). This history may have been a factor in the replacement of the system of preventive detention in the United Kingdom with control orders that are discussed in the next chapter. The current reliance on executive orders in the Unites States to detain "enemy combatants" can be viewed as an echo of the use of powers of internment in Northern Ireland. While the parameters of executive powers can still be limited by the courts, such powers are often much broader than legislative schemes that take into account due process considerations.

As suggested in Chapter 2, there are cycles in preventive detention and supervision schemes with certain groups being targeted at different times. This chapter has provided a broad overview of the laws relating to current preventive detention and supervision schemes and some of the relevant court decisions. If history is any guide, some will fall out of favour in due course with others emerging to take their place. For example, the Council of Australian Governments (2013: 68) has recommended that preventive detention laws in relation to suspected terrorists be repealed. On the other hand, the Northern Territory government has introduced its Serious Sex Offenders Bill 2013 into Parliament and the New South Wales government has foreshadowed expanding its preventive detention scheme to cover "high risk violent offenders" as well as serious sex offenders via its Crimes (Serious Sex Offenders) Amendment Bill 2013.

The next chapter turns to supervision and control orders in the community.

5

SUPERVISION, CONTROL, AND COMMUNITY TREATMENT ORDERS

INTRODUCTION: JOSEPH "JACK" THOMAS

Joseph "Jack" Terrence Thomas was born in Williamstown, a seaside suburb of Melbourne, Australia in 1973. He was interested in the performing arts and took ballet classes for some years. He enrolled to study dance at the Victorian College of the Arts, but was rejected as a dancer for being too stocky (Neighbour 2006). Thomas then became an apprentice chef and in his late teens began to look into different religious beliefs. He was introduced to Islam by his best friend from school and, after joining him in a fast for the month of Ramadan, he decided to convert.

Thomas was encouraged by his friends to marry a Muslim woman. After a short correspondence, Thomas flew to South Africa and married Maryati, the daughter of an Indonesian policeman, on the day they first met. Maryati had degrees in arts and information systems from Monash University in Australia and was studying in South Africa at the time of the marriage. They eventually set up home in the Melbourne suburb of Brunswick where Thomas, through his wife, became involved with members of the local Indonesian community, some of whom were followers of the group Jemaah Islamiyah ("Islamic Congregation") (Neighbour 2006).

Jemaah Islamiyah's aim is to establish a regional Islamic caliphate (a political system governed by a "caliph" or Islamic spiritual leader) in Southeast Asia. At the time Thomas became involved with the group, it had not yet turned to terrorist activities to pursue this aim. Jemaah Islamiyah began its involvement with terrorism after one of its founders, the late Abdullah Sungkar, established contact with al-Qaeda, the militant organization founded by Osama bin Laden. Through his contacts in Jemaah Islamiyah, Thomas became interested in the fight by the Taliban, the then rulers of Afghanistan, against the Northern Alliance, which comprised a number of anti-Taliban factions in the northeast corner of the country.

In March 2001, Thomas journeyed to Kabul, Afghanistan, with his family in order to join the Taliban's fight. Through his network in Melbourne, he was introduced to a Taliban commander and he was then sent to the training site, Camp Faruq, to undergo basic military training. Osama bin Laden frequently visited Camp Faruq and Thomas apparently saw him there three times and once shook hands with him (Neighbour 2006). Thomas spent a week on the frontline of the fight with the Northern Alliance, but did not take part in combat. He stayed in Afghanistan for another four months and had contact with the most senior al-Qaeda leaders.

After the terrorist attacks in the United States on September 11, 2001, Thomas organized for his wife and daughter to fly to Indonesia, but stayed behind to fight the Americans before fleeing into Pakistan after Afghanistan descended into chaos. He was escorted into Pakistan by al-Qaeda member, Abu Zubaida, who was known as a top recruiter for bin Laden. Thomas offered in return to "do some work" for Abu Zubaida (Neighbour 2006).

Thomas spent the following year in Pakistan staying in safe houses used by al-Qaeda and its Pakistani offshoot, Laskar-e-Toiba in Karachi and Lahore. Eventually, Thomas was captured by Pakistani authorities at an airport in Karachi as he tried to return to Australia with his passport that had been altered in an attempt to cover his movements. He had an airline ticket for travel to Australia and a little over $3,800AUD in cash. Thomas was kept in custody between January 4, 2003 and June 6, 2003.

Thomas later stated that he had been held for about two weeks on his own in a cell that was like a "dog kennel about the size of a toilet", with open bars and a gate that exposed him to the elements (*R v Thomas* 2006: para. [12]). He was blindfolded and hooded when interviewed by a Pakistani official and two Americans. On a number of occasions, the Pakistani officials told him: "We're outside the law. No-one will hear you scream" (*R v Thomas* 2006: para. [14]). He was then flown to Islamabad where he eventually had his first contact with an Australian official on January 22, 2003.

During the ensuing interviews, the Pakistani interrogators repeatedly told Thomas that his fate depended on his cooperation. If he cooperated he would be able to return to his family; if not, he would be kept there indefinitely. The Australians present made no attempt to distance themselves from these statements, but impliedly endorsed them. Thomas was not given the opportunity to contact a lawyer nor was he given the choice to remain silent.

There were six joint Australian Federal Police/Australian Security Intelligence Organisation interviews conducted over that period. Thomas admitted in an interview conducted by two members of the Australian

Federal Police on March 8, 2003 that he had altered his passport in order to conceal the amount of time he had spent in Pakistan because he was concerned that he might be asked about his associations and activities while he had been there. He also told the police that the ticket and money had been given to him by Khaled bin Attash, who was an associate of Osama bin Laden and a high-ranking member of al-Qaeda.

Thomas was eventually allowed to return to Australia on June 6, 2003. Some 17 months later, on November 18, 2004, Thomas was arrested and charged with two counts of intentionally providing resources to a terrorist organization, one count of receiving funds from a terrorist organization and possessing a falsified Australian passport. He was acquitted of the first two counts, but found guilty of receiving funds and possessing a falsified passport by a jury in the Supreme Court of Victoria on February 26, 2006. On March 31, 2006, he was sentenced to five years' imprisonment, with a minimum non-parole period of two years for receiving funds from a terrorist organization and given a concurrent sentence of one year's imprisonment for the possession offence (*DPP {C th} v Thomas* 2006).

Thomas' convictions were quashed by the Victorian Court of Appeal on August 18, 2006, after it found that his interview with the Australian Federal Police had not been voluntary and was unfair and contrary to public policy (*R v Thomas* 2006). The Court was of the opinion that the circumstances in which the interview was conducted amounted to pressure of a kind calculated to overbear Thomas' will and, therefore, the admissions made were not voluntary and accordingly inadmissible. After further submissions, on December 20, 2006, the Court of Appeal ordered a retrial (*R v Thomas (No 3)* 2006).

Ten days after Thomas' convictions were quashed, Jack Thomas became the first Australian citizen to be made the subject of an interim "control order" under Division 104 of the Criminal Code (Cth). A Federal Magistrate granted an interim control order on an application by the Australian Federal Police with the consent of the then Attorney-General, Philip Ruddock. The order was made *ex parte*, that is, without Thomas or any legal representative for him being present. The conditions of the interim control order included a curfew so that Thomas was confined to his house between midnight and 5 am, he had to report to police three days a week, was banned from leaving Australia without permission, and was restricted in what phones he could use. He was also prohibited from acquiring or manufacturing explosives. The condition that was widely reported by the media was that he was also banned from any contact with members of banned terrorist groups including Osama bin Laden whose whereabouts at that time were unknown. This control order was subjected to an appeal to the High Court of Australia, which is discussed below.

Control orders for suspected terrorists are but one example of a wide range of binding civil preventive orders. Peter Ramsay (2009: 109) has pointed out some general features of such orders:

- they are grounded in civil proceedings, or administratively with some judicial supervision;
- they are granted on satisfaction of broad and vaguely defined conduct;
- their terms may be any prohibition (or mandatory term in some cases) deemed necessary to prevent future instances of the broad and vaguely defined conduct on which they are grounded;
- breach of any of their terms is a criminal offence of strict liability.

These features certainly apply to control orders for suspected terrorists and a range of preventive orders existing in the United Kingdom such as antisocial behaviour orders (ASBOs), criminal ASBOs, risk of sexual harm orders, sexual offence prevention orders, violent offender orders, and serious crime prevention orders. The Home Office (2012) has recommended the enactment of two new civil orders: criminal behaviour orders and crime prevention injunctions. There are also informal non-legislative "contracts" available in England and Wales that are known as "acceptable behaviour contracts" (Brown 2012). Control orders are also increasingly being used in Australia to curb the activities of "bikie gangs" (McGarrity 2012).

Community treatment orders for those with severe mental illness do not fit the preventive mould in that they do not focus on prohibiting certain conduct, but mandate treatment. They may, however, contain restrictions such as setting out requirements for where the person is to live and limitations on his or her alcohol or drug consumption.

This chapter provides a broad overview of supervision orders for serious offenders, community treatment orders for those with severe mental illness, and ASBOs for those who have exhibited antisocial tendencies.

CONTROL ORDERS FOR SUSPECTED TERRORISTS

Only Australia and the United Kingdom have a system of control orders or measures in place for suspected terrorists. The Prevention of Terrorism Act 2005 (UK) came into force on March 11, 2005 and replaced the existing preventive detention scheme with control orders. This was a response to the House of Lords decision in *A and others v Secretary of State for the Home Department* (2004) in which seven justices held that the preventive detention provisions in the Anti-Terrorism, Crime and

Security Act 2001 were incompatible with the rights to liberty and non-discrimination. This case is explored in Chapter 7.

The control order regime set up in 2005 was abolished by the Terrorism Prevention and Investigation Measures Act 2011 after a review conducted in late 2010 (Home Office 2011) and replaced by "measures" that can still serve to restrict a person's liberty. In the time they were available, some 48 people were made subject to a control order and by the end of December 2010, there were eight people – all British citizens – on control orders (Home Office 2011: 36). The Home Office Review (2011: 37) pointed out that:

> Control order powers have always been controversial because they are imposed without the person on whom they are applied being convicted for the terrorist activity in which he is judged to be engaged, because of the use of closed material and because of the very intrusive restrictions that they can involve.

It concluded (2011: 39) that "an approach that scrapped control orders and introduced more precisely focused and targeted restrictions, supported by increased covert investigative resources, would mitigate risk while increasing civil liberties."

The terrorism prevention and investigation "measures" introduced by the 2011 Act in the United Kingdom are similar to control orders in that they impose restrictions in the absence of a criminal conviction or charge and "involve neither full disclosure nor the adversarial testing of accusations" (Walker and Horne 2012: 423). Some of the features of this scheme as set out in Schedule 1 of the 2011 Act are outlined in Table 5.1.

Under section 5, a two-year limit is placed on the imposition of measures on any individual. Any extension beyond two years must be based entirely on "new terrorism-related activity" (section 3(6)). Section 4(1) of the 2011 Act defines involvement in terrorism-related activity very broadly as any one or more of the following:

(a) the commission, preparation or instigation, of acts of terrorism;
(b) conduct which facilitates the commission, preparation or instigation of such acts, or which is intended to do so;
(c) conduct which gives encouragement to the commission, preparation or instigation of such acts, or which is intended to do so;
(d) conduct which gives support or assistances to individuals who are known or believed by the individual concerned to be involved in conduct falling within paragraphs (a) to (c) . . .

Table 5.1 Terrorism prevention and investigation measures under the Terrorism Prevention and Investigation Measures Act 2011 (UK)

Key elements	Legislative requirements
What kind of supervision Schedule 1	**Overnight residence measure** The Secretary of State may impose restrictions on the individual in relation to the residence in which the individual resides. In particular, [the Secretary of State may] impose:

(a) a requirement to reside at a specified residence;
(b) a requirement to give notice to the Secretary of State of the identity of any other individuals who reside (or will reside) at the specified residence;
(c) a requirement, applicable overnight between such hours as are specified, to remain at, or within, the specified residence.

Travel measure
The Secretary of State may impose restrictions on the individual leaving a specified area or travelling outside that area. The specified area must be one of the following areas:

(a) the United Kingdom (in any case);
(b) Great Britain (if the individual's place of residence is in Great Britain);
(c) Northern Ireland (if the individual's place of residence is in Northern Ireland).

Exclusion measure
The Secretary of State may impose restrictions on the individual entering a specified area or place, or a place or area of a specified description.

Movement directions measure
The Secretary of State may impose a requirement for the individual to comply with directions given by a constable in respect of the individual's movements (which may, in particular, include a restriction on movements).

Financial services measure
The Secretary of State may, in particular, impose any of the following requirements:

(a) a requirement not to hold any accounts, without the permission of the Secretary of State, other than the nominated account;
(b) a requirement to close, or to cease to have an interest in, accounts;
(c) a requirement to comply with specified conditions in relation to the holding of any account (including the nominated account) or any other use of financial services;
(d) a requirement not to possess, or otherwise control, cash over a total specified value without the permission of the Secretary of State. *(continued)*

Table 5.1 Continued

Key elements	Legislative requirements

Property measure: the Secretary of State may impose either or both of the following:

(a) restrictions on the individual in relation to the transfer of property to, or by, the individual; or
(b) requirements on the individual in relation to the disclosure of property.

The Secretary of State may, in particular, impose any of the following requirements:

(a) a requirement not to transfer money or other property to a person or place outside the United Kingdom without the permission of the Secretary of State;
(b) a requirement to give notice to the Secretary of State before transferring money or other property to a person or place outside the United Kingdom;
(c) a requirement to comply with any other specified conditions in relation to the transfer of property to, or by, the individual;
(d) a requirement to disclose to the Secretary of State such details as may be specified of any property that falls within sub-paragraph (3).

Electronic communication device measure

The Secretary of State may impose either or both of the following:

(a) restrictions on the individual's possession or use of electronic communication devices;
(b) requirements on the individual in relation to the possession or use of electronic communication devices by other persons in the individual's residence.

Association measure

The Secretary of State may impose restrictions on the individual's association or communication with other persons. The Secretary of State may, in particular, impose any of the following requirements:

(a) a requirement not to associate or communicate with specified persons, or specified descriptions of persons, without the permission of the Secretary of State;
(b) a requirement to give notice to the Secretary of State before associating or communicating with other persons (whether at all or in specified circumstances);
(c) a requirement to comply with any other specified conditions in connection with associating or communicating with other persons.

Work or studies measure

The Secretary of State may impose restrictions on the individual in relation to the individual's work or studies. The Secretary of State may, in particular, impose a requirement not to carry

Key elements	Legislative requirements

out – without the permission of the Secretary of State – specified work or work of a specified description, or specified studies or studies of a specified description.

Reporting measure
The Secretary of State may impose a requirement for the individual to report to such a police station, at such times and in such manner, as the Secretary of State may by notice require, and to comply with any directions given by a constable in relation to such reporting.

Photography measure
The Secretary of State may impose a requirement for the individual to allow photographs to be taken of the individual at such locations and at such times as the Secretary of State may by notice require.

Monitoring measure
The Secretary of State may impose requirements for the individual to cooperate with specified arrangements for enabling the individual's movements, communications, or other activities to be monitored by electronic or other means.

Who can order supervision
Schedule 1

Secretary of State, confirmed by the High Court.

Grounds for ordering supervision
ss 2–3

Imposition of terrorism prevention and investigation measures
The Secretary of State may by notice (a "TPIM notice") impose specified terrorism prevention and investigation measures on an individual if conditions A to E (below) are met.

Condition A is that the Secretary of State reasonably believes that the individual is, or has been, involved in terrorism-related activity (the "relevant activity").

Condition B is that some or all of the relevant activity is new terrorism-related activity.

Condition C is that the Secretary of State reasonably considers that it is necessary, for purposes connected with protecting members of the public from a risk of terrorism, for terrorism prevention and investigation measures to be imposed on the individual.

Condition D is that the Secretary of State reasonably considers that it is necessary, for purposes connected with preventing or restricting the individual's involvement in terrorism-related activity, for the specified terrorism prevention and investigation measures to be imposed on the individual.

Condition E is that the court gives the Secretary of State permission or the Secretary of State reasonably considers that the urgency of the case requires terrorism prevention and investigation measures to be imposed without obtaining such permission.

In *Secretary of State for the Home Department v BM* (2012), Justice Collins of the Administrative Court conducted the first review of a terrorism prevention measure under the 2011 Act. On January 13, 2012, the measure was imposed on BM, a 39-year-old British national, who had previously been the subject of a control order. Justice Collins upheld the measure and made some comments about the standard of proof that are explored in the next chapter.

The measure in *BM*'s case contained a restriction under Schedule 1 paragraph 1 of the 2011 Act that is entitled "Overnight residence measure." Paragraph 1(2) provides:

The Secretary of State may, in particular, impose any of the following:

(a) a requirement to reside at a specified residence; . . .
(b) a requirement to give notice to the Secretary of State of the identity of any other individuals who reside (or will reside) at the specified residence;
(c) a requirement, applicable overnight between such hours as are specified, to remain at, or within, the specified residence.

Justice Collins (2012: para. [51]) criticized the fact that there was no definition of "overnight" in the legislation and held (2012 para. [53]) that the term "should bear some relationship to the hours between which most people would regard it as reasonable to think that people might be at home, the evening having come to an end." He interpreted this to mean between the hours of 9 pm and 7 am.

There has not been a constitutional challenge to terrorism prevention and investigation measures to date and, given that the jurisprudence on previous control orders (outlined in Chapter 7) primarily dealt with the type of restrictions imposed rather than whether control orders of themselves breach the right to liberty, it may be that they will go unchallenged.

In Australia, control orders were introduced into the Criminal Code (Cth) by the Anti-Terrorism Act (No 2) 2005 (Cth). Only two people have been made the subject of control orders – Jack Thomas and David Hicks. Hicks, an Australian citizen, pleaded guilty to and was convicted by the United States Guantanamo Military Commission of providing "material support for terrorism," a war crime specified by the Military Commissions Act of 2006. He served part of his sentence in Australia and was made the subject of a control order after his release, but this expired in December 2008. The United States Court of Appeal for the District of Columbia Circuit subsequently ruled in *Hamdan v United States* (2012) that the conviction of Salim Hamdan be vacated on the grounds that providing material support for terrorism was not a war crime at the time he allegedly carried out certain activities that led to the charge and because the Military

Commissions Act could not be interpreted as sanctioning retroactive punishment for new crimes. The effect of this ruling on David Hicks' conviction is still being debated, given that he pleaded guilty to the charge.

Division 104 of the Criminal Code (Cth) permits a senior Australian federal police officer, subject to permission from the Commonwealth Attorney-General, to apply *ex parte* to a Federal Court for an interim control order for up to 12 months. The Court may issue an interim order if it is satisfied on the balance of probabilities that the restrictions imposed are "reasonably necessary, and reasonably appropriate and adapted, for the purpose of protecting the public from a terrorist act" (104.4(1)(d)). A full order may be made at a confirmation hearing at which the individual concerned must appear, although material may be withheld to avoid prejudice to national security or police operations.

Table 5.2 sets out some of the essential features of this scheme.

The restrictions that may be imposed include prohibiting the person from being in certain areas or places or from associating or communicating with certain individuals as well as requiring the person to stay at home during certain periods of the day or to wear a tracking device.

In *Thomas v Mowbray* (2007), the High Court of Australia was asked to consider whether the power to impose this interim control order on Jack Thomas under Division 104 of the Criminal Code (Cth) was constitutional. There were two main arguments proferred. The first was that Division 104 was invalid because it conferred a non-judicial power on a Federal Court contrary to Chapter III of the Constitution, which preserves the independence of the judiciary, by preventing the Federal Court from exercising a combination of judicial and non-judicial power (see on this point *R v Kirby; Ex parte Boilermakers' Society of Australia* 1956). Part of the reasoning behind this argument was that the restrictions imposed under control orders were inherently penal or punitive in nature despite not requiring a judicial determination of guilt. In relation to this argument, the majority of the High Court by five justices to two (Kirby and Hayne JJ dissenting) held that control orders were not incompatible with judicial involvement in terms of their procedure and preventive aims. Chief Justice Gleeson (*Thomas v Mowbray* 2007: 328–29) likened control orders to orders for bail or for apprehended violence orders, "both of which impose restrictions on the basis of [individuals'] likely future conduct, and are issued by courts on a regular basis" (see Hardy 2011: 5 on this point).

The second main argument was that Division 104 of the Criminal Code was invalid because it was not supported by section 51 of the Constitution. The Australian Constitution does not contain a specific power to make

Table 5.2 Control orders under the Australian Criminal Code

Key elements	Legislative requirements
What kind of supervision s. 104.5(3)	The obligations, prohibitions, and restrictions that the court may impose on the person by the [control] order are the following:

(a) a prohibition or restriction on the person being at specified areas or places;

(b) a prohibition or restriction on the person leaving Australia;

(c) a requirement that the person remain at specified premises between specified times each day, or on specified days;

(d) a requirement that the person wear a tracking device;

(e) a prohibition or restriction on the person communicating or associating with specified individuals;

(f) a prohibition or restriction on the person accessing or using specified forms of telecommunication or other technology (including the internet);

(g) a prohibition or restriction on the person possessing or using specified articles or substances;

(h) a prohibition or restriction on the person carrying out specified activities (including in respect of his or her work or occupation);

(i) a requirement that the person report to specified persons at specified times and places;

(j) a requirement that the person allow himself or herself to be photographed;

(k) a requirement that the person allow impressions of his or her fingerprints to be taken;

(l) a requirement that the person participate in specified counselling or education.

Grounds for ordering supervision s. 104.4

(1) The issuing court may make an order under this section in relation to the person, but only if:

(a) the senior AFP member has requested it in accordance with section 104.3;

(b) the court has received and considered such further information (if any) as the court requires;

(c) the court is satisfied on the balance of probabilities:

    (i) that making the order would substantially assist in preventing a terrorist act; or

    (ii) that the person has provided training to, or received training from, a listed terrorist organization; and

(d) the court is satisfied on the balance of probabilities that each of the obligations, prohibitions, and restrictions to be imposed on the person by the order is reasonably necessary, and reasonably appropriate and adapted, for the purpose of protecting the public from a terrorist act.

Key elements	Legislative requirements
	(2) In determining whether each of the obligations, prohibitions, and restrictions to be imposed on the person by the order is reasonably necessary, and reasonably appropriate and adapted, the court must take into account the impact of the obligation, prohibition, or restriction on the person's circumstances (including the person's financial and personal circumstances). (3) The court need not include in the order an obligation, prohibition, or restriction that was sought by the senior AFP member if the court is not satisfied as mentioned in paragraph (1)(d) in respect of that obligation, prohibition, or restriction.
Maximum duration s. 104.5(f) s. 104.16(d)	If the issuing court makes the interim control order, the order must . . . specify the period during which the confirmed control order is to be in force, which must not end more than 12 months after the day on which the interim control order is made. If the issuing court confirms the interim control order, the court must make a corresponding order that . . . specifies the period during which the order is to be in force, which must not end more than 12 months after the day on which the interim control order was made.

anti-terrorism laws, or even to make criminal laws more generally. The "defence power" in section 51(vi) of the Constitution states:

> The Parliament shall, subject to this Constitution, have power to make laws for the peace, order, and good government of the Commonwealth [ie. federal polity] with respect to:
>
> (vi) the naval and military defence of the Commonwealth and of the several States, and the control of the forces to execute and maintain the laws of the Commonwealth.

A majority of six justices to one (Justice Kirby dissenting) held that the threat posed by terrorism was of such a character and scope that the legislation enabling the making of an interim control order was validly enacted as a means of defending Australia within section 51(vi). Little time was spent on assessing whether the system of control orders was reasonably proportionate to meeting the threat posed by terrorism, with the implication being that this was self-evident (Santow and Williams 2012: 42).

Justice Kirby in his dissenting judgment analyzed the policy implications of control orders and concluded that the interim control order was not constitutional on a number of grounds. He was of the view (*Thomas v*

Mowbray 2007: 428) that control orders impinged upon "the basic rights to liberty of those made subject to them." He stated (2007: 432):

> [Division 104 of the Criminal Code] provides for the deprivation of liberty because of an estimate of some future act, not necessarily one to be committed by the person subject to the proposed order. To uphold the validity of that type of control order for which Div 104 of the Code provides would be to erode the well-founded assumption that the judiciary in Australia under federal law may only deprive individuals of their liberty on the basis of evidence of their past conduct . . . [Control orders] deny persons their basic legal rights not for what they have been proved to have done (as established in a criminal trial) but for what an official suggests that they might do or that someone else might do. To allow judges to be involved in making such orders, and particularly in the one-sided procedure contemplated by Div 104, involves a serious and wholly exceptional departure from basic constitutional doctrine unchallenged during the entire history of the Commonwealth.

Justice Kirby was the only High Court Justice willing to consider that issues concerning the deprivation of liberty must not be divorced from the broader context of the importance of principles protecting human rights. The result of the decision in *Thomas v Mowbray* is that control orders remain constitutionally valid in Australia and the Council of Australian Governments (2013: 54) has recommended that they should be retained.

In August 2007, a few days before the interim control order was due to expire, the Australian Federal Police decided not to apply to confirm the control order (Robinson 2007). Thomas was at that stage subject to bail conditions pending his retrial. He was retried in 2008 on the basis of comments he had made in an interview with Sally Neighbour in the ABC television programme "Four Corners" (Neighbour 2006), but he was convicted only of possessing a falsified passport (*R v Thomas (No 4)* 2008). On October 29, 2008, Thomas was sentenced to imprisonment for nine months for this conviction, but after taking into account time already served, the sentencing judge ordered him to pay a bond of $1,000 to be of good behaviour for the five days remaining of his sentence and he was released.

SUPERVISION OF OFFENDERS

There are a number of schemes that exist in common law jurisdictions that impose restrictions on offenders post-sentence. The whole concept of parole is based on an offender promising to abide by certain conditions of release from prison and submitting to the supervision of a parole officer, with any violation of the conditions resulting in the offender's return to prison.

In England and Wales, Multi-Agency Public Protection Arrangements (MAPPAs) were established under the Criminal Justice and Court Services Act 2000 and in Scotland, under the Management of Offenders, etc. (Scotland) Act 2005. The Scottish legislation dealt initially with arrangements for sex offenders and was later extended in 2008 to "restricted patients" (serious offenders whose mental illness was related to their offending). The legislation sets up Multi-Agency Public Protection Panels to coordinate services with the aim of reducing the risk of reoffending. MAPPAs initially required the police and probation services to cooperate in managing the risks posed by serious offenders in the community. This has since been extended to include "the prison service and there is a statutory duty for health, housing, social services, education, social security and employment services, youth offending teams and electronic monitoring providers to cooperate with multiagency protection panels" (Thomson 2011: 169). Evaluations of MAPPAs have identified some problems with insufficient administrative arrangements and the lack of a coordinator role in certain regions (Maguire *et al.* 2001; Kemshall *et al.* 2005).

As well as more traditional probation schemes, "[t]here has been a proliferation of legislation over the past 20 years in the United Kingdom, North America, and Australasia intended to provide greater protection of the public from high-risk sexual offenders" (Vess and Eccleston 2009: 271). These include sex offender registration schemes, extended supervision orders, and sexual offence prevention orders. Some of these schemes are outlined below together with specific forms of civil orders that can be used with the aim of preventing offences occurring even where there has been no conviction.

Sex Offender Registration Schemes

Sex offender registration schemes emerged in the United States during the early 1990s in response to high-profile cases, with other countries soon following suit (Harris and Lobanov-Rostovsky 2010; Thomas, T. 2011). In 1994, the United States federal government passed the Jacob Wetterling Crimes Against Children and Sexually Violent Offender Registration Act. This Act was named after an 11-year-old boy who was abducted at gun point in Minnesota and never found. This Act mandated the development of state registration schemes and required offenders who had been convicted of various criminal offences against children, or "sexually violent offences" against children or adults, to register their address with a state law enforcement agency. Community notification laws permitting the public dissemination of information about registered offenders were enacted in the United States from 1990, with Washington State's Community Protection Act 1990 being the first community notification scheme established.

In January 1996, the Wetterling Act was amended by the federal Megan's Law (42 USC § 13701) to require state law enforcement agencies to "release relevant information" about registered offenders "that is necessary to protect the public" (42 USC § 14071(d)). Megan's Law was named after Megan Kanka, a seven-year-old girl, who was raped and murdered by a neighbour who was a convicted child sex offender.

A registration scheme for sex offenders was introduced in the United Kingdom by the Sex Offenders Act 1997. This Act formed the basis of the Child Protection (Offenders Registration) Act 2000 (NSW), which in turn influenced the model registration legislation on which all Australian jurisdictions based their schemes (Victorian Law Reform Commission 2011: 15).

The aims of such sex offender registration schemes are to reduce the likelihood of sex offenders reoffending and to assist in the investigation and prosecution of any future offences. However, they may also serve to operate "as a source of information for child protection authorities about children who may be at risk of harm" (Victorian Law Reform Commission 2011: xi). It is difficult to measure the effectiveness of such schemes. As the Victorian Law Reform Commission (2011: 149) has observed:

> It is difficult to determine the impact of registration on offender behaviour, as distinct from the effect of other factors such as treatment and rehabilitation programs, sentencing practices and demographic change. Moreover, there has been very little research into this area.

Extended Supervision Orders

The post-sentence supervision of sex offenders is enabled by legislation in the Australian states of:

- New South Wales: Crimes (Serious Sex Offenders) Act 2006 ss 6–13;
- Queensland: Dangerous Prisoners (Sexual Offenders) Act 2003 s. 13;
- South Australia: Criminal Law (Sentencing) Act 1988 s. 24;
- Western Australia: Dangerous Sexual Offenders Act 2006 s. 17(1)(b); and
- Victoria: Serious Sex Offenders (Detention and Supervision) Act 2009 s. 9.

These schemes enable an order for continuing supervision to be made as sex offenders reach the end of their prison sentence. An order may contain a number of conditions including that the offender must report to and receive visits by certain specified individuals, must obey any curfews relating to leaving his or her residence at certain times, must not commit an offence or move to a new address without prior written consent. The Western Australian Dangerous Sexual Offenders Amendment Act 2012 introduced provisions enabling the electronic monitoring of sex offenders.

In *Attorney-General (Qld) v Francis* (2006: para. [39]), the Queensland Court of Appeal expressed a preference for supervision orders to be made over orders for preventive detention in prison:

> If supervision of the prisoner is apt to ensure adequate protection, having regard to the risk to the community posed by the prisoner, then an order for supervised release should, in principle be preferred to a continuing detention order on the basis that the intrusions of the [Queensland Act] upon the liberty of the subject are exceptional, and the liberty of the subject should be constrained to no greater extent than is warranted by the statute which authorized such constraint.

While these schemes are meant not only to protect the community but also to reintegrate offenders into the community, in Australia, there have been significant practical problems with finding suitable accommodation for offenders who are on extended supervision orders (McSherry and Keyzer 2010: 88ff). Some offenders are socially isolated and do not have any supports in the community. Others may have offended against family members making it inappropriate for them to return to live with them. This has led to special housing being set up for offenders just outside of, or in the state of Victoria, actually inside prison grounds. In Queensland, a number of buildings adjacent to the Wacol Prison Reserve (and only 20 metres from the prison) in outer-suburban Brisbane are used to house a number of offenders released on supervision orders. The buildings are surrounded by a 10-metre high barbed wire fence and the outside is patrolled by a dog squad officer.

In Victoria, those released on supervision orders may be housed in units within prison grounds, despite the premise of such orders being supervision in the community. A challenge to this practice was brought in the case of *Fletcher v Secretary to Department of Justice and Anor* (2006). The facts were that Robin Fletcher had been made the subject of an extended supervision order after completing a ten-year prison term for three counts of wilfully committing an indecent act with a child under the age of 16, one count of child prostitution, and one count of attempting to pervert the course of justice. One of the conditions of the order required him to live in a security unit forming part of the Ararat Prison which is three kilometres to the east of the township of Ararat in country Victoria. The nearest street to the Prison is approximately one kilometre away. The unit comprised ten cells and Fletcher lived in one of them. He could only leave the premises in the company of an approved escort.

After he instituted proceedings in the Supreme Court of Victoria for a judicial review of the order, Fletcher was moved from the secure unit to a separate unit, which was still inside the perimeter of the Ararat Prison. Justice Gillard (2006: para. [20]) pointed out:

> The new residence was located on a portion of land which was degazetted as a result of an Order in Council made on 27 July 2006. This no longer formed part of the Ararat Prison. However, the fact is that the area is within the walls of the Ararat Prison. The degazetted land was fenced off using cyclone fencing, and shade cloth screening on three sides, in order to provide privacy for any occupants and visitors. A house described as a "relocatable unit", comprising a two bedroom weatherboard dwelling with a small kitchen, bathroom and lounge-dining area, was erected on the site.

Justice Gillard found that despite the particular area no longer being gazetted as a prison, the unit was still behind the walls of the prison and Fletcher's freedom of movement was severely restricted. Accordingly, he held that the statutory power relating to residence was not lawfully exercised as it could not be said that Fletcher was living in the community.

As a result of this case, the Victorian government enacted the Serious Sex Offenders Monitoring (Amendment) Act 2006. This Act inserted sections 16(3A) and (3B) into the Serious Sex Offenders Monitoring Act 2005 (now repealed). These provisions set out that where a condition of an extended supervision order "required the person to reside at premises that are situated on land that is within the perimeter of a prison . . . but does not form part of the prison," the offender "must be taken for the purposes of this Act to have been released in the community and to be residing in the community while residing in accordance with that instruction or direction."

Section 133 of the current Serious Sex Offenders (Detention and Supervision) Act 2009 (Vic) enables the Governor in Council to appoint "any premises (including part of any building or place) other than a prison or police gaol to be a residential facility" with the result that many sex offenders on extended supervision orders are kept at "Corella Place" a

40-bed facility on degazetted land within the boundaries of Ararat Prison. In practice then, the Australian supervision schemes can in some instances be compared to the operation of the United States "inpatient" detention regimes where very few offenders have ever been released (La Fond 2005: 149).

A similar scheme to the Australian extended supervision schemes was introduced in New Zealand by the Parole (Extended Supervision) Amendment Act 2004. In that country, a person who has been convicted of certain sexual offences against children under the age of 16 may be supervised in the community for a period of up to ten years post-sentence. Section 107I(1) of the Parole Act 2002 (NZ) states:

> The purpose of an extended supervision order is "to protect members of the community from those who, following receipt of a determinate sentence, pose a real and ongoing risk of committing sexual offences against children or young persons."

The Chief Executive of the Department of Corrections may apply to the Court for an extended supervision order for those offenders deemed by the department to present sufficient risk to warrant extended supervision. Applications must be accompanied by a report from a "health assessor" such as from practising psychiatrists and registered psychologists. In practice, all eligible offenders are assessed for their risk of reoffending via the use of a seven-item risk assessment tool, the Automated Sexual Recidivism Scale (Skelton *et al.* 2006). (This was the scale used to assess Jacob Rangaita Peta's risk of reoffending in the case outlined in Chapter 3.) If the offenders score in the medium-high or high-risk category for further risk assessment, they are then individually assessed by department psychologists (Vess and Eccleston 2009: 273). Other risk assessment instruments may also be administered at this stage. Under section 107F(2) of the Parole Act 2002, reports concerning the offender must address:

(a) the nature of any likely future sexual offending by the offender, including the age and sex of likely victims;
(b) the offender's ability to control his or her sexual impulses;
(c) the offender's predilection and proclivity for sexual offending;
(d) the offender's acceptance of responsibility and remorse for past offending;
(e) any other relevant factors.

The Court must be satisfied that the person is likely to commit any of the relevant offences specified in the Act (Parole Act 2000 (NZ) s. 107I(2)). These range from indecency offences to sexual violation of those under the age of 16 and attempted sexual offences (Parole Act 2000 (NZ) s. 107B(2)). Once an extended supervision order is made, the Parole Board can also impose special conditions on the offender.

There has been little research to date as to the effect of extended supervision orders on reoffending. Danny Sullivan, Paul Mullen, and Michelle Pathé (2005) have pointed out that such schemes are expensive to implement and require the redirection of generally underfunded supervisory and clinical resources. It would seem that the success of such schemes depends on whether the supervision is based upon treatment and meeting the individual needs of the offender rather than just controlling and restricting behaviour.

Sexual Offence Prevention Orders and Risk of Sexual Harm Orders

In Canada and the United Kingdom, conditions may also be imposed on those considered at risk of sexual offending through various civil orders, a breach of which is a criminal offence. For example, in Canada, sections 810.1 and 810.2 of the Criminal Code allow a judge to impose a peace bond or recognizance for up to 12 months based on a reasonable fear that an individual might commit a sexual offence against a child under 14 years old. The risk need not be linked to a particular individual. A range of conditions can be made under such orders including directions to stay away from certain places or persons, requirements to report regularly to the police or corrections officials, drug and alcohol prohibitions and curfews. A breach of the order is punishable by a term of imprisonment of up to two years (Criminal Code s. 811).

The Sexual Offences Act 2003 introduced sexual offence prevention orders into the United Kingdom. Sexual offences prevention orders can be viewed as the successors to sex offender orders (introduced by section 2 of the Crime and Disorder Act 1998) and restraining orders (introduced by section 66 of the Criminal Justice and Court Services Act 2000) (Shute 2004). They are civil orders, a breach of which results in a criminal offence and may apply to those living in the community who have a previous conviction for an offence listed in Schedules 3 and 5 to the Act. Schedule 3 includes sexual offences such as rape, indecent assault, incest, bestiality, voyeurism, and offences relating to child prostitution and pornography. Schedule 5 contains a long list of offences from assault occasioning actual bodily harm to injuring persons by furious driving to endangering the safety of railway passengers. As Stephen Shute (2004: 425) points out, "[t]here seems to be no logic to this list. It is a hotchpotch, but one whose effect is to widen very considerably the range of offenders against whom a SOPO can be made."

There are three questions that the court generally considers in relation to the making of a sexual offences prevention order (*R v Mortimer* 2010; *R v Collard* 2005):

- Is the making of an order necessary to protect others from "serious sexual harm" (defined as "serious physical or psychological harm" caused by a sexual offence)?
- If some order is necessary, are the terms proposed nevertheless oppressive?
- Overall are the terms proportionate?

In *R v Smith (Steven)* (2012), it was held that the sexual offences prevention order was properly regarded as part of the total protective sentencing package and that it should not duplicate the effect of other sanctions to which the offender may be subject such as notification requirements, being released "on license," or being disqualified from working with children (Thomas, D.A. 2011).

Section 107(1)(b) of the Sexual Offences Act 2003 states that a sexual offences prevention order is to have effect for a fixed period of not less than five years. However, the "fixed period" may in reality be an indefinite one in that the order can be expressed to have effect until a further order is made (Moloney 2010: 1115). Any breach of an order without reasonable excuse is punishable by up to six months' imprisonment on summary conviction and up to five years' imprisonment on indictment (s. 113).

Risk of sexual harm orders, which aim to protect children from sexual harm, can be imposed on persons who have no convictions of any kind. They were introduced into England, Wales, and Northern Ireland by the Sexual Offences Act 2003 and in Scotland by the Protection of Children and Prevention of Sexual Offences (Scotland) Act 2005. Under section 123 of the 2003 Act and section 2 of the 2005 Act, a chief officer of police (a chief constable in Scotland) can bring an application where "it appears" that the person has on at least two occasions done a certain act and there is reasonable cause to believe that it is necessary for the order to be made. Section 123(3) of the Sexual Offences Act 2003 lists the relevant acts as:

(a) engaging in sexual activity involving a child or in the presence of a child;
(b) causing or inciting a child to watch a person engaging in sexual activity or to look at a moving or still image that is sexual;
(c) giving a child anything that relates to sexual activity or contains a reference to such activity;
(d) communicating with a child, where any part of the communication is sexual.

A similar provision exists in the Scottish Act (s. 2(5)).

Alison Cleland (2005: 204) points out that this section is very broad and that paragraph (c), for example, could encompass providing "health promotion material about safer sex and the prevention of sexually transmitted diseases" and thus the scheme could potentially apply to "youth workers, health promotion workers and school guidance and other staff giving information about sexual matters."

A magistrate or sheriff can make a risk of sexual harm order (which lasts for a fixed period of not less than two years) if satisfied that the person has done an act listed on at least two occasions and "it is necessary to make such an order, for the purpose of protecting children generally or any child from harm from the defendant" (s. 123(4)(b); s. 2(6)). Any prohibitions imposed under the order must keep this premise in mind.

Not surprisingly, risk of sexual harm orders were considered controversial prior to their introduction because they can be imposed on those with no previous convictions (Shute 2004). Perhaps because of this, it appears that they have been made only on rare occasions (Burdge 2011; Derby Telegraph 2012).

Antisocial Behaviour Orders and Criminal Antisocial Behaviour Orders

An ASBO prohibits an individual from certain actions that may or may not be criminal in nature. They were introduced in England, Scotland, and Wales by the Crime and Disorder Act 1998 and strengthened by the Anti-social Behaviour Act 2003 (England and Wales) and the Antisocial Behaviour, etc. (Scotland) Act 2004. The latter Act was particularly controversial in granting power to courts to grant an ASBO against a child under the age of 16. In England and Wales, ASBOs are issued by Magistrates' Courts and in Scotland by the Sheriff Courts.

The House of Lords in *R (McCann) v Crown Court at Manchester; Clingham v Kensington and Chelsea Royal London Borough Council* (2003) classified ASBO proceedings as civil in nature. The rationale for the introduction of ASBOs was set out by Lord Steyn (2003: 805–806):

> The aim of the criminal law is not punishment for its own sake but to permit everyone to go about their daily lives without fear of harm to person or property. Unfortunately, by intimidating people the culprits, usually small in number, sometimes effectively silenced communities. Fear of the consequences of complaining to the police dominated the thoughts of people: reporting incidents to the police entailed a serious risk of reprisals. The criminal law by itself offered inadequate protection to them. There was a model available for remedial legislation. Before 1998

Parliament had, on a number of occasions, already used the technique of prohibiting by statutory injunction conduct deemed to be unacceptable and making a breach of the injunction punishable by penalties . . . The unifying element is . . . the use of the civil remedy of an injunction to prohibit conduct considered to be utterly unacceptable, with a remedy of criminal penalties in the event of disobedience.

He concluded (2003: 808) that the "true purpose of the proceedings is preventative."

The decision in this case opened the way for hearsay evidence, which is prevented from use in criminal proceedings, to be used in ASBO applications. Jane Donoghue (2010: 133) has pointed out that interim ASBOs are usually obtained on the basis of hearsay evidence and that "applicant agencies in England and Wales are able to obtain a full ASBO based only on hearsay evidence." Interestingly, the House of Lords required a higher criminal standard of proof for the issuing of ASBOs than the civil standard of the balance of probabilities. This is discussed in Chapter 6.

The Antisocial Behaviour, etc. (Scotland) Act 2004 also introduced the Criminal Antisocial Behaviour Order (CRASBO) via inserting a new section 234AA into the Criminal Procedure (Scotland) Act (1995). A CRASBO may be made by either the sheriff court or the district court.

The definition of antisocial behaviour is the same for both ASBOs and CRASBOs (Antisocial Behaviour, etc. (Scotland) Act 2004, s. 143; Criminal Procedure (Scotland) Act 1995, s. 234AA(3)), namely that the person:

(a) acts in a manner that causes or is likely to cause alarm or distress; or
(b) pursues a course of conduct that causes or is likely to cause alarm or distress to at least one person who is not of the same household as him [or her].

Conditions under such orders may range from prohibiting noise during certain times of the day, entering certain places or associating with certain people to prohibiting the making of threats or committing assaults.

It is an offence to breach an ASBO or CRASBO. If a person breaches an ASBO they may be liable on summary conviction to a prison term not exceeding six months or to a fine not exceeding the statutory maximum or both. There is also the possibility of prosecuting a breach on indictment with a maximum prison sentence of five years, or an unlimited fine, or both.

Trish Pryce (2008: 278–79) has argued that CRASBOs can offer the courts a flexible form of sentence:

> If used appropriately and thoughtfully, such an order can be used to try and [sic] prevent offenders from ending up in situations which lead them to re-offending. The intention is not simply about prohibiting further criminal acts (although the orders can be used for this). Such orders can be used to try and [sic] help offenders to avoid situations which lead them to offend further.

ASBOs have been the subject of extensive criticism on the basis that they breach important due process principles (e.g., Ashworth *et al.* 1998; Squires and Stephen 2005; Simester and von Hirsch 2006; Squires 2008). Drawing on household survey data, Michael Tonry (2010: 399) suggests that there is a likelihood that ASBOs "increased rather than decreased citizens'" concern about antisocial behaviour.

In practice, the Home Office has pointed out (2012: 8) that the use of ASBOs declined from 4,122 in 2005 to 1,664 in 2010 and that "over half of ASBOs are breached at least once, with 42% of these being breached more than once." It has recommended the replacement of ASBOs with new measures to combat antisocial behaviour including a "Crime Prevention Injunction," which will be a purely civil order, with sanctions under civil rather than criminal law and with the burden of proof being the balance of probabilities rather than beyond reasonable doubt (Home Office 2012: 24). It has also suggested the introduction of a "Criminal Behaviour Order," which will be a civil order that can be made on conviction to require the offender to "undertake positive activities to address underlying activities" as well as to restrict certain behaviour (Home Office 2012: 26).

Violent Offender Orders and Serious Crime Prevention Orders

The Criminal Justice and Immigration Act 2008 introduced into England and Wales a similar regime to sexual offences prevention orders in relation to violent offenders. The police may seek an order from magistrates to control places visited and contact with other people (s. 102) if the person is someone who has been sentenced to 12 months' imprisonment in relation to causing grievous bodily harm, manslaughter, soliciting murder, or attempting or conspiring to murder (ss 98, 99). Under section 101, an order may be made if the person "acted in such a way as to make it necessary to make a violent offender order for the purpose of protecting the public from the risk of serious violent harm." The order lasts from two to five years, but is renewable (ss 98, 103).

The Serious Crime Act 2007 introduced serious crime prevention orders in England and Wales. Under section 8, the Director of Public Prosecutions, the Director of Revenue and Customs Prosecutions, and the Director of the Serious Fraud Office may make applications for Serious Crime Prevention Orders (SCPOs). The High Court and the Crown Court may make an SCPO if satisfied that the individual concerned has been involved in serious crime whether in England or Wales or elsewhere (s. 1(1)(a)). There must also be reasonable grounds to believe that the order "would protect the public by preventing, restricting or disrupting involvement by the person in serious crime in England and Wales" (s. 1(1)(b)). The term "serious crime," as set out in Part 1 of Schedule 1, includes trafficking in drugs, people, and arms; child sex offences; armed robbery: assault with intent to rob; money laundering; and corruption and bribery offences.

Sections 35 and 36 clarify that SCPO proceedings before the High Court and the Crown Court are civil in nature and that the standard of proof is the "civil standard of proof"; that is, the balance of probabilities is the test to be applied. Failing to comply with an SCPO without reasonable excuse is a criminal offence punishable by up to 12 months' imprisonment or a fine on summary conviction or up to five years' imprisonment on indictment (s. 25).

The aim of SCPOs is presumably to pre-empt criminal activities, but Andrew Picken (2009: 14) has pointed out that such a scheme may be encouraging the authorities to focus on guilt by association and suspicion rather than requiring criminal prosecutions based on the criminal standard of proof. The broad provision relating to future conduct has also been criticized as allowing the court to "engage in pure speculation" (Lorimer 2008: 56). As of February 2012, 89 Crown Court SCPOs had been issued (Serious Organised Crime Agency 2012).

Orders for Lifelong Restriction

Scotland has introduced a system of orders for lifelong restriction for those who are considered to pose a continuing risk to the public. This was in response to recommendations by the MacLean Committee on Serious Violent and Sexual Offenders, which was established in March 1999, to make proposals for the sentencing, management, and treatment of serious sexual and violent offenders who may present a continuing danger to the public. The MacLean Committee presented its report to the Scottish Parliament in June 2000 (Scottish Executive 2000) and public consultation followed. A White Paper (Scottish Executive 2001) was subsequently prepared that translated the MacLean recommendations into legislative proposals.

The Committee recommended orders for lifelong restriction as a method of controlling the behaviour of a small group of offenders, that control initially being of a custodial nature and then under supervision in the community. In this sense, it is a hybrid between indefinite sentencing and post-sentence supervision orders. The Committee also recommended the formation of a Risk Management Authority that was subsequently established under the Criminal Justice (Scotland) Act 2003. This Act inserted new provisions into the Criminal Procedure (Scotland) Act 1995, dealing with the powers of the Risk Management Authority and the procedures for orders for lifelong restrictions.

An order for lifelong restriction can be imposed only by the High Court. Before sentencing, once the court determines that certain risk criteria are met, it is required to make a risk assessment order. The risk criteria are set out in section 210E of the Criminal Procedure (Scotland) Act 1995 and require the court to consider whether:

> the nature of, or in the circumstances of the commission of, the offence of which the convicted person has been found guilty either in themselves or as part of a pattern of behaviour are such as to demonstrate that there is a likelihood that he [or she], if at liberty, will seriously endanger the lives, or physical or psychological wellbeing, of members of the public at large.

The risk assessment order provides for a risk assessor accredited by the Risk Management Authority to carry out a risk assessment and to prepare a risk assessment report (Darjee and Russell 2011). The purpose of the report is to assist the court to make an informed decision about the level of risk an offender poses to the community. If on the basis of this report and other evidence, the court is satisfied on the balance of probabilities that certain risk criteria are met, it must impose an order for lifelong restriction (Criminal Procedure (Scotland) Act 1995: s. 210F). Such an order is available for those convicted of a single offence but only if the offence is of a serious, violent, or life-endangering nature and the court is satisfied that the offender meets the statutory risk criteria.

What is interesting to note about the Scottish approach is that the scheme comes into play at the sentencing stage and depends on a specifically designed risk assessment process coordinated by a statutory body (McSherry and Keyzer 2010; Fyfe and Gailey 2011). As of March 2011, there had been 92 risk assessment orders completed and following these, 66 offenders had been given an order for lifelong restriction (Risk Management Authority 2011: 22). This has been referred to as a "tiny" amount in comparison to those sentenced to indeterminate sentences in England and Wales (Darjee and Russell 2011: 226).

Overall then, there are numerous schemes for the supervision of serious offenders, all of which aim at the prevention of future harm. While most flow from some form of offending, some such as the risk of sexual harm order can be imposed in the absence of any convictions. As with control orders for suspected terrorists, supervision orders are constitutionally legitimate, but may be criticized on human rights grounds, in particular their potential to breach the right to liberty. Human rights issues are explored in Chapter 7.

COMMUNITY TREATMENT ORDERS FOR INDIVIDUALS WITH SEVERE MENTAL ILLNESS

Community Treatment Orders (CTOs) differ from other control or supervision orders in that their primary purpose is to authorize the provision of involuntary psychiatric treatment outside hospital, rather than monitor or control certain behaviour. The general premise behind CTOs is that involuntary treatment in the community is less restrictive of people's rights than keeping them without consent in psychiatric facilities. This echoes the idea that community supervision orders for sex offenders is a less restrictive alternative than continuing detention in prison.

The criteria for making a CTO are similar to those for making an order for involuntary commitment that are set out in Chapter 4. Some mental health statutes also require that the treatment can be obtained in the community (see, for example, Mental Health Act 1990 (Ontario) s. 33.1; Mental Health (Compulsory Assessment and Treatment) Act 1992 (NZ), ss 27, 28; Mental Health Act 1983 (England and Wales) s. 17A(5); and Mental Health Act 1997 (NSW) ss 13–14, 53). In the United States, CTOs are generally made by a court or tribunal, whereas in Australia, New Zealand, Canada, and the United Kingdom, psychiatrists are able to make them.

The duration of CTOs ranges from three months (in Western Australia) to six months e.g., in California, England and Wales, Ontario, and New Zealand) to a year (for example, in New South Wales, South Australia, and Victoria) with the majority being renewable after a review by a tribunal.

Those who are subject to a CTO are usually required to keep taking medication and accept home visits from a community psychiatric nurse who will monitor their mental health (Dawson 2008). If the person refuses treatment, he or she may be returned to hospital in order for the required treatment to be administered there.

143

However, CTOs may sometimes go further than solely imposing certain medication. Mary Donnelly (2008: 784) points out:

> A CTO may also prescribe or restrict certain kinds of behaviour, e.g. it may tell a person where to live or restrict her alcohol or drug consumption. Depending on the nature of the CTO model employed, failure to comply with treatment or other conditions in the order may result in the patient being involuntarily detained (either automatically or following a separate hearing). Thus, CTOs attempt to combat the relatively uncontrolled environment of everyday life and to introduce a greater degree of control over individuals' behaviour without the wholesale restriction of an institutional setting.

CTOs have been an accepted part of the mental health systems in Australia and New Zealand for over two decades (Dawson 2005, 2008, 2010). They were introduced in Victoria by the Mental Health Act 1986 (Vic) with other states gradually following suit and in New Zealand by the Mental Health (Compulsory Assessment and Treatment) Act 1992 (NZ). They are a much newer feature of mental health law in European jurisdictions (Donnelly 2008). In Australasia, the rate of use of CTOs varies substantially. A 2009 study estimated their use to range from approximately 55 per 100,000 in Victoria, 44 for New Zealand, and 37 for New South Wales down to 10 in Western Australia (Burns and Dawson 2009). A more recent study has put these figures as approximately 99.8 per 100,000 in Victoria, followed by 61.3 in Queensland, 56.1 in the Northern Territory, 51.3 in South Australia, 48.6 in Western Australia, 46.4 in New South Wales, and 30.2 in Tasmania (Light et al. 2012). Many factors affect these rates including differences in mental health service culture and the adequacy of funding for community care (Dawson 2007).

Scotland introduced CTOs via the Mental Health (Care and Treatment) (Scotland) Act 2003 and these came into effect in October 2005. CTOs were subsequently introduced in England and Wales, via the Mental Health Act 2007, which amended the Mental Health Act 1983.

In Canada, all provinces with the exception of New Brunswick and the three territories (Canadian Medical Association 2010) authorize the use of CTOs or variations such as extended leave provisions. Ontario was the first province to introduce CTOs in 2000 when its Mental Health Act 1990 was amended by Bill 68, which was known as Brian's Law in honor of Brian Smith, a sports broadcaster who was shot dead in 1995 by a person who was diagnosed with untreated paranoid schizophrenia. The majority of states in the United States also have some legislative scheme for involuntary outpatient commitment (Swartz and Swanson 2004).

Virginia Aldige Hiday (2003) makes the point that the concept behind CTOs is not new in that there have long been non-legislative schemes for the provisional release of individuals from psychiatric institutions. In England and Wales, for example, the use of leave from hospital under section 17(1) of the Mental Health Act 1983 created a form of community treatment programme. The decision in *R v Hallstrom; Ex parte W (No 2)* (1986) limited the use of such leave by holding that the practice of admitting those who had been involuntarily committed overnight so as to renew and extend their use was unlawful. This decision set the scene for a debate about whether community treatment orders should be introduced in England and Wales. The Mental Health (Patients in the Community) Act 1995 (England and Wales) introduced supervised discharge, which entailed no power to force medical treatment upon a person who was not consenting, but enabled people to be escorted by police officers to treatment clinics. This was not seen as going far enough and, hence, in 2007, CTOs were introduced into England and Wales amid a great deal of controversy (Lawton-Smith 2008).

As well as criticisms of the human rights implications of CTOs, their use has been criticized as emphasizing "[r]eliance on medication-only regimes with minimal psychosocial intervention" (Brophy and McDermott 2012: 9). There have also been concerns that CTOs serve a "social control function" in targeting certain individuals who are perceived as "dangerous" (Brophy et al. 2006: 472).

Rachel Churchill and colleagues (2007) conducted a review of the international findings on community treatment orders and concluded that there was little evidence to support the effectiveness of CTOs. They did find, however (2007: 109), that:

> [t]here is remarkable consistency in the characteristics of patients on CTOs across jurisdictions in very different cultural and geographic settings. [They are] typically males, around 40 years of age, with a long history of mental illness, previous admissions, suffering from a schizophrenia-like or serious affective illness, and likely to be displaying psychotic symptoms, especially delusions at the time.

A recent study by Tom Burns and colleagues (2013) has suggested that CTOs do not reduce the rate of readmission of those diagnosed with psychosis.

While a number of court cases in various jurisdictions have dealt with challenges to the use of or restrictions under CTOs, there have not been any challenges to the constitutionality of CTO schemes. This may be because they are viewed through the lens of treatment rather than control.

CONCLUSION

Five years and nine months since he was arrested at Karachi airport, Jack Thomas walked out of court a free man. Ultimately he was not convicted of any terrorist activity and the interim control order that was imposed on him did not get to the confirmation stage. His lawyer, Rob Stary (2011), described Thomas as "an inconsequential figure in the war on terror", opining that "The [Thomas] case was designed to send a clear message, particularly to any home-grown convert, that if you express any jihadist ideology and subscribe to fundamentalist Islam, you will be crushed – crime or no crime."

The Home Office (2011: 36) has pointed out that in relation to suspected terrorists, "control orders can mean that prosecution and conviction (a principal purpose of our counter-terrorism work) becomes less not more likely." Nevertheless, the power to restrict suspected terrorists' daily lives and activities through terrorism prevention and investigations measures and control orders remains an option in the United Kingdom and Australia.

This chapter has outlined some of the numerous schemes for the supervision of serious offenders as well as control orders for suspected terrorists. All these schemes aim at the prevention of future harm. While most flow from some form of offending, some orders may be imposed in the absence of any convictions. The main advantage of supervision and control orders is that they enable the police to monitor the whereabouts of offenders and suspected terrorists. The conditions attached to such orders may aid in reducing (re)offending. However, these schemes are expensive and resource intensive particularly given that many versions of these orders can last for years or for the life of the offender in the case of Scotland's orders for lifelong restriction. The conditions set out in such orders can be so highly restrictive that they may severely limit the opportunities for normal day-to-day interaction for the person concerned.

Community treatment orders for those with severe mental illness are in a slightly different category in that they are concerned with continued treatment rather than supervision or control, but they can have restrictions of liberty attached to them. David Oaks (2011: 189), for example, describes community treatment orders as "an example of the expansion of coerced psychiatric treatment from the back wards of locked psychiatric institutions, to the front porch of our own homes in our own neighbour-hoods" and that "[a]ll involuntary psychiatric procedures can feel unjust, because an individual is losing their liberty due to a psychiatric diagnosis, rather than because of violating a law created by duly elected representatives that is fairly applied to everyone equally."

Supervision, control, and community treatment orders are all considered to be constitutionally valid despite breaching human rights such as the right to liberty. While they are, therefore, "lawful," they raise issues concerning the balance between the use of state powers to protect the community and the infringement of human rights. This is taken up further in Chapter 7. The next chapter turns to the question of legal requirements for proving risk for both preventive detention and supervision schemes.

6

PROVING RISK IN PREVENTIVE DETENTION AND SUPERVISION PROCEEDINGS

INTRODUCTION: THE McCANN BROTHERS

Sean, Joseph, and Michael McCann lived in a housing estate in Beswick, Manchester. They were aged 16, 15, and 13, when their neighbours complained to the police that the brothers had been engaging in abusive and threatening behaviour and causing criminal damage. The Chief Constable met with members of the Manchester City Council to see what could be done to stop the brothers' behaviour. They decided to apply for antisocial behaviour orders (ASBOs) under section 1 of the Crime and Disorder Act 1998. These orders were granted by a stipendiary magistrate and an appeal, which was heard in the form of a rehearing, was dismissed by the Crown Court. Among other matters, the orders prohibited each of the brothers from entering the Beswick area and "using or engaging in any abusive, insulting, offensive, threatening or intimidating language or behaviour in any public place in the City of Manchester" for a minimum of two years (*R (McCann) v Crown Court at Manchester; Clingham v Kensington and Chelsea Royal London Borough Council* 2003: 815).

The evidence against Sean, Joseph, and Michael consisted of both direct evidence from neighbours as well as anonymous hearsay evidence (that is, evidence based on what others have said to the witness) by neighbours and the police. Defence counsel appealed to the House of Lords. They argued that ASBO proceedings should be considered as criminal rather than civil proceedings on the basis that orders could result in a criminal penalty. The evidence on which the ASBOs were made, including hearsay evidence not allowed in a criminal court, was required only to meet civil standards of proof.

The characterization of proceedings as civil or criminal is important because it affects the issue as to whether:

- a high standard of proof applies (the highest being the criminal standard of proof beyond reasonable doubt);

- the scheme can be applied retrospectively;
- specific rules of evidence apply; and
- the restrictions available under the scheme breach the right not to be punished twice for an offence (often referred to as double jeopardy).

This chapter explores how legal proceedings have been characterized in relation to preventive detention and supervision orders and what standard of proof (if any) applies as well as some of the important evidentiary rules for expert evidence. The House of Lords decision in *McCann*'s case is an unusual one and is discussed below. First, however, the possible combinations of civil and criminal proceedings and the standard of proof are explored.

THE STANDARD OF PROOF

In court proceedings, the *burden* of proof deals with which party bears the duty to prove a particular issue, whereas the *standard* of proof relates to the quantum or level of proof; that is, how much evidence is required for a decision to be made. The standard of proof in criminal proceedings – "beyond reasonable doubt" – is commonly defined and contrasted by its antimony, the standard of proof in civil proceedings, the "balance of probabilities." The Privy Council observed in *Ferguson v The Queen* (1979: 882):

> The time-honoured formula [in criminal proceedings] is that the jury must be satisfied beyond reasonable doubt . . . attempts to substitute other expressions have never prospered. It is generally sufficient and safe to direct a jury that they must be satisfied beyond reasonable doubt so that they feel sure of the defendant's guilt.

"Feeling sure" is a vague instruction, but any attempt by a judge to elaborate on the notion of beyond reasonable doubt in Australia or the United Kingdom by resort to mathematical analogies or percentages may provide grounds for appeal (Bronitt and McSherry 2010: 139). Penny Darbyshire (2001: 974) observes that in practice:

> Juries have immense difficulty in understanding "beyond reasonable doubt". Depending on how it is interpreted by the judge, they may equate it with 51–100 per cent proof. Modern lay persons are used to evaluating probability in percentages. English research findings confirm real jurors' accounts that when

the judge uses the word "sure", some or even the majority of jurors will equate [beyond reasonable doubt] with absolute proof.

In comparison, the Supreme Court of Canada in *R v Lifchus* (1997) has held that it is insufficient for juries to be told that the standard of beyond reasonable doubt was a familiar concept determined by its ordinary meaning. The Court emphazised (1997: 333) that judges should draw a link between the standard of proof and the presumption of innocence, with a reasonable doubt being described as "a doubt based on reason and common sense which must be based upon the evidence or lack of evidence" (see also Ferguson, 2000: 262–63).

The civil standard of proof, the balance of probabilities, although suggestive of 51 out of 100 per cent, has traditionally been case- or context-dependent. Sometimes it is equated with "reasonable satisfaction" (as opposed to "feeling sure"), but this is dependent on the circumstances of the particular case. Sir Owen Dixon observed in *Briginshaw v Briginshaw* (1938: 361–62):

> Reasonable satisfaction is not a state of mind that is attained or established independently of the nature and consequence of the fact or facts to be proved. The seriousness of an allegation made, the inherent unlikelihood of an occurrence of a given description, or the gravity of the consequences flowing from a particular finding are considerations which must affect the answer to the question whether the issue has been proved to the reasonable satisfaction of the tribunal.

More recently, however, the House of Lords in *Re B (Children) (Care Proceedings: Standard of Proof)* (2008) cast doubt on the notion that the balance of probabilities is case-dependent. It held that there was a clear distinction between the criminal and civil standards of proof and that "neither the seriousness of the allegation nor the seriousness of the consequences should make any difference to the standard of proof to be applied in determining the facts" (para. [70] per Baroness Hale of Richmond).

Along with the balance of probabilities, however interpreted, there have been numerous versions of the standard of proof used in court and tribunal proceedings, particularly in the United States, including:

- reasonable suspicion;
- reasonable belief;
- some credible evidence;
- substantial evidence;
- the preponderance of evidence;
- clear and convincing evidence.

This brief overview of standards of proof indicates that it can be difficult to pinpoint the quantum of evidence needed to make a decision in court or tribunal proceedings. When a person's liberty is at stake, it would seem that a high standard of proof should be required, but this has not necessarily been the case in relation to preventive detention regimes.

There are many possible combinations for classifying proceedings relating to preventive detention and supervision orders. The schemes discussed in this book have been variously classified as:

- criminal proceedings with a non-criminal standard of proof;
- criminal proceedings with no set standard of proof;
- civil proceedings with the criminal standard of proof;
- civil proceedings with a non-criminal standard of proof;
- civil proceedings with no set standard of proof.

None of the schemes discussed have been categorized as criminal proceedings with the criminal standard of proof, presumably because criminal proceedings with the criminal standard of proof is connected to the criminal trial process and is seen as closely tied to the presumption of innocence. The other combinations, however, have been used and these are discussed below.

Criminal Proceedings but a Non-Criminal Standard of Proof

Section 40 of the Dangerous Sexual Offenders Act 2006 (WA) states that "[p]roceedings under this Act or on an appeal under this Act, are to be taken to be criminal proceedings for all purposes." This means that the rules of evidence apply as for criminal trials, and, as Justice Murray stated in *State of Western Australia v Alvisse (No 2)* (2007: para. [5]) that "[t]he proceedings are adversarial. It is not an enquiry by the court. The court conducts itself in the ordinary way, making its judgment upon the basis of evidence adduced by the applicant and the respondent."

Heather Douglas (2008: 870) has pointed out that in practice "even though proceedings are described as 'criminal' in Western Australia, this appears to have little effect on the way that decisions are made." This may be because a non-criminal standard of proof applies to these proceedings. Section 7(2) of the Western Australian Act requires the Director of Public Prosecution to adduce "acceptable and cogent evidence" and satisfy the court "to a high degree of probability" that there is an unacceptable risk that if the person concerned were not subject to a continuing detention order or a supervision order, the person would commit a serious sexual offence. It may also be because the legislation mandates the court to consider reports from two psychiatrists who have assessed the offender as well as "other medical, psychiatric, psychological, or other assessment" (s. 7(3)(b)). Hence the focus is on opinion evidence rather than the evidence of witnesses which may give rise to problems of hearsay.

The standard of a "high degree of probability" is also used in the preventive detention and supervision laws in Queensland and New South Wales. How this has been interpreted is discussed below.

Criminal Proceedings but No Set Standard of Proof

As with the Western Australian preventive detention and supervision scheme, proceedings under the New Zealand scheme of extended supervision orders have also been characterized as criminal in nature. In *Belcher v Chief Executive of the Department of Corrections* (2007) the New Zealand Court of Appeal held that an extended supervision order is a criminal penalty that was intended by the legislature to apply retrospectively. It held that this was inconsistent with the Bill of Rights Act 1990 (NZ), but it also held that it did not have jurisdiction to make a declaration of inconsistency. An application for leave to appeal was dismissed by the Supreme Court of New Zealand in *Belcher v Chief Executive of the Department of Corrections* (2007).

Despite the finding in *Belcher*'s case that an extended supervision order is a criminal penalty, the Court of Appeal subsequently ruled that the criminal standard of proof was not required. In *McDonnell v Chief Executive of the Department of Corrections* (2009: para. [75]), the Court of Appeal stated that "[t]he fact that ESOs are a penalty and the proceedings are therefore criminal does not require the criminal standard of proof that applies in criminal trials to be applied."

Section 107I(2) of the Parole Act 2002 (NZ) gives the Court power to make an ESO if it is "satisfied . . . that the offender is likely to commit any . . . relevant offences . . ." The Court of Appeal in *McDonnell*'s case approved the approach taken by John Hansen and Panckhurst JJ of the High Court of New Zealand in *Chief Executive of the Department of Corrections v McIntosh* (2004: paras [20]–[21]). Justices Hansen and Panckhurst had adopted the meaning given to "satisfied" in the context of a sentence of indefinite detention, as set out in *R v Leitch* (1998: 428):

> "The need to be 'satisfied' calls for the exercise of judgment by the sentencing Court. It is inapt to import notions of the burden of proof and of setting a particular standard, eg beyond reasonable doubt."

Thus, in New Zealand, there is no set civil or criminal standard of proof for the making of an extended supervision order. As Gledhill (2011: 94) states, it "is simply a matter of [the court] reaching a judicial conclusion as to [the likelihood of the commission of a further offence], rather than applying a particular standard of proof."

Civil Proceedings with the Criminal Standard of Proof

Returning to the facts set out at the beginning of this chapter, the House of Lords in *R (McCann) v Crown Court at Manchester; Clingham v Kensington and Chelsea Royal London Borough Council* (2003) classified ASBO proceedings as civil in nature, yet went on to hold that the criminal standard of proof should apply.

Lord Steyn stated (2003: 812) that "[h]aving concluded that the relevant proceedings are civil, in principle it follows that the standard of proof ordinarily applicable in civil proceedings, namely the balance of probabilities, should apply." However, he went on to hold (2003: 812) that "pragmatism dictates that the task of magistrates should be made more straightforward by ruling that they must . . . apply the criminal standard." Why applying the standard of beyond reasonable doubt is more straightforward than applying the standard of the balance of probabilities is not fully explained. Lord Steyn implies (2003: 812) that the beyond reasonable doubt standard will be satisfied by requiring magistrates *"to be sure* that the defendant has acted in an anti-social manner" (emphasis in original.)

Lord Hope of Craighead (2003: 825) pointed to the "serious consequences" of ASBOs as requiring a higher standard of proof than the balance of probabilities. He stated (2003: 826) that "the condition . . . that the defendant has acted in an anti-social manner raises serious questions of fact, and the implications for him of proving that he has acted in the way are also serious." The other Lords agreed with the use of the criminal standard of proof without detailing their reasons.

The use of the criminal standard of proof in civil proceedings has also been accepted in relation to post-sentence preventive detention and supervision schemes in the United States. Courts must be satisfied "beyond reasonable doubt" that the offender is a sexually violent predator who more probably than not will reoffend if released.

In *Kansas v Hendricks* (1997), the United States Supreme Court was asked to consider the nature of the proceedings under the Kansas Sexually Violent Predator Act (1994). Although the legislature had declared the Act to be a "civil" statute (§ 59-26a01), the Kansas Supreme Court (*Re Hendricks* 1996: 132) held that the trial court should employ the standard of "beyond reasonable doubt" to determine whether Hendricks was a sexually violent predator.

Leroy Hendricks' qualifying offending occurred ten years before the Kansas Sexually Violent Predator Act was passed. He argued that because the Kansas Supreme Court had held that the criminal standard of proof applied, the proceedings were criminal in nature and thus could not be applied retrospectively.

The majority (1997: 361) cited *Allen v Illinois* (1986: 368) as setting out the rule that categorizing a particular proceeding as civil or criminal is a question of statutory construction. The majority (1997: 361) stated that "[n]othing on the face of the statute suggests that the legislature sought to create anything other than a civil commitment scheme designed to protect the public from harm." It found (1997: 361) that Leroy Hendricks had not provided "the clearest proof" that the scheme was so punitive in its purpose that the manifest intent to deem the scheme as civil in nature was negated. The majority stated (1997: 361–62):

> As a threshold matter, commitment under the Act does not implicate either of the two primary objectives of criminal punishment: retribution or deterrence. The Act's purpose is not retributive because it does not affix culpability for prior criminal conduct. Instead, such conduct is used solely for evidentiary purposes, either to demonstrate that a "mental abnormality" exists or to support a finding of future dangerousness. In addition, the Kansas Act does not make a criminal conviction a prerequisite for commitment – persons absolved of criminal responsibility may nonetheless be subject to confinement under the Act.

Given that the scheme was interpreted as civil in nature, it could, therefore, apply retrospectively. The majority did, however, provide a significant limitation on what needed to be proved beyond reasonable doubt by requiring that the individual concerned must not only be dangerous, but also "dangerous beyond control" (1997: 357). In *Kansas v Crane* (2002: 415), the Court upheld the "dangerous beyond control" interpretation of the legislation, while stating that there may be a "considerable overlap" between difficulty in controlling behaviour and "defective understanding or appreciation."

In *Selig v Young* (2001), the United States Supreme Court also held that the Washington scheme for the detention of sexually violent predators was civil in nature. This case concerned Andre Brigham Young who had been detained after the conclusion of his sentence for six rapes. Young argued that while the law might be valid on its face, it was punitive in its effect. He urged the Court to apply the approach to the characterization of the law that was endorsed by a majority of the Supreme Court in

Allen v Illinois (1986) – that it was necessary for the Court to recognize the practical effect of the legislation, which was to detain people indefinitely in prison-style conditions.

The majority in *Selig v Young* held that the clearest proof of punitive conditions would be required to disprove the legislature's stated intention, and that Young had not satisfied that burden. The majority noted that the Washington State law required adequate care and individualized treatment and that detainees were at liberty to bring civil suits to enforce Washington State's statutory obligations to provide this care and treatment. The majority thus accepted the stated objectives of Washington's law as preventive and rehabilitative and found that the civil commitment regime did not offend the constitutional guarantees against retrospectivity and double jeopardy. As a result, State legislatures have been careful not to draft legislation that appears to be punitive. Instead, the laws are expressed as preventive measures to reduce the risk posed by dangerous offenders rather than to serve as punishment for specific crimes.

In relation to suspected "unlawful enemy combatants" under the United States Military Commissions Act (2006) (10 USC § 949), before a vote is taken on the findings, the military judge must instruct the commission members "that the accused must be presumed to be innocent until his [or her] guilt is established by legal and competent evidence beyond reasonable doubt." The rules of evidence echo those of federal criminal procedure, but military commission proceedings are not the same as criminal trial proceedings because there is no jury, proceedings may be closed to the public (10 USC § 949d) and hearsay evidence may be admitted (10 USC § 949a(b)(3)(d)(as amended)). The proceedings, therefore, do not fit clearly within either a civil or criminal model, but have given rise to a specific branch of military law (Schleuter 2008; Elsea 2010). What is clear though is that the criminal standard of proof is used in the proceedings, however defined.

Civil Proceedings with a Non-Criminal Standard of Proof

A number of the schemes discussed in this book fall within the category of civil proceedings with a non-criminal standard of proof. The United States Supreme Court in a unanimous opinion in *Addington v Texas* (1979) rejected an argument that the evidentiary standard in civil commitment proceedings relating to individuals with severe mental illness should be "beyond a reasonable doubt." The Court noted (1979: 425) that "civil commitment for any purpose constitutes a significant deprivation of liberty that requires due process protection." It also stated (1979: 427) that "the individual's interest in the outcome of a civil commitment proceeding is of such weight and gravity that due process requires the state to justify confinement by proof more substantial than a mere preponderance of the evidence." However, the Court went on to hold that civil commitment is not fundamentally punitive and that it "can in no sense be equated with a criminal prosecution" (1979: 428). It settled (1979: 433) on a standard of proof of "clear and convincing evidence" of dangerousness. It rejected the criminal standard of proof on the basis that "given the uncertainties of psychiatric diagnosis, it may impose a burden the state cannot meet and thereby erect an unreasonable barrier to needed medical treatment" (1979: 432).

In Australia, hearings relating to the involuntary detention and treatment of those with severe mental illness are also civil in nature, but the standard of proof is generally that of the balance of probabilities. In *Re the Appeal of MM* (1987: 5), the Mental Health Review Board of Victoria stated:

> if a person is lawfully involuntarily detained in a psychiatric inpatient service pursuant to the relevant provisions of the Mental Health Act 1986 it is not for the purposes of punishment but because the legislature has decided that in certain circumstances persons who are mentally ill should be detained and treated either for their own good or for the protection of the public. Proceedings to determine whether that involuntary detention should continue must, therefore, be regarded as civil rather than criminal in nature . . . It is a legal truism that the standard of proof normally required in civil proceedings is the balance of probabilities. That is the standard which the Board proposes to apply.

The Mental Health Review Board of Victoria's *Members Manual* (2006: para. 4.3.2) describes the balance of probabilities as meaning "on the basis of the material before the Board, is it more likely than not that X version of the facts is correct rather than Y version."

In *S v State Administrative Tribunal of Western Australia {No 2}* (2012), the Supreme Court of Western Australia held, in the context of guardianship legislation, that administrative tribunals should apply the standard set out by Sir Owen Dixon in *Briginshaw v Briginshaw* (1938: 361–62) and in particular, take into account, the "gravity of the consequences flowing from a particular finding." In *S*'s case, it was held that the absence of witnesses together with the absence of a process to verify the information given in a guardianship hearing amounted to a denial of procedural fairness. In the context of supervision orders for those found not guilty of a crime by reason of mental impairment, the Court of Appeal of the Supreme Court of Victoria has also recently held that the principle in *Briginshaw*'s case is applicable: *NOM v Director of Public Prosecutions & Ors* (2012).

A different standard of proof based on probability is used in the Australian laws relating to preventive detention and supervision in Queensland, New South Wales, and Western Australia. The Queensland and New South Wales laws refer to the proceedings as civil in nature (Crimes (Serious Sex Offenders) Act 2006 (NSW), s. 21) and the standard of proof as that of "a high degree of probability" that the offender is a serious danger to the community based on "an unacceptable risk" of reoffending (Crimes (Serious Sex Offenders) Act 2006 (NSW), ss 9(2), 17(2), 17(3); Dangerous Prisoners (Sexual Offenders) Act 2003 (Qld), s. 7). Despite proceedings in Western Australia being criminal in nature, the "high degree of probability test" is also used pursuant to section 7(2)(b) of the Dangerous Sexual Offenders Act 2006 (WA).

What a "high degree of probability" actually means has been the subject of some judicial interpretation. In *Director of Public Prosecutions (WA) v D* (2010: para. [13]), Justice Hasluck described this as "more than a finding on the balance of probabilities, but less than a finding of proof beyond reasonable doubt." This interpretation had previously been accepted by Steytler P and Buss JA in *Director of Public Prosecutions (WA) v GTR* (2008 para. [34]). Similarly, the New South Wales Court of Appeal stated in *Cornwall v Attorney-General for New South Wales* (2007: para. [21]):

> The expression "a high degree of probability" indicates something "beyond more probably than not"; so that the existence of the risk, that is the likelihood of the offender committing a further serious sex offence, does have to be proved to a higher degree than the normal civil standard of proof, though not to the criminal standard of beyond reasonable doubt.

The situation in New South Wales, however, has been somewhat confusing because the original section 17 required that the court be satisfied to a high degree of probability that the offender was *likely* to commit a further serious sex offence if he or she was not kept under supervision before making an extended supervision or continuing detention order. In *Tillman v Attorney-General (NSW)* (2007: 461), Giles and Ipp JJA decided that the close proximity of the words "high degree of probability" and "likely" inferred that Parliament intended the standard of proof to denote a higher degree of probability than "likely," the latter being interpreted as denoting "a degree of probability at the upper end of the scale, but not necessarily exceeding 50 per cent." In comparison, President Mason (2007: 450) preferred that "likely" be interpreted as meaning "more probable than not." He stated (2007: 451):

> The common law's presumption in favour of the liberty of the subject underpins the predictive inquiry to be undertaken and

further explains why this opaque legislation should be interpreted strictly in the sense that the available, tighter meaning of "more probable than not" should be chosen for "likely."

President Mason (2007: 451) also observed that the standard of proof that the court be satisfied to a high degree of probability "falls somewhere between a slight preponderance and satisfaction beyond reasonable doubt." In a subsequent case, *Winters v Attorney-General (NSW)* (2008: para. [2]), President Mason stated that he was bound by what the majority had decided in *Tillman*'s case in relation to the word "likely" – that is, it meant "a degree of probability at the upper end of the scale, but not necessarily exceeding 50 per cent."

The New South Wales legislation was subsequently amended by Schedule 1 of the Crimes (Serious Sex Offenders) Amendment Act 2010 to remove the word "likely" from sections 17(2) and (3). The legislation now requires the court to be "satisfied to a high degree of probability that the offender poses an unacceptable risk of committing a serious sex offence if he or she is not kept under supervision." Schedule 1 of the Crimes (Serious Sex Offenders) Amendment Act 2010 also inserted a new section 17(3A) which states:

> The Supreme Court is not required to determine that the risk of a person committing a serious sex offence is more likely than not in order to determine that the person poses an unacceptable risk of committing a serious sex offence.

This reflects the majority decision in *Tillman*'s case.

The notion of probability is bypassed in schemes relating to the preventive detention and supervision of suspected terrorists. Instead, the key terms justifying the initial preventive detention of suspected terrorists are generally that of a suspicion or belief "on reasonable grounds" that the individual concerned is a terrorist or will engage in a terrorist act. For example, under section 105.4 of the Australian Criminal Code (Cth) the application for a "preventative detention order" may be made where "there are reasonable grounds to suspect" the person concerned will engage in or is planning a terrorist act. In the United Kingdom, under section 3 of the Terrorism Prevention and Investigation Measures Act 2011, a measure can be made on condition that the Secretary of State "reasonably believes" that the person has been or is involved in terrorism-related activity.

What is actually meant by a belief or suspicion on reasonable grounds is open to debate. In *Secretary of State for the Home Department v BM* (2012), Justice Collins of the Administrative Court considered the requirement that for terrorism prevention and investigation measures, the Secretary of State must reasonably believe that the individual has been involved in terrorism-related activity. He stated (2012: para. [4]) that "[r]easonable belief is a higher standard than having reasonable grounds for suspicion." However, a reasonable belief does not equate to a standard on the balance of probabilities. Justice Collins went on to state (2012: para. [34]):

> It is entirely consistent with the view that for the belief to be reasonable it must be shown that the material provided justified the belief that the state of affairs did exist whether or not subsequent investigations or testing in court shows that it did not. The reality is, as I have said, that to found a reasonable belief that a subject is or has been involved in [terrorism-related activity] and that a [terrorism prevention and investigation measure] is necessary does not involve the requirement to establish involvement in specific [terrorism-related activity] to any higher standard than that which can properly give rise to such a belief. No doubt some facts which go to forming the belief will be clearly established, others may be based on an assessment of the various pieces of evidence available. But there is certainly no requirement that particular [terrorism-related activity] needs to be established to the standard of at least more probable than not.

Hence, a reasonable belief is considered to be a lesser standard of proof than the balance of probabilities (see also Clarke 2008: 234), although it appears to impose a higher threshold than a reasonable suspicion.

A standard of "reasonable suspicion" is the lowest of possible standards that have been used in this area and coincides with the general standard relating to arrest and warrants. There have been some judicial opinions on the term "suspicion" in criminal cases. In the English Court of Appeal case of *Shaaban bin Hussein v Chong Fook Kam* (1970: 948), Lord Devlin stated that "[s]uspicion" is "a state of conjecture or surmise where proof is lacking" and in the South Australian Supreme Court case of *Tucs v Manley* (1985: 461), Jacobs J stated that a "reasonable suspicion" "does not necessarily imply that it is well-founded or that the grounds for suspicion must be factually correct." From these statements, it can be gleaned that the word "suspicion" has been interpreted as describing a mental state that need not be based on "proof."

The concepts of both "belief" and "suspicion" are tempered by an objective gloss, that of "reasonableness." As set out in Table 4.3 in Chapter 4, in some of the Australian states' legislation relating to the preventive detention of suspected terrorists, the standard is for the judge to be satisfied of the necessity for detention "on reasonable grounds." Of course the notion of reasonableness has been criticized as meaning different things to different people at different times. Geoffrey Alpert and William Smith (1994) have pointed out that the police have not been aided by vague standards of "reasonableness" guidelines in relation to the use of force. The same can be said of reasonableness in relation to both belief and suspicion.

In Australia, in relation to interim control orders, section 104.4(1) of the Criminal Code (Cth) requires that:

> (c) the court is satisfied on the balance of probabilities:
>
>> (i)   that making the order would substantially assist in preventing a terrorist act; or
>>
>> (ii)   that the person has provided training to, or received training from, a listed terrorist organisation; and
>
> (d) the court is satisfied on the balance of probabilities that each of the obligations, prohibitions and restrictions to be imposed on the person by the order is reasonably necessary, and reasonably appropriate and adapted, for the purpose of protecting the public from a terrorist act.

Under section 104.14(4)(d) the court may then confirm the interim control order without variation if it "is satisfied on the balance of probabilities that the order was properly served on the person in relation to whom the order is made." Under section 104.15, the interim control order then ceases to be in force and the confirmed control order begins to be in force.

Schemes that are characterized as civil in nature, therefore, vary markedly in the non-criminal standard of proof required, ranging from a reasonable suspicion or belief to clear and convincing evidence through to a high degree of probability.

Civil Proceedings and No Set Standard of Proof

One sex offender scheme is an anomaly in not having any set standard of proof. Sections 9(1) and 35(1) of the Serious Sex Offenders (Detention and Supervision) Act 2009 (Vic) do not refer to any probability standard in relation to extended supervision and detention orders, but require the court simply to be "satisfied" in relation to the "unacceptable risk" of reoffending.

Previously, section 11 of the Serious Sex Offenders Monitoring Act 2005 (Vic), as with the preventive detention scheme in New South Wales, required the court to be satisfied to a high degree of probability that the offender was likely to commit a relevant offence before making an extended supervision order. In *TSL v Secretary to the Department of Justice* (2006), the Victorian Court of Appeal held that the decision to make an order should proceed in two stages. First, the court must be satisfied that "there is a high degree of probability that the offender will commit a relevant offence" (2006: para. [38]); and second, if the court is so satisfied, it must decide whether to exercise its discretion to order an extended supervision order. Callaway AP (with whom Buchanan JA and Coldrey AJA agreed) stated (2006: para. [11]) that there was no reason to consider that "a high degree of probability" had to be more than 50 per cent.

Subsequently, in *RJE v Secretary to the Department of Justice & Ors* (2008), Maxwell P and Weinberg JA disagreed with this interpretation. They stated (2008: para. [21]):

> we consider that in this context 'likely to commit' means 'more likely than not to commit.' That is, the Court must be satisfied that there is a greater than 50 per cent chance that a relevant offence will be committed if the offender is released unsupervised. The previous decision of this Court in TSL, holding that a less than 50 per cent chance might suffice for this purpose, should not be followed. . . .

In a separate judgment, Nettle JA agreed with this interpretation of "likely."

The Victorian government took immediate action to counteract this interpretation. It passed the Serious Sex Offenders Monitoring Amendment Act 2009 that introduced subsection (2B) into section 11 of the Serious Sex Offenders Monitoring Act 2005. This stated:

> For the avoidance of doubt, subsection (1) [setting out the standard of proof] permits a determination that an offender is likely to commit a relevant offence on the basis of a lower threshold than a threshold of more likely than not.

Later in 2009, the Victorian scheme of extended supervision orders for sex offenders was replaced by a scheme of both post-sentence detention and supervision. In replacing the earlier legislation with the Serious Sex Offenders (Detention and Supervision) Act 2009, it was clear that the legislature rejected the Court of Appeal's approach in *RJE*'s case and intended that a low standard of proof apply.

Sections 35(4) and 36(2) of the 2009 Act now state that "an offender poses an unacceptable risk of committing a relevant offence even if the likelihood that the offender will commit a relevant offence is less than a likelihood of more likely than not." This reflects the earlier Court of Appeal decision in *TSL*'s case that a less than 50 per cent chance that the offender will commit a relevant offence will suffice. While there is no set standard as such other than requiring the court to be "satisfied" there is an "unacceptable risk" of reoffending, it is clear that the Victorian government intended that evidence of risk be easily proved.

The Importance of a High Standard of Proof

Having a civil standard of proof, however phrased, or no set standard of proof provides courts and tribunals with a great deal of discretion. This is compounded in proceedings where written reasons for decisions are not made or are not publicly available. Terry Carney and colleagues (2011: 196) have pointed out that in their research observing how mental health tribunals reached decisions:

> the *appearance* was that these decisions were frequently based on the tribunal members' acceptance of the limited information available to the tribunal, dominated by the clinical perspectives in the file, and that conflicting views raised by consumers or others present were downplayed.

Michael Perlin (2000) has argued that civil commitment practice has elements of what he refers to as "sanism," an irrational prejudice that contributes to and reflects social attitudes towards those with severe mental illness such as that they are dangerous and lack decision-making capacity. He states (2012: 5) that sanism is "sustained and perpetuated by our use of a false 'ordinary common sense' and heuristic reasoning in an unconscious response to events both in everyday life and in the legal process (refs omitted)."

Allowing courts and tribunals too much discretion in relation to the weight to be placed on evidence of risk does bring with it the possibility that decision-makers will resort to this problematic notion of "common sense" reasoning. Justice Michael Kirby in *Chappel v Hart* (1998: 269) pointed out that resort to "common sense" is "at best an uncertain guide involving subjective, unexpressed and undefined extra-legal values." How much extra-legal values infuse decisions concerning the civil commitment of those with severe mental illness is difficult to ascertain given the lack of a body of reported decisions in this field, but Ian Freckelton (2010: 204) has warned that the lack of formality in Mental Health Tribunal hearings brings with it the danger that it "can become a licence for lack of clinical and decision-making rigour, over-ready judgmentalism and paternalism." He has suggested that in relation to mental health tribunal hearings, "extra-legislative factors" such as "lacking insight" and "non-compliance" with treatment have an overly important role to play in satisfying the standard of proof (Freckelton 2005, 2010).

What is important to keep in mind is that preventive detention and supervision schemes ultimately affect a person's liberty. Denise Meyerson (2009: 533) argues that "[t]he lower we require the likelihood of harm to be and the lower we require our degree of confidence in the predictions [of risk] to be, the higher the risk of the erroneous deprivation of liberty."

She argues that it should not be sufficient to prove the prediction of risk on the balance of probabilities,

> because setting the procedural burden at that level would impose an equal risk of error on the person who poses a risk of harm and the community. Imposing such a symmetrical risk of error could only be justified if a false negative were as regrettable as a false positive, but . . . this is not the case.

Grant Morris (1999: 81) writes that "for an individual to be deprived of liberty without having transgressed society's criminal laws, the harm posed by the individual must be great and its probable occurrence must be extremely high." He points out (1999: 82) that "[h]owever problematic the Kansas Sexually Violent Predator Act, at least it imposes upon the state a burden of proving beyond a reasonable doubt that the individual meets the statutory criteria." He argues that in relation to the civil commitment of those with severe mental illness, the burden should be on the State to prove beyond a reasonable doubt that there is a 90 per cent probability that violence, suicide, or self-inflicted harm will occur within six months. Morris' intention is to make civil commitment of those with severe mental illness difficult to achieve. Setting a 90 per cent probability of harm, however, may not be acceptable to judges who have traditionally shied away from mathematical conceptions of probability.

It is interesting, however, that courts have been prepared to set a standard of proof beyond reasonable doubt in relation to ASBOs and the preventive detention of sexually violent predators. The imposition of a criminal standard of proof in civil proceedings may seem to be counterintuitive in principle, but it does serve to curtail the use of orders that have serious repercussions for personal liberty.

The criminal standard of proof, or failing that, a standard of a "high degree of probability" interpreted as meaning more than the civil standard of the balance of probabilities would help circumscribe the scope of preventive detention and supervision schemes. It is perhaps understandable that law enforcement officers might need a lower standard such as reasonable belief for the initial detention of persons suspected of being terrorists, but judges making detention or control orders in relation to suspected terrorists should require a higher quantum of evidence than the existing "reasonable belief" or "balance of probabilities" standards.

Imposing a high standard of proof will help ensure that evidence of risk is rigorously examined and people are not unnecessarily deprived of their liberty. However, as exemplified by the Victorian government's approach to the interpretation of the standard of "a high degree of probability" as less than a 50 per cent probability, it appears that some governments intend for as many individuals as possible to be detained and supervised on the basis of community protection. While judicial interpretation may impose high standards of proof where legislative provisions are unclear, the legislature ultimately determines what standard decision-makers must apply.

THE RULES OF EXPERT EVIDENCE

The rules of evidence in general are related to matters of proof. Some of the tribunal and court proceedings discussed above such as those related to the involuntary detention of persons with severe mental illness are not bound by the rules of evidence. This allows proceedings to be informal and enables those the subject of the proceedings to take an active part.

As outlined in Table 4.3 of Chapter 4, the judicial proceedings relating to the preventive detention of suspected terrorists are closed proceedings and most of the Australian jurisdictions have penalties for the disclosure of information about them. Because these are civil proceedings, hearsay evidence may be admitted, but it is up to the decision-maker to decide what weight to give to that evidence.

In civil hearings, courts, administrative agencies, and tribunals are under a duty to comply with the legal requirements of procedural fairness, sometimes referred to as "natural justice" (O'Connor *et al.* 2006: Ch. 3). This involves a duty to adopt fair procedures that are appropriate and relevant to the circumstances of the particular case. In general, the doctrine of procedural fairness means that the more serious the consequences of a decision, the higher the standard of proof required.

There are two rules of procedural fairness:

* The hearing rule whereby a decision-maker must give the affected persons an opportunity to state his or her case; and
* The bias rule whereby the decision-maker must be impartial and have no personal interest in the matter to be decided.

Sometimes the first rule can be displaced by legislation. For example, as mentioned in Chapter 5, Jack Thomas was made the subject of an interim control order despite his not being present at the hearing. This was because Division 104 of the Criminal Code (Cth) enables interim control orders to be made *ex parte* without the person concerned being present. Section 104.14(4) of the Criminal Code (Cth) states that a court can confirm an interim control order in the absence of the person concerned or his or her representative.

In relation to mental health tribunal hearings, any evidence of potential harm to self or others by those with severe mental illness is generally presented by treating clinicians and their opinions are often based upon their own "observations and experiences" (Winick 2003: 28), rather than being based on actuarial risk assessment instruments. In relation to the preventive detention and supervision of suspected terrorists, the language of risk is not used at all and expert evidence by mental health practitioners is not generally considered. However, as outlined in Chapter 3, this situation may be changing.

Proceedings relating to serious offenders that require expert testimony from psychiatrists and/or psychologists are subject to the rules relating to expert evidence. The law of evidence provides that it is only expert witnesses who may give evidence based on their opinions (Freckelton 2008). Section 25(1) of the Evidence Act 2006 (NZ), for example, sets out that the court must be able to obtain "substantial help" from the expert opinion in understanding other evidence in the proceedings or in ascertaining any fact necessary for the relevant decision (see further Freckelton and Selby 2009). There are various codes of conduct in existence in relation to expert evidence. For example, in New Zealand, psychiatrists and psychologists must comply with the Code of Conduct for Expert Witnesses contained in schedule 4 to the High Court Rules.

In order to be able to give admissible opinion evidence, psychiatrists and psychologists need to have specialized current knowledge about a specific area. Ian Freckelton and Hugh Selby (2009: para. 10.5.40) observe that for psychiatrists and psychologists:

> to give oral evidence in the witness box about an area, they must be in a position to demonstrate convincingly that they have specialised knowledge about it that is up-to-date and of real substance. The more sub-specialised the area and the more it is controversial, in a practical sense the more onerous will be the burden.

In Australia, New Zealand, and the United Kingdom, there is uncertainty as to whether it is the expert's opinions in the context of his or her specialization or the reliability of the "scientific" research upon which it is based that determines whether or not he or she falls within the necessary area of expertise. Ian Freckelton (2008: 207) states that "if it appears that if an expert's views are out-of-step with the preponderance of opinion within the intellectual marketplace, they may not be admissible."

In *R v Luttrell* (2004: para. [25]), the English Court of Appeal noted that law in that jurisdiction will not consider expert evidence properly admissible if it is "based on a developing new brand of science or medicine ... [it must be] accepted by the scientific community as being able to provide accurate and reliable opinion." However, it went on to state (2004: para. [34]):

> In established fields of science, the court may take the view that expert evidence would fall beyond the recognised limits of the field or that methods are too unconventional to be regarded as subject to the scientific discipline. But a skill or expertise can be recognized and respected, and thus satisfy the conditions for admissible expert evidence, although the discipline is not susceptible to this sort of scientific discipline.

Thus, in England, while reliability might be relevant to the admissibility of evidence, it does not constitute a criterion for it. This also appears to be the case in Australia and New Zealand.

Since the 1990s, the focus of decisions in the United States and Canada has been upon the reliability of scientific techniques and theories as the predominant criterion for admissibility (Freckelton and Selby 2009). In the United States, the Supreme Court ruling in *Daubert v Merrell Dow Pharmaceuticals Inc* (1993) prohibits expert testimony "unless its basis has been subject to some sort of verification process, ideally including the generation of error rates that provide the fact finder with a sense of how much weight to give to the testimony" (Slobogin 2011a: 44). The Federal Rules of Evidence (2010: 401) state that evidence is probative if it has "any tendency to make the existence of any fact that is of consequence to the determination of the action more probable or less probable than it would be without the evidence." On this basis, Christopher Slobogin (2007: 117) observes that expert evidence of risk "virtually always satisfies this test" because predictions of risk generally "exceed chance or random selection." The Federal Rules of Evidence (2010: 403) also set out that evidence may still be inadmissible if it has the potential for prejudicing, biasing, or over-influencing the jury.

What then does this mean for expert evidence by psychiatrists and psychologists concerning the risk of future harm? The answer is complicated by the fact that testimony given by psychiatrists and psychologists may be viewed as a combination of evidence based on education, training, and experience ("non-scientific") and evidence based on verifiable experimentation by way of risk assessment instruments ("scientific") (Bernstein 1995).

It is clear that in relation to post-sentence preventive detention and supervision schemes, expert psychiatric and psychological evidence based on risk assessment instruments is admissible. In *Woods v Director of Public Prosecutions (WA)* (2008: para. [53]), President Steytler and Associate

Justice Buss of the Supreme Court of Western Australia pointed out that "[p]sychiatric evidence that is sought to be adduced in any proceedings may, in a particular case, be based on scientific tests or scientific publications and data." They held (2008: para. [60]) that the psychiatrists who had given evidence on risk in proceedings seeking a supervision order "were entitled to base their opinions and evidence on the so-called 'assessment instruments' referred to them by them." They went on to state (2008: para. [60]):

> In any event, it is apparent from the psychiatrists' reports and evidence that the assessment tools on which they relied were generally accepted by psychiatrists engaged in the assessment of sexual offenders and the prediction of recidivism, subject to the limitations (including the application of the tools to the indigenous Australian population) which were acknowledged by them.

Any limitations of the particular instruments used, therefore, goes to the weight to be placed on them in making the decision. As Murray AJA stated in *Woods'* case (2008: para. [228]):

> expert psychiatric evidence . . . and the reports made by psychiatrists, is admissible evidence. . . . Whether such evidence carries weight as acceptable and cogent evidence, and the extent to which it may fall short of that, is a matter for the judgment of the court. All that is required is the court "have regard" to it.

Judges can thus be viewed as the gatekeepers in relation to the admissibility of expert evidence and they have considerable discretion as to the weight that should be attached to such evidence. After examining how evidence of the risk of future harm has been accepted by Australian courts in a range of matters, David Ruschena (2003: 129) writes that "the vast majority of cases find no problem with the proof of likelihood of future offending." The ethical perspectives relating to whether and how expert evidence of risk should be given are discussed in Chapter 8.

CONCLUSION

With the exceptions of the schemes in Western Australia and New Zealand, the preventive and supervision regimes discussed in this book have generally been viewed as part of the civil justice system, opening the way for a low standard of proof, the availability of retrospective operation, and the acceptance of their being seen as preventive rather than punitive in nature. Even where such schemes are characterized as criminal in nature, it appears that because the proceedings are dependent on expert opinion evidence and use a lesser standard of proof than "beyond reasonable doubt," the hearings are markedly similar in practice to those characterized as civil in nature.

The schemes characterized as requiring civil proceedings vary markedly in the non-criminal standard of proof required, ranging from a reasonable suspicion or belief to clear and convincing evidence through to a high degree of probability. Some schemes use no set standard at all. Some proceedings are bound by the rules of evidence and others are not. There is a question as to whether this actually matters. The United States Supreme Court in *Addington v Texas* (1979: 425–26) admitted to "a belief that the varying standards tend to produce comparable results" in deprivation of liberty schemes because of the amount of judicial discretion involved.

The admissibility of expert evidence should not be confused with the standard of proof that needs to be satisfied. Expert evidence of risk may be admissible, but it is still up to the court or the tribunal to decide whether that evidence satisfies the requisite legal test.

Where the expert evidence of psychiatrists and psychologists on risk is called for, courts have generally held such evidence to be admissible, but judges have retained discretion as to how much weight to place upon it.

Michael Barnett and Robert Hayes (2008: 59) point out in relation to schemes enabling the post-sentence detention and supervision of sex offenders:

> Civil commitment schemes are likely to create difficulties in developing a consistent approach to the standard of proof because the proceedings themselves are artificially hybrid. Their aim is to generally require a standard of proof lower than the criminal standard of beyond reasonable doubt but to require, on at least issues directly bearing on continuing detention, a standard higher than merely on the balance of probabilities because detention involves the loss of liberty.

Certainly at present there is a lack of consistency in the type of proceedings, the standard of proof, and the evidentiary rules that apply to preventive detention and supervision schemes. While it may be unrealistic to believe that a consistent approach can ever be achieved across the different schemes, imposing a high standard of proof and strict compliance with the rules of procedural fairness and expert evidence may help ensure that evidence of risk is rigorously examined and people are not unnecessarily deprived of their liberty.

Part III

HUMAN RIGHTS AND
ETHICAL ISSUES

7

HUMAN RIGHTS ISSUES

INTRODUCTION: ROBERT JOHN FARDON

Robert John Fardon was born in 1949 in Murwillumbah, a country town in far northeastern New South Wales. His parents separated when he was very young and he was raised by his father who often left him in the care of an aunt and uncle on a farm. Fardon described his father as a chronic alcoholic who was absent for lengthy periods either working as a labourer or serving time in prison. When his father was around, he often brutally punished Fardon. He abused Fardon's dog and eventually shot it in front of him. He also gave alcohol to Fardon when he was only five or six. At the age of 12, Fardon was expelled from school after punching a teacher. He then worked on the farm or in other labouring jobs.

When he was 14, Fardon left the farm after a physical fight with his father. He lived on the streets, working as an occasional farm hand and hanging out with a motor cycle gang.

In later years, Fardon told mental health practitioners that when he was seven, he was sexually abused by an older cousin who was intellectually impaired and that this continued for about three or four years until he could defend himself. Fardon complained to his aunt and uncle and to his father but was not believed. He claimed also to have been sexually abused by other cousins and an adult member of the family. He told one mental health professional that he first had heterosexual sex at the age of about 11 when his father brought a woman home from a pub to have sex with him. He was about 13 or 14 when he had sex with a girl of the same age.

When Fardon was 18, he pleaded guilty and was convicted of the attempted "unlawful carnal knowledge" of a girl aged under ten, but was released on a three-year good behaviour bond. Over the next decade or so, he was convicted of various offences including theft, drink driving, and one count of assault occasioning bodily harm. He was dependent on alcohol and took a range of illicit drugs. When he was about 27, Fardon married and had two sons. The marriage broke down and he lost contact with his sons who were placed in foster care and then adopted.

On October 8, 1980, Fardon pleaded guilty to charges of rape and indecent dealing with a 12-year-old girl and the wounding of her 15-year-old sister. Fardon was 29 when he committed these offences. The sentencing judge described the rape as "brutal" and the circumstances as "somewhat horrific," but he noted that because the offences were of a sexual nature, they could be described as out of character (see *Attorney-General (Qld) v Fardon* 2003: para. [37]). Fardon served eight years of a 13-year sentence for these offences.

Within 20 days of being released on parole, Fardon raped, sodomized, and assaulted a woman with whom he had gone to a flat to obtain heroin. On June 30, 1989, he was sentenced to 14 years' imprisonment.

There was contradicted evidence that Fardon told a sentence management support officer on March 12, 1998 that he wanted to stay in prison until he died and he would kill an officer or another prisoner to stay there (*Attorney-General (Qld) v Fardon* 2003: para. [41]).

Fardon's term of imprisonment was due to expire on June 29, 2003. Two days before this date, an interim detention order was granted under the Dangerous Prisoners (Sexual Offenders) Act 2003 (Qld). An appeal to the Queensland Court of Appeal against this order was dismissed (*Attorney-General (Qld) v Fardon* 2003). As detailed in Chapter 4, Fardon then appealed to the High Court of Australia which, by a majority of six judges to one, held that the Queensland Act was valid (*Fardon v Attorney-General (Qld)* 2004). This decision opened the door for the post-sentence preventive detention of sex offenders in Australia (McSherry 2005).

Fardon was released on a supervision order in 2007 (*Attorney-General v Fardon* 2006). In 2008, he was charged with raping a 61-year-old woman with intellectual disabilities on the Gold Coast and sentenced to ten years' imprisonment, but this was overturned on appeal: *R v Fardon* (2010). In this case, there was evidence that Fardon had known the complainant for many years and that they had been sexual partners on other occasions. There was also evidence that the alleged offending conduct concerned a non-consensual act of digital penetration in the course of consensual sexual activity, which apparently ended when the complainant told him he was hurting her.

Another supervision order was made on May 20, 2011, but this was rescinded by the Queensland Court of Appeal (*Attorney-General (Qld) v Fardon* 2011). The Court of Appeal ordered that Fardon remain in custody for an indefinite term for "care, control or treatment" under the Dangerous Prisoners (Sexual Offenders) Act 2003 (Qld).

As explored in Chapter 1, offenders like Robert Fardon present significant challenges for governments, particularly in the light of community condemnation and fear of sex offenders. Often governments will defend preventive detention regimes on the basis that a balance needs to be struck between competing human rights because the rights of one person may represent a threat to another. The protection of the community must be balanced against the maintenance of individual human rights such as the right to liberty.

The concept of human rights has had a long history, arising as a result of religious movements and the development of nation states, with "a crucial influence in the formative stages of human rights . . . [being] that of natural law as developed by European thinkers such as John Locke and Thomas Hobbes during the Enlightenment period" (Brems 2001: 17). The development of international human rights *law*, however, can largely be traced back to the end of World War II with the founding of the United Nations in 1945 and the adoption in 1948 by the United Nations General Assembly of the Universal Declaration of Human Rights. Although the Declaration was not intended to be a legally binding document, its preamble made it clear that it provided "a common standard of achievement for all peoples and all nations" (para. 8).

Since the end of World War II, there has been a "tremendous evolution of international human rights law" (Baderin and Ssenyonjo 2010: 4) in the form of significant international conventions such as the International Covenant on Civil and Political Rights and the International Covenant on Economic, Social and Cultural Rights. These were adopted in 1966 and came into force in 1976 as well as regional conventions in Europe, America, and Africa and country-specific human rights legislation.

This chapter explores some of the decisions of the United Nations Human Rights Committee and the European Court of Human Rights concerning preventive detention regimes. It focuses on the human rights that may be breached under international human rights law by preventive detention regimes, in particular the right to liberty and the effect of decisions made at an international level on domestic human rights compliance. The preventive detention of Robert Fardon was the subject of a significant decision by the United Nations Human Rights Committee. Other courts and commentators have also questioned the scope of the preventive detention of individuals with mental illness and suspected terrorists on the basis of violations of human rights.

The next section sets out the international human rights framework that governs the states that have ratified international covenants and conventions. This is followed by an analysis of the right to liberty and how various human rights bodies such as the United Nations Human Rights Committee and the European Court of Human Rights have interpreted it. The next section then analyses some of the other relevant human rights before considering what effect international human rights jurisprudence may have on domestic compliance.

THE INTERNATIONAL HUMAN RIGHTS FRAMEWORK

What is often referred to as the International Bill of Rights comprises three United Nations documents: the Universal Declaration of Human Rights, the International Covenant on Civil and Political Rights, and the International Covenant on Economic, Social and Cultural Rights. Together they constitute the "definitive contemporary statement of human rights" (McBeth *et al.* 2011: 3).

The Preamble to the Universal Declaration of Human Rights recognizes the "inherent dignity and inalienable rights of all members of the human family." The International Covenant on Civil and Political Rights sets out a range of individual rights, including the "inherent right to life" (Article 6). The International Covenant on Economic, Social and Cultural Rights focuses on the obligations of states to recognize certain rights such as the right to work (Article 6) and the "right of everyone to education" (Article 23). Civil and political rights are sometimes referred to as "negative" rights, meaning freedom from state interference, while economic, social, and cultural rights are referred to as "positive" rights as they place obligations on States Parties to ensure certain rights are upheld. The division between civil and political rights on the one hand and economic, social, and cultural rights on the other has diminished over time with newer treaties such as the Convention on the Rights of Persons with Disabilities incorporating both sets of rights.

Since the adoption of the International Bill of Rights, "human rights have progressively developed into a universal value system" (Baderin and Ssenyonjo 2010: 12) and the protection of such rights is now a key issue for the international community. In terms of a hierarchy of human rights law, states can be bound by treaties at both the international and regional level. For example, the United Kingdom has ratified both the International Bill of Rights and the European Convention for the Protection of Human Rights and Fundamental Freedoms, which means it is bound by both these treaties.

There are four main regional treaties:

- The European Convention for the Protection of Human Rights and Fundamental Freedoms was adopted on November 4, 1950 and entered into force on September 3, 1953 (This Convention is usually referred to as the European Convention on Human Rights).
- The American Convention on Human Rights was adopted on November 22, 1969 and entered into force on July 18, 1978.
- The African Charter on Human and Peoples' Rights was adopted on June 27, 1981 and entered into force on October 21, 1986.

- The Arab Charter on Human Rights was adopted first in 1994, with a revised version adopted on May 22, 2004 and entered into force on March 15, 2008.

In 2000, the European Union also adopted the Charter of Fundamental Rights of the European Union which, as it is a non-binding document, will not be explored in this chapter.

The United States and Canada, being members of the Organization of American States, signed the American Convention but neither country has ratified it. In comparison, the African Charter has been ratified by all 53 members of the African Union. Larry Gostin and Lance Gable (2004: 47–48) point out that regional human rights systems:

> have created additional fora for the protection and promotion of human rights, often through more direct means. Courts and commissions established at a regional level have granted individuals the ability to redress human rights grievances that have not been dealt with appropriately at the domestic level or to challenge domestic policies and practices that violate human rights norms.

Countries may also have specific Charters or Bills of Rights. Canada has its Charter of Human Rights and Freedoms and the United States has the Bill of Rights that is the name given to the first ten amendments to the United States Constitution. These rights are "entrenched" which means that they cannot be modified or repealed by the country's legislature through normal legislative procedure. This may explain why these countries have not ratified the American Convention on Human Rights.

In the United Kingdom, the Human Rights Act 1998 is not entrenched in that it can be altered through legislative amendments. It does, however, form part of a regional human rights system which means that disputes concerning human rights may be heard by the European Court of Human Rights.

Australia has never had a national bill of rights or Charter although the Australian Capital Territory and the State of Victoria have enacted human rights legislation. New Zealand has a Bill of Rights Act 1990 and, like the United Kingdom Act, it is an ordinary statute that can be amended by Parliament. Neither Australia nor New Zealand is part of a regional human rights system as the Asia-Pacific region does not have a human rights treaty or a regional mechanism for the protection of human rights (see McBeth *et al*. 2011: 311ff for the reasons why there is no such treaty).

The United Nations Human Rights Committee monitors the implementation of the International Covenant on Civil and Political Rights by its States Parties. The Human Rights Committee publishes its interpretation of the content of human rights provisions. These are known as "general comments" and, as outlined below, this Committee can examine individual complaints concerning alleged violations of the Covenant by States Parties who have signed the First Optional Protocol to the Covenant. For states that have ratified the European Convention, the European Court of Human Rights can hear complaints from individuals against their own states for alleged violations of the rights set out in this Convention.

There may also be specific conventions that are relevant to persons who have been detained on the basis of the prevention of harm to the community:

- The Convention on the Rights of Persons with Disabilities entered into force on May 3, 2008. While neither "disability" nor "persons with disabilities" are defined, Article 1 of that Convention states that the latter term "includes those who have long-term . . . mental . . . impairments which in interaction with various barriers may hinder their full and effective participation in society on an equal basis with others." It is this Convention that is relevant to those with severe mental illness and it is shaping the scope of mental health laws in many countries (McSherry 2008; McSherry and Weller 2010).
- Similarly, persons detained under anti-terrorism prevention laws have rights under the International Bill of Rights and other human rights instruments including the Convention against Torture and Other Cruel, Inhuman or Degrading Treatment or Punishment that was adopted on December 10, 1984 and entered into force on June 26, 1987.
- Persons detained without charge are also covered by the Standard Minimum Rules for the Treatment of Prisoners that were adopted by the First United Nations Congress on the Prevention of Crime and the Treatment of Offenders in 1955 (rule 95).

So where do preventive detention and supervision schemes fit into this framework of international human rights? In the Supreme Court of New South Wales decision of *Kable v Director of Public Prosecutions* (1995: 376), Associate Justice Mahoney warned that preventive detention schemes "may infringe – and certainly will create the danger of infringement of – the basic human rights which should underlie the laws of a modern democratic society."

The next section focuses on the right to liberty and seminal decisions by the United Nations Human Rights Committee and the European Court of Human Rights that have set out the circumstances in which preventive detention schemes are in breach of this right.

THE RIGHT TO LIBERTY

The right to liberty is a core human right. At the international level this right is set out in:

- Article 9 of the Universal Declaration of Human Rights;
- Article 9 of the International Covenant on Civil and Political Rights; and
- Article 14 of the Convention on the Rights of Persons with Disabilities.

On a regional and domestic level the right is set out in:

- Article 5 of the European Convention on Human Rights;
- Article 7 of the American Convention on Human Rights;
- Section 7 of the Canadian Charter of Rights and Freedoms;
- the 14th amendment to the United States Constitution; and
- Section 22 of the New Zealand Bill of Rights Act 1990.

In the United Kingdom, the Human Rights Act 1998 incorporates Article 5 of the European Convention on Human Rights into domestic law via a Schedule to that Act.

Article 9 of the Universal Declaration of Human Rights states: "[n]o one shall be subjected to arbitrary arrest, detention or exile." This is expanded upon by Article 9(1) of the International Covenant on Civil and Political Rights which provides:

> Everyone has the right to liberty and security of the person. No one shall be subjected to arbitrary arrest or detention. No one shall be deprived of his [or her] liberty except on such grounds and in accordance with such procedure as are established by law.

In its General Comment No 8 on the general application of Article 9, the United Nations Office of the High Commissioner for Human Rights (1982), which was established under the International Covenant on Civil and Political Rights, made the following statement:

> The Committee points out that paragraph 1 [of Article 9] is applicable to all deprivations of liberty, whether in criminal cases or in other cases such as, for example, mental illness, vagrancy, drug addiction, educational purposes, immigration control etc (para. 1).

What the term "arbitrary" means in Article 9 is open to debate. On a narrow interpretation, arbitrary detention could simply mean not according to legislative procedure. However, Claire Macken (2005) argues that arbitrary detention means more than "unlawful" detention. It imposes an additional higher requirement above unlawfulness. That is, "arbitrary" could be taken to mean unreasonable or unjust. Exploring the background *travaux préparatoires* of the International Covenant on Civil and Political Rights, Parvez Hassan (1973) reveals that the drafters gave a distinct meaning to the word. He points out (1973: 179) that in the Report of the Third Committee, the majority stated that an arbitrary act was one which violated justice, reason, *or* legislation.

Article 5(1) of the European Convention on Human Rights makes it clear that the right to liberty is not an absolute one. It states:

1. Everyone has the right to liberty and security of person.
    No one shall be deprived of his liberty save in the following cases and in accordance with a procedure prescribed by law:

    (a) the lawful detention of a person after conviction by a competent court;
    (b) the lawful arrest or detention of a person for non-compliance with the lawful order of a court or in order to secure the fulfilment of any obligation prescribed by law;
    (c) the lawful arrest or detention of a person effected for the purpose of bringing him [or her] before the competent legal authority of reasonable suspicion of having committed an offence or when it is reasonably considered necessary to prevent his [or her] committing an offence or fleeing after having done so;
    (d) the detention of a minor by lawful order for the purpose of educational supervision or his [or her] lawful detention for the purpose of bringing him [or her] before the competent legal authority;
    (e) the lawful detention of persons for the prevention of the spreading of infectious diseases, of *persons of unsound mind*, alcoholics or drug addicts, or vagrants; (emphasis added)
    (f) the lawful arrest or detention of a person to prevent his [or her] effecting an unauthorized entry into the country or of a person against whom action is being taken with a view to deportation or extradition.

Two points are worth noting. First, there is no mention of detention for the purposes of community protection under these exceptions. Second, the inclusion of a reference to the lawful detention of "persons of unsound mind" indicates that the drafters of the Convention were aware of the existence of mental health legislation that enabled the involuntary detention of those with mental illness and they considered that detention under such laws was not in itself arbitrary. In *Enhorn v Sweden* (2005: para. [43]), the European Court of Human Rights observed:

> There is a link between all those persons [listed in Article 5(1)(e) in that they may be deprived of their liberty either in order to be given medical treatment or because of considerations dictated by social policy, or on both medical and social grounds. It is therefore legitimate to conclude from this context that a predominant reason why the Convention allows the persons mentioned . . . to be deprived of their liberty is not only that they are dangerous for public safety but also that their own interests may necessitate their detention.

The European Court of Human Rights did not explain the concept of being "dangerous for public safety," but other cases from this Court suggest that certain restrictions apply to the scope of detention laws in relation to individuals with severe mental illness.

It is useful to examine some of the decisions made at the international law level relating to preventive detention and the right to liberty as they relate to offenders, individuals with severe mental illness, and suspected terrorists.

Offenders

At both the international and regional levels, schemes enabling the *post-sentence* preventive detention in prison appear to violate the right to liberty. However, preventive detention ordered *at the time of sentence* may be justified if certain requirements are satisfied. In this regard, there are some significant decisions made by both the United Nations Human Rights Committee and the European Court of Human Rights.

The United Nations Human Rights Committee

As set out in Chapter 4, the majority of the High Court of Australia in *Fardon v Attorney-General (Qld)* (2004) held that the Queensland legislation enabling post-sentence preventive detention was constitutional. Thus, Robert Fardon's continued detention in prison was lawful according to Australia's domestic law. However, this High Court decision is irrelevant to the question of whether or not continuing detention in prison is in breach of *international* human rights law. Accordingly, in 2006, Fardon instructed the Prisoners' Legal Service of Queensland to initiate a communication to the United Nations Human Rights Committee on the basis that his continued detention breached international human rights law (Keyzer and Blay 2006).

The First Optional Protocol to the International Covenant on Civil and Political Rights enables an applicant to file a communication with the Human Rights Committee, which oversees the operation of the Covenant. Australia ratified the First Optional Protocol in September 1991 and in so doing recognized the competence of the Human Rights Committee "to receive and consider communications from individuals subject to its jurisdiction who claim to be victims of a violation by that State Party of any of the rights set forth in the Covenant" (First Optional Protocol Art 1).

Rule 90(f) of the Rules of Procedure of the Human Rights Committee provides that for a communication to be admissible, a Working Group of the Committee must be satisfied that "the individual has exhausted all available domestic remedies." As the High Court had upheld the Queensland legislation, this was so in *Fardon*'s case. A separate communication was also filed in relation to Kenneth Davidson Tillman, who was the first person to be preventively detained in prison in New South Wales under the equivalent legislation, the Crimes (Serious Sex Offenders) Act 2006 (NSW). Both communications were filed in 2007 and the Human Rights Commission delivered its views in March 2010.

The main arguments raised in both the Fardon and Tillman communications dealt with the right to liberty under Article 9(1) and the right not to be punished again for an offence under Article 14(7) of the International Covenant on Civil and Political Rights. The Human Rights Committee made a number of observations in both decisions concerning Article 9(1) and did not consider it necessary to examine the matter separately under Article 14(7). The concept of double punishment is explored later in this chapter.

The Human Rights Committee had indicated in previous decisions that to avoid being arbitrary, detention must be (a) "reasonable," (b) "necessary in all circumstances of the case," and (c) "proportionate to achieving the legitimate ends of the State party" (Keyzer 2009). Additionally, if a state could achieve its purpose through less invasive means than detention, detention may be considered arbitrary (Keyzer 2009).

On this point, the main argument raised in the communications was that continued detention in prison is a disproportionate response to the aim of rehabilitating sex offenders and that supervision in the community should be viewed as a less invasive means of achieving this end.

Eleven of the 13 members of the Human Rights Committee agreed that both schemes were in violation of Article 9(1). They pointed to four significant factors leading to their conclusion:

(1) The continued detention in prison "amounted to a fresh term of imprisonment which . . . is not permissible in the absence of a conviction" (*Re Fardon v Australia* 2010: para. [7.4(1)]; *Re Tillman v Australia* 2010: para. [7.4(1)]).

(2) Because imprisonment is penal in nature, both Fardon's and Tillman's continued detention in prison amounted to a "new sentence" which meant they suffered a heavier penalty than that applicable at the time the offences were committed. This is prohibited under Article 15(1) of the International Covenant on Civil and Political Rights (*Re Fardon v Australia* 2010: para. [7.4(2)]; *Re Tillman v Australia* 2010: para. [7.4(2)]).

(3) The procedures under the Acts, being civil in nature, did not meet the due process guarantees under Article 14 of the International Covenant on Civil and Political Rights "for a fair trial in which a penal sentence is imposed" (*Re Fardon v Australia* 2010: para. [7.4(3)]; *Re Tillman v Australia* 2010: para. [7.4(3)]).

(4) Because of the problematic nature of the concept of feared or predicted dangerousness, "the Courts must make a finding of fact on the suspected future behaviour of a past offender which may or may not materialize." Accordingly, the onus was on the State to demonstrate that rehabilitation could not have been achieved by "means less intrusive than continued imprisonment *or even detention*" (emphasis added, *Re Fardon v Australia* 2010: para. [7.4(4)]; *Re Tillman v Australia* 2010: para. [7.4(4)]).

The final paragraph referring to rehabilitation by means less intrusive than "continued imprisonment or even detention" is not explained, but this could be a reference to detention in specifically built "halfway" houses for sex offenders such as those at Wacol in Queensland or at Ararat in Victoria. Alternatively it could mean "detention" in a broad sense via restrictions on liberty through supervision conditions.

In both decisions, the Human Rights Committee requested that the State provide it with information within 180 days as to the remedy taken to give effect to its views. The Australian government did not respond within this time limit. On September 6, 2011, the Australian government filed a five-page document, setting out the reasons why both Fardon and Tillman remained in prison and stating that it rejected the Human Rights Committee's finding that there were less restrictive means available to achieve the purposes of the New South Wales and Queensland legislation other than detention in prison. The statement pointed out that both men had failed to attend rehabilitation programmes while incarcerated and that there were no intensive treatment and rehabilitation options available in the community for either Tillman or Fardon. The response stated (para. 18):

Australia stresses that the community has a legitimate expectation to be protected from these offenders, and at the same time, that authorities owe these offenders a duty to try and [sic] rehabilitate them. The purpose of these schemes is not to indefinitely detain serious sex offenders, but rather to ensure as far as possible that their release into the community occurs in a way that is safe and respectful of the needs of both the community, and the offenders themselves.

The statement concluded with the observation that the New South Wales and Queensland governments did not consider any further action needed to be taken. Thus, despite the Human Rights Committee's finding that Fardon and Tillman's continued imprisonment breached their right to liberty under international human rights law, the Australian government has clearly signalled that there will be no changes made to current preventive detention schemes. The Australian government is effectively indicating that it places a higher value on protecting the community from the possibility of what sex offenders might do if they are released at the end of their sentences, than it does on Australia's record and reputation of upholding human rights. The Australian government's refusal to abide by the findings of the Human Rights Committee is revisited later in this chapter.

The European Court of Human Rights

On the regional scale, the European Court of Human Rights has also held that post-sentence preventive detention breaches the right to liberty under Article 5 of the European Convention on Human Rights. Much of the European jurisprudence in this area concerns the system of indefinite and preventive detention in Germany. Hans-Jörg Albrecht (2012: 44–45) describes the German criminal justice system as "two-track" in that is has punishment in the form of fines or imprisonment on conviction for offences as well as "measures of rehabilitation and protection of public security which can be added to a prison sentence (preventive detention) or replace prison sentences (committal to a psychiatric hospital)."

In 1998, Article 67d of the German Criminal Code was amended to enable the indefinite detention of physically aggressive and sex offenders at the time of sentence. The Criminal Code was further amended in 2002, to allow preventive detention to be ordered after an offender had completed two-thirds of the prison term so that evidence could be gathered to support a finding that the offender was dangerous. The trial judge at the time of sentence could thus delay an eventual order of preventive detention. On July 28, 2004 the Federal legislature enacted the Introduction of Retrospective Preventive Detention Act (Gesetz zur Einführung der nachträglichen Sicherungsverwahrung), which entered into force on July 29, 2004. This introduced Article 66b into the Criminal Code, which enables preventive detention to be ordered retrospectively if there is evidence that the convicted person presents a significant danger to the general public in the sense that he or she is liable to commit serious offences by which the victims would be seriously harmed. Christopher Michaelsen (2012: 152) writes in relation to the latter amendment:

> This form of preventive detention could be ordered in cases where new evidence became available during the prison term and which was considered to warrant further detention. This option meant that the offender was unable to predict whether or not preventive detention was going to be ordered at the end of his or her prison term.

In *M v Germany* (2010) and *Grosskopf v Germany* (2010), the European Court of Human Rights did not consider that preventive detention that had been ordered *at the time* of sentence was in itself a breach of the right to liberty. Rather, in order to find a breach, the Court found it necessary to consider issues in relation to the causal connections between the respective offenders' convictions and deprivations of liberty as well as the relevant law that applied at the time they were sentenced (see Drenkhahn *et al.* 2012 and Slobogin 2012a for a full analysis of *M*'s case).

However, in *Haidn v Germany* (2011), the European Court of Human Rights held that the applicant's *post-sentence* preventive detention did breach his right to liberty. The main reason for this was that the detention in prison had been ordered retrospectively and so was not foreseeable. The Court stated (2011: para. [96]) that:

> in order to be "lawful", the detention must conform to the substantive and procedural rules of national law, which must, moreover, be of a certain quality and, in particular, must be foreseeable in its application, in order to avoid all risk of arbitrariness.

Following these rulings by the European Court of Human Rights, Germany's Federal Constitutional Court, the Bundesverfassungsgericht (BVerfG) subsequently reconsidered the system of preventive detention in the decisions known as *Preventive Detention Cases I and II* (BVerfG 2011a) that were handed down on May 4, 2011.

The two cases known as *Preventive Detention I* concerned two men who were subject to preventive detention orders at the time of their sentences, but these orders had been made before the 1998 laws. At that time, there was a ten-year cap upon such orders. Both men had been preventively detained for longer than ten years and the question was whether the original orders could be prolonged.

The two cases known as *Preventive Detention II* concerned two men who were subject to retrospective detention orders under the 2004 amendments. All four applicants relied on the European Court of Human Rights decisions, arguing that the provisions of the German Constitution (the "Basic Law") should be interpreted in the light of this jurisprudence. They argued that the orders for preventive detention contravened the fundamental right to liberty protected under Article 2(2) in conjunction with Article 104(1) of the Basic Law.

The BVerfG allowed all four complaints, concluding that the orders had breached the applicants' right to liberty. They clarified that the Basic Law should be interpreted in a manner compatible with international law. The European Convention and the judgments of the European Court of Human Rights were viewed as providing interpretative guidance in relation to the Basic Law.

The BVerfG ordered that the provisions that were declared unconstitutional could remain until the entry into force of new legislation to be enacted prior to May 31, 2013. It did not go so far as to declare *all* forms of preventive detention unconstitutional, but held that the serious encroachment upon the right to liberty that preventive detention constitutes could be justified only if it is subject to a review of proportionality and if strict requirements were satisfied. As Hans-Jörg Albrecht (2012: 52) points out, the decision means that preventive detention "can be tolerated only under the condition that preventive detention is implemented in a way differing significantly from the implementation of prison sentences."

The BVerfG stressed that the underlying rationale for preventive detention was the minimization of danger through a therapeutic regime aimed at reducing the deprivation of liberty to that which was absolutely necessary. It, therefore, called upon the legislature to develop a "liberty-oriented overall concept of preventive detention aimed at therapy" (Michaelsen 2012: 163). This decision was confirmed by the BVerfG in a subsequent decision handed down on June 8, 2011 (BVerfG 2011b).

Interestingly, the BVerfG considered that preventive detention could be prolonged or ordered retrospectively if the individual fell within the categories of persons set out in Article 5(1)(e) of the European Convention including an individual considered to be of "unsound mind" (BVerfG 2011a: paras 144, 151). Why this may be the case is explored in the next section.

Overall, it is clear from an international human rights law perspective that *post-sentence* preventive detention laws violate the right to liberty. As mentioned in Chapter 1, orders for the indefinite detention of offenders made at the time of sentence may be easier to justify as they are closely tied to the finding of guilt for an offence and also because the offender knows from the start of the sentence that it is indefinite, but subject to review processes. On the other hand, post-sentence preventive detention orders are harder to justify because they are based on what the offender *might* do in the future.

Supervision orders in relation to offenders also raise concerns about the violation of the right to liberty, but have not been subject to the same level of scrutiny at the international level as preventive detention regimes. Presumably, these orders can be justified if there are sufficient procedural safeguards attached to them. Control orders are considered later in this chapter.

Individuals with Severe Mental Illness

International human rights discourse has influenced the shaping of modern mental health laws in many developed countries where mental health statutes now generally include references to rights. During the 1980s in the United Kingdom, Larry Gostin's concept of a "new legalism," which led to the introduction of procedural safeguards in mental health laws including the regulation of treatment by psychiatrists, drew on the European Convention on Human Rights (Fennell 2010: 16). The "new legalism" was reflected in the Mental Health Act 1983, which contained increased rights to challenge detention and to seek review of involuntary detention. In Canada, provincial mental health laws since the 1970s have "placed a new emphasis on procedural fairness, improved procedures for assessing capacity, and enhanced protections for the autonomy and self-determination of persons with mental illness" (Zuckerberg 2010: 300). In the United States, mental health law reforms have emerged as a part of civil rights law (Petrila 2010). Similarly, the United Nations Principles for the Protection of Persons with Mental Illness and the Improvement of Mental Health Care which were adopted in 1991 influenced the move towards emphasizing rights in Australian mental health laws throughout the 1990s. This has led to the development of a "rights analysis instrument" to measure the rights compliance of mental health legislation in the six Australian states and two territories (Watchirs 2005).

The European Court of Human Rights decisions on the detention of persons of "unsound mind"

The European Court of Human Rights has developed significant jurisprudence relating to Article 5(1)(e) of the European Convention on Human Rights that makes an exception to the right to liberty for "persons of unsound mind." A number of decisions have specified the minimum conditions necessary for the lawful deprivation of liberty on the basis that the person is of unsound mind.

In *Winterwerp v The Netherlands* (1979), the European Court of Human Rights held that the applicant's involuntary detention and treatment in a psychiatric hospital in accordance with Dutch emergency procedure breached Article 5(1)(e). The Court declared (1979: para. [39]) that the term "persons of unsound mind" could not be given a definitive interpretation, but that it needed to be established via medical expertise:

> In the Court's opinion, except in emergency cases, the individual concerned should not be deprived of his [or her] liberty unless he [or she] has been reliably shown to be of 'unsound mind'. The very nature of what has to be established before the competent national authority – that is, a true mental disorder – calls for objective medical expertise. Further, the mental disorder must be of a kind or degree warranting compulsory confinement. What is more, the validity of continued confinement depends upon the persistence of such a disorder.

Subsequent decisions have confirmed that "persons of unsound mind" cannot be deprived of their liberty unless three minimum conditions are established. First, they must be "reliably shown to be of unsound mind; secondly, the mental disorder must be of a kind or degree warranting compulsory confinement; thirdly, the validity of continued confinement depends upon the persistence of such a disorder" (*Stanev v Bulgaria* 2012: para. [145]; see further Bartlett *et al.* 2007; Weller 2013: 133ff.) The European Court of Human Rights also clarified that there must be procedural safeguards for the detention of those who are "compliant" with treatment, but who lack the capacity to consent to it. In *HL v The United Kingdom* (2004), the European Court of Human Rights considered the case of HL, who had autism since birth and who was detained in the Intensive Behavioural Unit at Bournewood Hospital in England. In March 1994, HL lived with two paid carers, Mr. and Mrs. E, while the hospital remained responsible for his care and treatment. From 1995 onwards, HL attended a day-care centre on a weekly basis.

On July 22, 1997, while HL was at the day-care centre, he became agitated and started banging his head against the wall. He was taken to the accident and emergency unit at the hospital and was admitted as an inpatient. A doctor considered making HL an involuntary patient, but decided not to because he was compliant and did not resist being admitted. It was not until December 12, 1997 that HL was released back into Mr. and Mrs. E's care.

The question as to whether HL's detention in hospital had been lawful went through the English court system and eventually came before the European Court of Human Rights. It held that HL's detention had breached the right to liberty set out in Article 5(1) of the European

Convention on Human Rights. It found that HL had been deprived of his liberty because he had been under continuous supervision and had not been free to leave (2004: para. [91]). Further, he was of unsound mind in that he was "suffering from a mental disorder of a kind or degree warranting compulsory confinement which persisted during his detention between 22 July and 5 December 1997" (2004: para. [101]). Ultimately, the main issue was whether or not HL's detention could be considered "lawful" in the sense of avoiding "arbitrariness" (2004: para. [119]). The court found that the detention was not lawful in this sense because of the lack of any fixed procedural rules governing HL's detention. In particular, there was a lack of any requirement for the clinical assessment of the continuation of the disorder warranting detention (2004: para. [120]). The court did not order monetary compensation for the detention, but did order that HL's costs be paid by the State.

The effect of this decision was to reinforce that "informal" admission procedures were not appropriate for those individuals who lack the capacity to consent to treatment, but who are compliant with it. Subsequently, Schedule A1 was added to the Mental Capacity Act 2005 (England and Wales) by Schedule 7 of the Mental Health Act 2007 (England and Wales). This Schedule, which entered into force on April 1, 2009, sets out a new system relating to certain individuals detained in hospitals and care homes for the purpose of treatment (Bruckard and McSherry 2009).

More recently, in *Sŷkora v the Czech Republic* (2012), the European Court of Human Rights held that a lack of adequate procedural safeguards for the detention without consent of a Czech national, Milan Sŷkora, in a psychiatric institution for 20 days amounted to a breach of the right to liberty under Article 5(1) of the European Convention on Human Rights. In that case, Mr. Sŷkora had been detained during a time when a guardian had been appointed for him without his knowledge and without judgment being served on him. The guardian consented to the detention without ever meeting or even consulting with Mr Sŷkora. The court ordered the government to pay Mr Sŷkora EUR 20,000 for non-pecuniary damage.

It is clear, then, that at the regional level in Europe, the preventive detention of those of "unsound mind" does not violate the right to liberty provided that certain conditions are met.

At the international level, however, the coming into force of the Convention on the Rights of Persons with Disabilities reignited a debate as to whether or not mental health laws should be abolished on the basis that they are discriminatory and that they violate the right to liberty.

The right to liberty under the Convention on the Rights of Persons with Disabilities

Article 14(1) of the CRPD provides:

> States Parties shall ensure that persons with disabilities, on an equal basis with others:
>
> (a) Enjoy the right to liberty and security of person;
> (b) Are not deprived of their liberty unlawfully or arbitrarily, and that any deprivation of liberty is in conformity with *the law, and that the existence of a disability shall in no case justify a deprivation of liberty* (emphasis added).

The main debate has been about the meaning of the words "the existence of a disability shall in no case justify a deprivation of liberty." These words can be interpreted to mean that laws enabling the involuntary detention of individuals with disabilities should be abolished. Alternatively, they can be read down to mean that "the existence of a disability *alone*" does not justify such laws.

During the drafting of Article 14, some states advocated that it should clearly state that any deprivation of liberty should not be "solely" based on disability (Third Session of the Ad Hoc Committee 2004). This approach would leave it open to allow detention where other criteria such as the need for treatment or dangerousness coexisted with a criterion of disability. This approach seems to be consistent with the statement made by the European Court of Human Rights in *Stanev v Bulgaria* (2012: para. [146]) that:

> the detention of a mentally disordered person may be necessary not only where the person needs therapy, medication or other clinical treatment to cure or alleviate his [or her] condition, but also where the person needs control and supervision to prevent him [or her], for example, causing harm to himself [or herself] or other persons.

In contrast to this approach, the World Network of Users and Survivors of Psychiatry argued that the introduction of the word "solely" would:

> open the door for States to deprive persons with disabilities of their liberty for being "a danger to society," which is discriminatory because persons without disabilities are not subject to the same standard. If there is no crime, a State cannot lock up [a] person who is not considered mentally ill or intellectually disabled. [Those with disabilities] should not be subject to a different standard (Third Session of the Ad Hoc Committee 2004).

On this point, however, those who are mentally ill or intellectually disabled are not the only persons subject to detention in the absence of a crime. As set out in Chapter 1, there are laws in place that enable the "civil" detention of certain individuals including those who have infectious diseases or are addicted to drugs or who are seeking asylum. Of course the groups of individuals that form the subject matter of this book are all subject to "civil" rather than "criminal" detention.

Ultimately, the word "solely" was not included in Article 14 and there are now numerous statements that indicate mental health legislation enabling involuntary detention of those with mental impairments breaches this Article. For example, the Annual Report of the United Nations High Commissioner of Human Rights (United Nations Human Rights Council 2009: 48) stated that "[l]egislation authorising the institutionalisation of persons with disabilities on the grounds of their disability without their free and informed consent must be abolished." It stated (2009: 49) that the legal grounds for detention of any person must be "de-linked from the disability and neutrally defined so as to apply to all persons on an equal basis." Any such statements from the High Commissioner, however, are not legally binding.

Perhaps of more significance are two statements by the United Nations Committee on the Rights of Persons with Disabilities. This Committee monitors the implementation of the Convention on the Rights of Persons with Disabilities. In response to Tunisia's report to the Committee, the Committee recommended (United Nations Committee on the Rights of Persons with Disabilities 2011a: para. 25) that Tunisia "repeal legislative provisions which allow for the deprivation of liberty on the basis of disability, including a psychosocial or intellectual disability." The United Nations Committee on the Rights of Persons with Disabilities (2011b: para. 36) reiterated this position in response to a report by Spain, stating that Spain must:

> repeal provisions that authorize involuntary internment linked to an apparent or diagnosed disability; and adopt measures to ensure that health-care services, including all mental-health-care services, are based on the informed consent of the person concerned.

The United Nations Special Rapporteur on Torture has also called for an "absolute ban on all forced and non-consensual medical treatments against persons with disabilities" (United Nations Human Rights Council 2013: para. 89 [b]).

When ratifying the Convention, Australia included a declaration which is a form of "interpretative announcement." This differs from a reservation that may serve to limit the legal effect of certain provisions in a Treaty (Kaczorowska 2010: 105ff). Australia's Declaration included the statement that "the Convention allows for fully supported or substituted decision-making arrangements" (Canada made a similar statement when ratifying the Convention) and that "the Convention allows for compulsory assistance or treatment of persons, including measures taken for the treatment of mental disability, where such treatment is necessary, as a last resort and subject to safeguards."

Interestingly, Australia's Declaration refers only to "compulsory assistance or treatment" and is silent as to involuntary *detention* for the purposes of treatment. However, the reference to compulsory treatment suggests that it is unlikely in the short term that mental health legislation as it currently exists will be repealed in Australia. This is despite the fact that the international statements interpreting Article 14 indicate that mental health laws enabling the involuntary detention of those with mental impairments are in breach of the right to liberty.

There is no significant jurisprudence on whether community treatment orders breach the right to liberty. As set out in Chapter 4, the involuntary treatment of those with mental impairments may occur either in hospitals or through "community treatment orders" that compel recipients to accept prescribed medication and treatment for mental illness while living in the community. John Dawson (2005: 82) argues that community treatment orders do not breach the right to liberty providing that:

- the regime covers only 'persons of unsound mind';
- the person's condition is assessed regularly by persons with appropriate medical expertise;
- fair and speedy review procedures are provided, under which the patient may be discharged from involuntary treatment by a process independent of treating clinicians; and
- only a 'proportionate' response is permitted to the condition and risks presented by the person.

In summary, at the international level, it has traditionally been assumed that the detention of those of "unsound mind" does not breach the right to liberty if certain minimum conditions are satisfied. This is now being challenged by recent interpretations of Article 14 of the Convention on the Rights of Persons with Disabilities. It may be that the preventive detention of those with severe mental illness will need to be rethought in response to the United Nations Committee's statements.

Suspected Terrorists

As with the preventive detention of serious offenders, the framework for international human rights law in relation to preventive detention of suspected terrorists also involves the application of the right to liberty under Article 9 of the International Covenant on Civil and Political Rights.

In its General Comment No 8 on the right to liberty and security, the United Nations Office of the High Commissioner for Human Rights (1982: para. 4) stated:

> [I]f so-called *preventive detention* is used, for reasons of public security ... it must not be arbitrary, and must be based on grounds and procedures established by law ... information of the reasons must be given ... and court control of the detention must be available ... as well as compensation in the case of a breach.

Thus preventive detention for public security may be justified, but only if subject to stringent safeguards. The effect of international human rights law on the preventive detention of suspected terrorists may vary according to the circumstances in which the detention is taking place. Claire Macken (2011: 16–17) points out that there are four main circumstances in which the preventive detention of a suspected terrorist may occur:

(1) in peacetime;
(2) as a public emergency short of war, in which states derogate from the right to liberty;
(3) as part of armed conflict of an international character;
(4) as past of armed conflict of a non-international character.

The laws explored in Chapter 4 have generally been concerned with the preventive detention of suspected terrorists under the first circumstance of "peacetime." However, the original preventive detention regime for suspected terrorists in the United Kingdom was couched as falling within the second circumstance. This affects the ability of states to "derogate" from their obligations under international human rights law because of the existence of a state of emergency and this is explored further below.

The third circumstance has been particularly relevant to the detention of suspected terrorists in the United States. The third and fourth circumstances bring into play international humanitarian law, which is sometimes referred to as the "laws of war," embodied in four Geneva Conventions that apply to "armed conflict."

Sometimes the distinction between the first and second circumstances may be blurred in relation to perceived threats of terrorism. Article 4(1) of the International Covenant on Civil and Political Rights states:

> In time of public emergency which threatens the life of the nation and the existence of which is officially proclaimed, the States Parties to the present Covenant may take measures derogating

from their obligations under the present Covenant to the extent strictly required by the exigencies of the situation, provided that such measures are not inconsistent with their other obligations under international law and do not involve discrimination solely on the ground of race, colour, sex, language, religion or social origin.

If there is an emergency threatening the life of the nation, states may thus derogate from certain rights such as the right to liberty, but Article 4(2) goes on to clarify that certain rights are non-derogable, such as the right of the individual detained to seek prompt judicial review of the lawfulness of the detention. In determining whether a public emergency threatens the life of the nation, Conte (2010: 545–47) points to four observations that arise from the jurisprudence in this field:

- The derogation can apply to distinct areas rather than the entire territory of the State;
- The crisis or emergency must be actual or imminent;
- The crisis or emergency must threaten the continued organised life of the community; and
- The crisis or emergency must be exceptional in that it cannot be dealt with under normal measures.

As mentioned in Chapter 4, the Anti-Terrorism, Crime and Security Act 2001 (UK) was enacted two months after the terrorist attacks that occurred on September 11, 2001 in the United States. Section 30 allowed for the making of derogation orders by the United Kingdom from Article 5(1) of the European Convention on Human Rights relating "to the detention of a person where there is an intention to remove or deport him [or her] from the United Kingdom." Accordingly, the Human Rights Act 1998 (Designated Derogation) Order 2001 came into force on November 13, 2001. This order stated:

> There exists a terrorist threat to the United Kingdom from persons suspected of involvement in international terrorism. In particular, there are foreign nationals present in the United Kingdom who are suspected of being concerned in the commission, preparation or instigation of acts of international terrorism, of being members of organisations or groups which are so concerned or of having links with members of such organisations or groups, and who are a threat to the national security of the United Kingdom.
>
> As a result, a public emergency, within the meaning of Article 15(1) of the Convention, exists in the United Kingdom.

Pursuant to this state of public emergency, Part 4 of the Anti-Terrorism, Crime and Security Act 2001 (UK) allowed for the Home Secretary to detain indefinitely any non-British citizen who was suspected of being a terrorist, pending deportation, even if such a deportation would be prohibited. Between 2001 and 2003, 16 foreign nationals were detained and held at Belmarsh Prison using these powers.

Interestingly, no other State Party to the European Convention considered it necessary to take measures to combat terrorism via a derogation from the right to liberty. Whether or not there was in fact a state of public emergency has been debated (Bates 2005: 275). A challenge was brought to the legality of the preventive detention regime under the Anti-Terrorism, Crime and Security Act 2001 by nine foreign nationals who had been detained without charge in Belmarsh Prison as suspected international terrorists. This challenge was eventually heard by the House of Lords in *A and others v Secretary of State for the Home Department* (2004).

In relation to the state of emergency derogation, the applicants referred to ministerial statements in October 2001 and March 2002 that: "[t]here is no immediate intelligence pointing to a specific threat to the United Kingdom, but we remain alert, domestically as well as internationally" and that "it would be wrong to say that we have evidence of a particular threat" (2004: para. [21]). Seven members of the House of Lords held that, while a "public emergency threatening the life of the nation" could be said to exist, the preventive detention provisions could not be said to be "strictly required" by that emergency and that the provisions were incompatible with the rights to liberty and non-discrimination. Only one judge, Lord Hoffman, found that the derogation was unlawful on the ground that there was no "war or other public emergency threatening the life of the nation" within the meaning of Article 15 of the European Convention on Human Rights. He stated (2004: para. [96]):

> This is a nation which has been tested in adversity, which has survived physical destruction and catastrophic loss of life. I do not underestimate the ability of fanatical groups of terrorists to kill and destroy, but they do not threaten the life of the nation. Whether we would survive Hitler hung in the balance, but there is no doubt that we shall survive Al-Qaeda. The Spanish people have not said that what happened in Madrid, hideous crime as it was, threatened the life of their nation. Their legendary pride would not allow it. Terrorist violence, serious as it is, does not threaten our institutions of government or our existence as a civil community.

Lord Hoffman agreed with the seven judges in the majority that the preventive detention provisions violated the right to liberty. Only one judge, Lord Walker of Gestingthorpe, found that the preventive detention provisions in Part 4 of the Act to be "proportionate, rational and non-discriminatory" (2004: para. [209]).

Article 15 of the European Convention on Human Rights requires that any measures taken by a member state in derogation of its obligations under the Convention should not go beyond what is "strictly required by the exigencies of the situation." The majority of judges found that the preventive detention scheme was not "strictly required" on the basis that it was disproportionate to the threat posed and discriminatory. In particular, the majority was concerned that the scheme applied only to "deportable aliens" and disregarded any threat posed by United Kingdom nationals. It also meant that some individuals could be deported to another country where they would be at liberty to plan activities that could be prejudicial to public security in the United Kingdom. Finally, there was a concern that the legislation was drafted so broadly that it could apply to individuals suspected of involvement with inter-national terrorist organizations that did not fall within the scope of the derogation.

Five years later, in *A and others v the United Kingdom* (2009), the Grand Chamber of the European Court of Human Rights heard an application by 11 of the Belmarsh detainees alleging that they had been unlaw-fully detained and did not have adequate remedies at their disposal. Like the House of Lords, it held that the derogating measures were dispropor-tionate in that they discriminated unjustifiably between nationals and non-nationals.

After the House of Lords decision, the preventive detention provisions were repealed and replaced by control orders under the Prevention of Terrorism Act 2005. These were in turn abolished by the Terrorism Prevention and Investigation Measures Act 2011 and replaced by "meas-ures" that can still serve to restrict a person's liberty.

In relation to control orders under the 2005 Act, the jurisprudence concerning the right to liberty has largely focused on the type of restric-tions imposed rather than whether control orders of themselves breach this right. For example, in *Secretary of State for the Home Department v JJ and others* (2006), the England and Wales High Court of Justice heard an application by six Iraqi men who were subject to control orders in England. The men argued that the control orders breached their right to liberty under Article 5 of the European Convention on Human Rights. Their control orders included 18-hour curfews, limitations on the places they could go in their six hours outside their place of residence, the impo-sition of electronic monitoring tags, and being prevented from attending any prearranged meeting with a person unless that person had been cleared by the Home Office.

In quashing these prevention orders, Justice Sullivan stated (2006: para. [73]):

> I am left in no doubt whatsoever that the cumulative effect of the obligations has been to deprive the respondents of their liberty in breach of Article 5 of the Convention. I do not consider that this is a borderline case. The collective impact of the obligations . . . could not sensibly be described as a mere restriction upon the respondents' liberty of movement. In terms of the length of the curfew period (18 hours), the extent of the obligations, and their intrusive impact on the respondents' ability to lead anything resembling a normal life, whether inside their residences within the curfew period, or for the 6-hour period outside it, these control orders go far beyond the restrictions in those cases where the European Court of Human Rights has concluded that there has been a restriction upon but not a deprivation of liberty.

The Secretary of State subsequently issued new orders with 14-hour curfews, and appealed the Court's finding. When the Court of Appeal dismissed the appeal, the Secretary of State appealed further to the House of Lords. This appeal was also dismissed by a majority of three justices to two (*Secretary of State for the Home Department v JJ and others* 2008). The majority, however, made it clear that they upheld the control order regime in general, and that they would accept curfews of less than 18 hours.

The Home Office remained committed to control orders for some time despite judicial curtailment. The Home Office considered that control orders "offer valuable protection where neither prosecution nor deportation is immediately viable and are more cost-effective than surveillance" (Walker 2011: 324). However, a subsequent review conducted in late 2010 (Home Office 2011) led to their abolition and the introduction of "terrorism prevention and investigation measures" that have yet to be tested under international human rights law.

The human rights jurisprudence in relation to suspected terrorists thus indicates that preventive detention and control orders or like measures may be justifiable providing they amount to a proportionate and necessary response to the terrorist threat.

OTHER RELEVANT HUMAN RIGHTS

While the right to liberty is probably the most obvious right that may be breached by preventive detention regimes, other rights may also be affected. The *Fardon* and *Tillman* communications raised a number of issues concerning the post-sentence preventive detention of sex offenders. Although the United Nations Human Rights Committee did not need to determine such issues, the Committee's finding that such detention violated the right to liberty touched on certain other rights. This section concentrates on the right to a fair hearing that is pertinent to all groups of individuals which are the focus of this book. Other rights affected include the right not to be subject to double punishment and the right not to be subject to retrospective laws, which are relevant to post-sentence preventive detention regimes.

The Right to a Fair Hearing

Article 14 of the International Covenant on Civil and Political Rights guarantees the general right to a "fair and public hearing by a competent, independent and impartial tribunal established by law," in both criminal and civil proceedings. It then specifies a number of procedural safeguards such as the presumption of innocence.

The principle of procedural fairness is relevant to any scheme that seeks to supervise or preventively detain serious offenders, those with severe mental illness or suspected terrorists. This is because procedural fairness requires safeguards to ensure that hearings carried out under the scheme operate in a way that is fair to the person being detained or supervised. Such safeguards could include periodic reviews, rights of appeal, and access to an independent tribunal.

Principle 1(6) of the United Nations Principles for the Protection of Persons with Mental Illness and the Improvement of Mental Health Care (1991) requires that any decision relating to a lack of "legal capacity" must be made "only after a fair hearing by an independent and impartial tribunal established by domestic law." Accordingly, mental health laws in many countries establish mental health tribunals to oversee decisions concerning the involuntary detention of individuals with severe mental illness (Carney *et al*. 2011). However, as indicated above, an argument can be made pursuant to Article 14 of the Convention on the Rights of Persons with Disabilities that legislation enabling the deprivation of liberty on the basis of disability should be abolished. If this occurred then any hearings enabling such a deprivation would violate the rights of this Convention.

The reality is, however, that most States Parties to the Convention on the Rights of Persons with Disabilities will continue, at least in the short term, to have tribunal oversight of detention decisions. While most of these tribunals are "mandated to proceed without undue formality and regard to technicalities" (Freckelton 2010: 204), procedural fairness is essential to their proper functioning (Carney *et al*. 2011).

In relation to post-sentence preventive detention schemes, the United Nations Human Rights Committee stated in the *Fardon* and *Tillman* decisions that the schemes in Queensland and New South Wales did not meet the due process guarantees under Article 14 of the International Covenant on Civil and Political Rights "for a fair trial in which a penal sentence is imposed" (*Re Fardon*, 2010: para. [7.4(3)]; *Re Tillman*, 2010: para. [7.4(3)]). This was of course dependent on the notion that detention in prison amounts to punishment, a notion that was not accepted by the majority of the High Court of Australia in *Fardon v Attorney-General (Qld)* (2004). For example, Justices Callinan and Heydon stated (2004: 654):

> [The Queensland Act] is intended to protect the community from predatory sexual offenders. It is a protective law authorising involuntary detention in the interests of public safety. Its proper characterisation is as a protective rather than a punitive enactment.

In relation to the preventive detention of suspected terrorists and control orders, the right to a fair hearing may be violated by the secrecy provisions surrounding such schemes. In *R v H* (2004: para. [23]), the House of Lords commented:

> The problem of reconciling an individual's right to a fair trial with such secrecy as is necessary in a democratic society in the interests of national security or the prevention or investigation of crime is inevitably difficult to resolve in a liberal society governed by the rule of law.

Both Article 14(1) of the International Covenant on Civil and Political Rights and Article 6(1) of the European Convention on Human Rights allow for the exclusion of the public and the press for reasons of national security, but only "to the extent strictly necessary in the opinion of the court in special circumstances where publicity would prejudice the interests of justice" (Article 14(1)). There is also an exception to the disclosure of all information to the accused in matters of public security. The European Court of Human rights stated in *Jasper v United Kingdom* (2000: para. [52]):

> the entitlement to disclosure of relevant evidence is not an absolute right. In any criminal proceedings, there may be competing interests, such as national security or the need to protect witnesses at risk of reprisals or keep secret police methods of investigation of crime, which must be weighed against the

rights of the accused. In some cases it may be necessary to withhold certain evidence from the defence so as to preserve the fundamental rights of another individual or to safeguard an important public interest.

Article 5(4) of the European Convention on Human Rights sets out the right "to take proceedings by which the lawfulness of . . . detention shall be decided speedily by a court." In *A and others v the United Kingdom* (2009), the Grand Chamber of the European Court of Human Rights unanimously held that this right had been breached in relation to the suspected terrorists who had been preventively detained under Part IV of the Anti-Terrorism, Crime and Security Act 2001. The Court held that the evidence on which the State relied to support the allegations made against four of the Belmarsh detainees was largely to be found in "closed material" and was, therefore, not disclosed to the men or their lawyers. The Court held that the detainees must be provided with sufficient information about the allegations against them to enable them to give effective instructions to the special advocate.

This decision had a bearing on the regime enabling control orders of suspected terrorists. The case of *Secretary of State for the Home Department v MB and AF* (2007) concerned the making of control orders against MB who was suspected of arranging to go to Iraq to fight against coalition forces and AF who was thought to be associated with Islamic extremists. The members of the House of Lords considered that the issue of a fair hearing was fact-specific and remitted the matter to the Administrative Court for reconsideration. Lord Bingham, however, stated (2007: para. [41]) that because MB had simply been confronted by an unsubstantiated assertion by the Security Services, he had not been given "a substantial measure of procedural justice, or that the very essence of the right to a fair hearing had been impaired." He made a similar finding in relation to AF (2007: para. [146]) on the basis that there had been no clear or significant allegations of involvement in terrorist-related activity disclosed in the control order proceedings against AF.

In the subsequent case of *Secretary of State for the Home Department v AF and another* (2009), which was decided after the European Court of Human Rights decision in *A and others v the United Kingdom*, the House of Lords agreed that if a person is subject to a control order and challenges its validity, that person must be given sufficient information to enable him or her to give effective instructions to the special advocate.

In situations where preventive detention and supervision regimes are considered lawful, the right to a fair hearing can operate as an effective check on the procedures used within those regimes.

The Right Not to be Subject to Double Punishment

Article 14(7) of the International Covenant on Civil and Political Rights states that "[n]o one shall be liable to be tried or punished again for an offence for which he [or she] has already been finally convicted or acquitted in accordance with the law and penal procedure of each country." In Australia, the term "double jeopardy" has been held to apply not only to the determination of guilt, but also to the quantification of punishment (*Rohde v Director of Public Prosecutions* 1986: 128–129; *Pearce v The Queen* 1998: 628).

The Dangerous Prisoners (Sexual Offenders) Act 2003 (Qld) was challenged in the High Court of Australia in *Fardon v Attorney-General (Qld)* (2004) on the basis that the court making the order under this Act was "*required* to have regard to the prior offences of a person in determining whether he should be a prisoner or not in circumstances where no crime has been committed" (Keyzer *et al.* 2004: 250). Justice Gummow was the only judge in the majority in the High Court case to deal with this argument and he did so briefly. He found that the Act did not breach the "double jeopardy" rule as it relates to sentencing because it did not punish Robert Fardon twice or increase the punishment for the offences for which he was convicted.

In the *Fardon* and *Tillman* communications, it was argued that a post-sentence preventive detention scheme dependent on a finding of guilt that involves imprisonment must be seen as a form of punishment above and beyond that of the sentence already served. This was the approach taken by Justice Kirby in his dissenting judgment when he stated (*Fardon* 2004: 644, footnotes omitted):

> Effectively, what is attempted involves the second court in reviewing, and increasing, the punishment previously imposed by the first court for precisely the same *past* conduct. Alternatively, it involves the second court in superimposing additional punishment on the basis that the original maximum punishment provided by law, as imposed, has later proved inadequate and that a new foundation for additional punishment, in effect retrospective, may be discovered in order to increase it.

The United Nations Human Rights Committee agreed with this approach, finding that post-sentence detention in prison "amounted to a fresh term of imprisonment which . . . is not permissible in the absence of a conviction" (*Re Fardon*, 2010: para. [7.4(1)]; *Re Tillman*, 2010: para. [7.4(1)]). In the Committee's view, the continued detention amounted to double punishment and was another factor on which to find that the right to liberty had been violated.

The Right Not to be Subject to Retrospective Laws

Article 15(1) of the International Covenant on Civil and Political Rights states that "[n]o one shall be held guilty of any criminal offence on account of any act or omission which did not constitute a criminal offence, under national or international law, at the time when it was committed." This right is also set out in Article 7(1) of the European Convention on Human Rights and is particularly salient in relation to post-sentence preventive detention regimes for serious offenders.

One view of the reasons for the principle against retrospectivity was expressed by Toohey J in *Polyukhovich v The Commonwealth of Australia and Another* (1991: 688–89):

> Protection against retroactive laws protects a particular accused against potentially capricious state action. But the principle also represents a protection of a public interest. This is so, first, in the sense that every individual is, by the principle, assured that no future retribution by society can occur except by reference to rules presently known; and secondly, it serves to promote a just society by encouraging a climate of security and humanity.

It is arguable that preventive detention schemes do not set up new criminal offences and do not impose additional punishment where the purpose of such schemes is community protection. On this view, the principle of retrospectivity does not apply.

However, in many instances the legislation introducing post-sentence preventive detention was enacted *after* the offender was originally sentenced. The European Court of Human Rights and the BVerfG decisions regarded the imposition of a penalty upon the accused that was not foreseen when the detention first began as crucial in finding that post-sentence detention violated the European Convention on Human Rights.

Of all the preventive detention and supervision schemes examined in this book, it is undoubtedly post-sentence preventive detention that has been regarded as clearly violating international human rights. Yet, such schemes continue to exist. The next section turns to the gap between principles and reality when it comes to implementing human rights compliance in individual countries.

INTERNATIONAL HUMAN RIGHTS LAW AND DOMESTIC COMPLIANCE

Both Article 9(5) of the International Covenant on Civil and Political Rights and Article 5(5) of the European Convention on Human Rights provide for a right to compensation for unlawful detention. However, in many instances, the challenge is primarily made in order to stop the detention and to reform the law rather than to seek compensation. This section explores what a finding that preventive detention breaches international human rights law means in reality.

Decisions of the United Nations Human Rights Committee are not legally binding (Blay and Piotrowicz 2000), which means that States Parties to international conventions can dispute or ignore the Committee's findings. As noted already, this is what occurred in relation to Australia's response to the *Tillman* and *Fardon* communications. In contrast, decisions of the European Court of Human Rights are binding in international law. The implementation of the Court's judgments is supervised by the Committee of Ministers, which represents all 47 Council of Europe states. However, the effect on domestic laws of the European Court of Human Rights decisions may largely depend on the willingness of individual states to abide by those decisions.

As most of the States Parties to the European Convention on Human Rights have incorporated the Convention into their own national laws, either through constitutional provision, statute, or judicial decision, it is arguable that this jurisprudence is more effective in rectifying human rights breaches than decisions by the United Nations Human Rights Committee. Certainly, the German Federal Constitutional Court (BVerfG) cases, *Preventive Detention Cases I and II* (BVerfG 2011a), indicate the willingness of domestic courts to take seriously the jurisprudence of the European Court of Human Rights.

Nevertheless, many national courts do not accept that they are bound by European Court of Human Rights decisions. In 2002, for example, 21 European constitutional courts declared that they were not bound by such decisions, although a large majority stated that they were influenced by them (Alen and Melchior 2002). In this way, the BVerfG's approach to preventive detention can be viewed as being influenced by the European Court of Human Rights decisions rather than fully compliant with them. As Kirstin Drenkhahn and colleagues (2012: 176) point out, the decisions of the BVerfG make it clear that at the national level, decisions of the European Court of Human Rights rank below that of German "Basic Law," but that the latter's jurisprudence can serve "as an aid to the interpretation of the content and reach of fundamental rights and principles of the rule of law contained in the Basic Law." The BVerfG's decision still allows for the continuing operation of post-sentence preventive detention until May 31, 2013 and preventive detention schemes are still permissible, although in a more restricted way. Christopher Michaelsen (2012: 166) points out that the European Court of Human Rights decision may influence how other preventive detention schemes are viewed in Austria, Denmark, France, Italy, Liechtenstein, San Marino,

Slovakia, Switzerland, and the United Kingdom, although "preventive detention may be qualified as an additional penalty in one State, and as a preventive measure in another."

Jurisprudence having an influence rather than being binding is still better than having no influence at all. Because the Human Rights Committee decisions are not binding on domestic courts, and because of community concerns about certain groups of individuals, it can be argued that these decisions ultimately have little impact on government policies and the interpretation of preventive detention legislation. For example, in *WBM v Chief Commissioner of Police* (2010: para. [49]), Justice Kaye of the Supreme Court of Victoria, in dealing with an application for a declaration that the applicant should not be a registered sex offender under the Sex Offenders Registration Act 2004 (Vic), referred to the Human Rights Committee in rather unflattering terms:

> That Committee does not perform the same judicial role, which is performed by the courts of this state. In particular, it is not the independent judicial arm of a parliamentary democracy, the other arms of which are the legislature and the executive. Further, it is fair to observe that the majority of the members of that Committee do not come from countries which have the same system of democracy as ours, or indeed any system of representative democracy at all. The opinions of that Committee, to which I was referred, involve the expressions by the Committee of value judgments in a manner and to an extent which is at odds with the traditional judicial function of the courts of this State and this nation.

On the other hand, Justice Atkinson of the Queensland Supreme Court stated in a footnote to her judgment in *Attorney-General (Qld) v Waghorn* (2010) that the decision of the United Nations Human Rights Committee in the *Fardon* communication "serves to emphasise the respect for human rights that ought be applied by this court when giving effect to the [Queensland legislation]." She reiterated this point in *Attorney-General (Qld) v Beattie* (2010) and stated that the Human Rights Committee decision in *Fardon* supported the need for regular reviews of detention orders as part of the constraints that ought to be placed on post-sentence preventive detention.

Freckelton and Keyzer (2010: 345–54) have also been optimistic in arguing that the "Australian states that have adopted re-imprisonment policies will now need to devise and implement risk management policies aimed at rehabilitation in the community."

The potential of international human rights jurisprudence in shaping preventive detention schemes may ultimately depend to some extent on the rights culture of the State concerned. As indicated above, Australia does not have a federal Bill or Charter of Rights and to some extent, the influence of human rights discourse on judicial decision-making is still in the process of development. In comparison, the German Federal Constitutional Court's willingness to engage with the decisions of the European Court of Human Rights in declaring post-sentence preventive detention to be in breach of the right to liberty may be partly explained by the modern-day importance of the protection of fundamental rights in that country given its history. The effect of international human rights decisions on domestic laws is thus dependent on the willingness of the State concerned to abide by such decisions.

CONCLUSION

Robert John Fardon is but one of a number of individuals who attract community condemnation. His harsh upbringing and the physical and probable sexual abuse he experienced as a child might be viewed as setting the scene for his subsequent brutal sexual attacks on his victims. Nevertheless, when the community condemns such crimes, it is simpler for governments to respond by focusing resources on preventive detention regimes on the basis of the protection of the community rather than on identifying and implementing social measures to prevent offending in the first place.

In terms of a "balance" between community protection and individual human rights, when it comes to serious offenders, many members of the public might argue that the scales must be tipped in favour of community protection because such offenders have forfeited their entitlement to their human rights due to the nature of the crimes committed. Justice John Barry of the Supreme Court of Victoria once observed (Barry 1969: 78):

> The public image of a prison as a place of degradation where it is right and proper that inmates should be repressed and debased is still strong. In the public mind . . . a prison is a place where people who have done wicked things are kept apart and held in subjection, so that they will not contaminate law-abiding citizens.

The extinction or suspension of human rights, sometimes referred to as "civil death," was once seen as a necessary consequence of conviction. However, the Preamble to the Universal Declaration of Human Rights in recognizing the "inherent dignity and inalienable rights *of all members of the human family*" (emphasis added) makes it clear that human rights are not selective. Offenders do not forfeit their human rights when they commit a crime.

At the international level, post-sentence preventive detention of sex offenders has been held by both the United Nations Human Rights Committee and the European Court of Human Rights to breach the right to liberty. Post-sentence preventive detention also violates the right to a fair trial, and the rights not to be subject to double punishment and retrospective laws. Nevertheless, states such as Australia remain unwilling to abide by the decisions of international human rights bodies and it may be a slow process for human rights frameworks to be accepted by governments.

The human rights status regarding other preventive detention and supervision schemes is complex. The detention of those of "unsound mind" has been held by the European Court of Human Rights not to breach the right to liberty providing that certain minimum conditions are satisfied, although this is now being challenged by recent interpretations of Article 14 of the Convention on the Rights of Persons with Disabilities. The preventive detention and control of suspected terrorists may also be lawful providing stringent conditions are applied. The right to a fair trial requires safeguards to ensure that hearings carried out under such schemes operate in a way that is fair to the person being detained or supervised.

Ultimately, international human rights law can provide a framework for preventive detention and supervision schemes that helps ensure a balance between individual rights and community protection. Given the potential arbitrariness of preventive detention schemes, it is preferable that supervision, control, or treatment orders that provide certain restrictions in a community setting be given priority. However, given that all such schemes are based on the risk of future harm, mental health practitioners need to consider the ethics of providing risk assessments for schemes that breach the right to liberty. The next chapter considers a number of ethical perspectives in this regard.

8

THE ETHICS OF FORENSIC RISK ASSESSMENT

INTRODUCTION: LESSONS FROM HISTORY

On May 9, 1944, a 12-year-old girl was admitted to the Heidelberg University Psychiatric Hospital for participation in a research programme examining the heredity of psychological traits (Roelcke *et al.* 2001). Since the age of nine, she had been housed at the nearby Schwarzacherhof asylum because her family were unable to cope with her aggressive behaviour.

Professor Carl Schneider, who held the Chair of Psychiatry and Neurology at the University of Heidelberg from 1933 to 1945, diagnosed the girl as having "spinal paralysis," although the cover of her file noted that the diagnosis was "idiocy" (Roelcke *e al.* 2001: 289). One of the research team, psychiatrist Julius Dreussen noted on May 31, 1944 (Roelcke *et al.* 2001: 289):

> Examination impossible because of active resistance which it is not possible to correct. Slaps do not help; has to be sedated. Is then placed in the corner for more than two hours, where . . . it [sic] looks up at the examiner, and cries and scratches when he approaches.

In June, the girl was returned to the asylum, her mother apparently having been told that the girl could not be cured. The next month, the girl's mother was told the asylum was to be closed. She wrote to Dr. Dreussen (Roelcke *et al.* 2001: 289) stating that: "It is my ardent wish that the poor child may find peace . . . Could you not take the child to Heidelberg and let her fall asleep there?"

Dr. Dreussen told the mother that he would take the matter in hand. The girl was transferred to another asylum at Eichberg and on August 4, 1944, the parents were told the girl had died.

This story is one of three case studies set out in an article by Volker Roelcke, Gerrit Hoendorf, and Maike Rotzoll (2001) that explores Professor Carl Schneider and his research team's association with the "euthanasia" programme that involved the mass murder of more than 100,000 individuals with mental and intellectual impairments in Nazi Germany as part of the National Socialists' social and health policy.

In July 1933, a few months after he seized power, Adolf Hitler pushed through the Cabinet the Law for the Prevention of Progeny of Hereditary Disease, which was enacted on January 1, 1934. This allowed the compulsory sterilization of individuals with mental illness, "mental retardation," epilepsy, severe alcoholism, as well as other individuals deemed to be genetically inferior by the Genetic Health Court (Hassenfeld 2002). Irwin Hassenfeld (2002: 186) writes that the "enforced eugenics programme, commencing in 1934, sterilized 50,000 German citizens a year. It is commonly believed that the sterilization process was a critical link in the process leading to the holocaust." Strous (2006: 31) states that "[o]f the 300,000 to 400,000 who were sterilized, roughly 60% were considered to have some form of mental illness."

On September 1, 1939, Hitler issued an order calling for the killing of those with disabilities. The "action" (the German word "aktion" can be interpreted as an official "operation" or "action") against children was organized by the Federal Board for the Scientific Registration of Hereditary or Other Severe Congenital Diseases and it is estimated that 5,000 children were killed as a result (Meyer 1988).

The "action" against adults with disabilities was known as Action T4 after the central office in charge of the programme situated at No 4 Tiergartenstrasse in the centre of Berlin. The Director of Action T4 was Dr. Werner Heyde, the Wurzburg Professor of Psychiatry. Hassenfeld (2002: 187) describes the procedure:

> [U]nder a program called "Economic Planning Registration" the medical department of the Ministry of the Interior distributed questionaires seeking information (diagnosis, length of stay, extent of disability etc.) on all institutionalized patients. A completed questionaire was sent to three of thirty psychiatric consultants to T4, many of whom were university professors. The consultants independently decided whether the patient should be allowed to live or be put to death. In cases of disagreement the final determination was made by Dr Heyde. By August, 1941, 70,000 patients had been gassed as a result of this program.

After the euthanasia programme was officially ended in 1941, it nevertheless continued in an unofficial manner until 1945 with an estimated

206

130,000 individuals starved, poisoned, neglected, and shot to death in German psychiatric institutions (Strous 2011: 165).

Why some psychiatrists became actively involved in the T4 programme while some resisted (Lifton 1986: 80–89) and others were indifferent is difficult to ascertain. Mary Seeman (2005) posits that the move from "Fürsorge" meaning care for the ill individual to "Vorsorge" meaning prior care or preventive medicine as a driving force in health care during the Nazi era provided a context for the eugenic and euthanasia programmes. Whatever the causes of the T4 programme, what is important to recognize here is that the murder of those with disabilities during this period was legally sanctioned. The law was used as a tool for the removal and death of those considered to be undesirable.

In the Australian High Court case of *Fardon v Attorney-General (Qld)* (2004: paras [188]–[189]), the dissenting judge, Justice Michael Kirby, sounded a warning about the parallels between laws enacted in Germany in the 1930s and post-sentence preventive detention laws for sex offenders:

> One pattern of intrusion into judicial functions may be observed in what occurred in Germany in the early 1930s. It was provided for in the acts of an elected government. Laws with retroactive effect were duly promulgated. Such laws adopted a phenomeno-logical approach. Punishment was addressed to the estimated character of the criminal instead of the proved facts of a crime. Rather than sanctioning specified criminal conduct, the phenomenological school of criminal liability procured the enact-ment of laws prescribing punishment for identified criminal archetypes. . . .
>
> This shift of focus in the criminal law led to a practice of not releasing prisoners at the expiry of their sentences. By 1936, in Germany, a police practice of intensive surveillance of discharged criminals was replaced by increased utilisation of laws permitting "protective custody" . . . Offenders for whom such punishments were prescribed were transferred from civil prisons to other institutions, such as lunatic asylums, following the termination of their criminal sentence. Political prisoners and "undesirables" became increasingly subject to indeterminate detention [footnotes omitted].

While the crimes of Nazi Germany may seem irrelevant to current preventive detention and supervision policies and practice, the involvement of mental health practitioners in the euthanasia programme nevertheless casts a shadow over the ethical duties of mental health practitioners in relation to the politics of social control. David Weisstub and Julio

Arboleda-Flórez (2000: 195) point to other instances of the misuse of psychiatry in the former Soviet Union and Cuba where the "use of psychiatry as punishment" occurred. Deidre Greig (1997: 238) refers to history showing "that the health professions are not immune from adjusting their role in line with emerging political forces." She makes the point (1997: 238) that "[w]hat is important is that this adjustment should be done with an understanding of history and the cultural changes which have influenced the way problems are conceptualized."

Perhaps as a response to past transgressions, there is a wealth of material on psychiatric ethics that seeks to ensure that psychiatrists and other mental health practitioners avoid becoming mere instruments of state power. Some of this material will be explored in this chapter.

There has also been debate about the ethics of the therapeutic relationship in mental health care and whether there is a distinctive ethics of psychiatry (Radden 2002, 2004). Jennifer Radden (2002: 53–54), for example, argues that psychiatry has three features that call for a special ethical framework:

- the nature of the therapeutic relationship that she views as a "treatment tool, analogous to the surgeon's scalpel";
- the fact that patients are vulnerable to "exploitation, dependence, and inherent inequality" because of their "diminished judgement, the stigma, and controversy associated with their condition, and the salient place of gender in psychiatry"; and
- the "therapeutic project" that aims to "restore some earlier level of functioning and to relieve debilitating signs and symptoms."

Radden's call for a special ethics for psychiatry has been criticized (Crowden 2003), but it is interesting to note that there has been increasing concern about the ethics of the psychiatric profession. There is less material on the role of psychologists in this regard, although this is now beginning to be explored (e.g., Ward and Syversen 2009).

This chapter is concerned with the ethics of engaging in risk assessment and giving risk assessment testimony before courts and tribunals in the light of the concerns that have been raised with risk assessment techniques and the potential violations of human rights that may occur with preventive detention and supervision regimes. As Robin Ion and Dominic Beer (2003: 240) point out:

> [m]ental health care does not take place in a vacuum. It influences, and is influenced by, the society in which it is practiced. As such, it is essential that mental health workers have an understanding of the sociopolitical context in which care takes place and of the potential for their work to be subverted for political ends.

THE ETHICAL CONCERNS WITH RISK ASSESSMENT TECHNIQUES AND TESTIMONY

The term "ethics" is sometimes used to refer to professional rules and guidelines, but it is most commonly understood as a branch of moral philosophy (Kämpf et al. 2009). Annegret Kämpf and colleagues (2009: 11) describe the study of ethics as attempting to understand:

- whether there are universal moral claims, values or principles in human behaviour;
- what ethics means in general (meta-ethics) or specific contexts (applied ethics); and
- whether ethics can constitute a framework to guide moral behaviour (normative ethics).

This chapter is primarily concerned with the second question of what ethics means in the specific context of risk assessment for the purposes of preventive detention and supervision of serious offenders and individuals with severe mental illness. The discussion, however, will be of relevance to the preventive detention of suspected terrorists should mental health practitioners be called upon to assess the risk of violence in that context. Adrian Grounds (2004), for example, has highlighted the ethical difficulties that face psychiatrists who may be involved in conducting assessments of those individuals captured in armed conflicts or counter-terrorism operations who are detained at the United States detention camp located within Guantanamo Bay Naval Base, Cuba.

As explored in the previous chapter, post-sentence preventive detention of sex offenders has been held by both the United Nations Human Rights Committee and the European Court of Human Rights to breach a number of rights, including the right to liberty, the right to a fair trial, the right not to be subject to double punishment, and the right not to be subject to retrospective laws. However, the human rights status regarding other preventive detention and supervision schemes is not as clear-cut. Chapter 3 explored the history and current status of risk assessment techniques, pointing out that the use of risk assessment instruments and clinical judgment may have a role in clinical environments, but another level of criticism overlays their use in the legal system.

In the light of these concerns about potential breaches of human rights and the imperfect nature of risk assessment techniques, what ethical approaches should guide mental health practitioners? There is a range of ethical approaches that may be taken to any particular problem (Kämpf et al. 2009). One of the approaches used most frequently in the medical field is the principle-based approach (Beauchamp and Childress 2001).

Thomas Beauchamp and James Childress' theory of ethics is based on four clusters of principles termed "beneficence," nonmaleficence, justice, and autonomy. Thomas Beauchamp (2007: 7) points out that these principles derive from a "common morality" that is "applicable to all persons in all places, and all human conduct is rightly judged by its standards." Ten elements constitute this common morality, namely that people should:

- not kill;
- not cause pain or suffering to others;
- prevent evil or harm from occurring;
- rescue persons in danger;
- tell the truth;
- nurture the young and dependent;
- keep promises;
- not steal;
- not punish the innocent;
- treat all persons with equal moral consideration (Beauchamp 2007: 7).

While these elements are seen as of common interest in realizing the objectives of morality, the four principles derived from these elements are not absolute, but allow for exceptions and are subject to modification and reformulation (Beauchamp 2007: 8). The principle of nonmaleficence requires that no harm be caused to the patient, or client, and thus can be viewed as requiring mental health practitioners to eliminate or minimize any potential for damage (Koocher and Keith-Spiegel 2008). On the other hand, the principle of justice that requires the fair distribution of benefits, risks, and costs and respecting the equality of all humans may require that the interests of third parties be taken into account in specific areas of practice.

Applying ethical theories to practice often requires weighing up fundamental moral principles that may be difficult for those not trained in moral philosophy. Professional codes of ethics are a relatively recent phenomenon (Bloch and Pargiter 2009: 151ff) that aim to help professionals find a framework for practical use. They consist of rules created by a professional body that attempt to define the ethical standards of the profession concerned and set out what is considered to be good practice. Codes of ethics are not prescriptive in identifying right or wrong solutions to specific problems, but provide guidance to the professions as to what values should be considered in certain circumstances (Kämpf et al. 2009). Professional bodies may also issue guidelines that provide minimum standards for practice.

Of course, a general knowledge of the relevant code of ethics is insufficient for ethical practice. As Rael Strous (2011: 162) points out "[i]n 1931 the German medical society developed a code of medical ethics which at the time was considered one of the most advanced, if not the most advanced, in the world." This code had little effect on the conduct of certain doctors in Nazi Germany, despite the requirement that it be well understood at the time.

When ethical dilemmas occur in practice, Samuel Knapp and Leon VandeCreek (2003) identify five steps derived from the different ethical approaches:

- identify the problem;
- develop alternatives;
- evaluate the alternatives;
- implement the best option;
- evaluate the results.

This chapter is primarily concerned with steps two and three. The fourth and fifth steps are largely dependent on what Shane Bush, Mary Connell, and Robert Denny (2006) refer to as personal beliefs and values. The problem under consideration is what position mental health practitioners should take in assessing and providing evidence of risk when a person's liberty is at stake. There are three possible alternative approaches to this problem.

The first approach is to take the extreme view that it is *always* ethical to engage in risk assessment and to give risk assessment testimony even in the knowledge that it will lead to human rights breaches. The reasoning behind this approach is that mental health practitioners must always perform their job and leave any ethical justifications to other professionals. Thomas Grisso and Paul Appelbaum (1992: 630) have outlined this position as being one that leaves "questions of justification to the courts and society to determine, not the mental health professional." Thus, it is for Parliament to create laws restricting the liberties of individuals and for mental health practitioners to comply with what is legally required of them in this regard.

To some extent this approach reflects a belief that mental health practitioners should abide by whatever the law requires and not become political activists for fear of violating the boundaries of their professions. Rael Strous (2007a: 12) points to the involvement of psychiatrists in sterilization and euthanasia programmes during the Nazi regime as an example of psychiatrists allowing "the political mood to influence their professional practice." He writes (2007a: 12) that "[m]any psychiatrists at the time maintained that they had an inherent responsibility more than other medical professions to be involved in community and political affairs."

However, the main problem with blindly accepting what the law requires, particularly where the law is unjust, is that it leaves the door open for mental health practitioners to become agents of state control. While Strous (2007a: 15) states that "political activism is dangerous and unprofessional," he advocates upholding professional standards of conduct embodied in professional codes of ethics. He writes (2007a: 15):

> Standing up for the rights of patients is included within [the] rubric of moral instincts, particularly when these rights are encroached upon due to a political process such as budget and service cuts or when human rights violations directly affect patient care.

The approach that it is always ethical to engage in risk assessment and giving risk assessment testimony where liberty is at stake also ignores the obligations placed on mental health practitioners through various codes of ethics to comply with ethical standards and even to seek changes in laws when they are contrary to the best interests of individuals. For example, section 3 of the American Psychiatric Association's *Principles of Medical Ethics* states that physicians "shall respect the law and also recognize a responsibility to seek changes in those requirements which are contrary to the best interests of the patient" (American Psychiatric Association 2010).

Under Standard 1.02 of the American Psychological Association's (2003) *Ethical Principles of Psychologists and Code of Conduct*, psychologists are required to make known their concern about conflicts between their ethical responsibilities and the law. Guideline 1.02 of the American Psychological Association's (2011) *Specialty Guidelines for Forensic Psychology* also requires forensic practitioners "to identify, make known, and address real or apparent conflicts of interest in an attempt to maintain the public confidence and trust, discharge professional obligations, and maintain responsibility, impartiality, and accountability." Similarly, in New Zealand, Principle 4.1.5 of the *Code of Ethics for Psychologists Working in Aotearoa/New Zealand* developed by a special Code of Ethics Review Group (2002) states that "[p]sychologists have a responsibility to speak out and/ or act in a manner consistent with the . . . principles of this Code if they believe policies, practices or regulations of the social structures within which psychologists work, seriously ignore or oppose any of the principles of this Code."

Rael Strous (2007b: 6) states that a major lesson arising from psychiatry during the Nazi era is that it is of "paramount value" that psychiatrists act as "moral agents in the interests of patients." Blindly following what the law dictates clearly does not meet the relevant ethical standards of the mental health professions.

There are two other possible approaches to the problem under consideration. One is to take the view that it is never ethical to engage in risk assessment where a person's liberty is at stake, while a less extreme, more nuanced approach is to believe that it can be ethical in certain circumstances. These approaches are explored below.

Risk Assessment for the Purpose of Preventive Detention and Supervision is Never Ethical

The involvement of mental health practitioners in preventive detention and supervision regimes gives rise to the ethical dilemma sometimes referred to as "dual loyalty." The International Dual Loyalty Working Group (2002) describes this as follows:

> The problem of dual loyalty – simultaneous obligations, express or implied, to a patient and to a third party, often the state – continues to challenge health professionals. Health professional ethics have long stressed the need for loyalty to people in their care. In the modern world, however, health professionals are increasingly asked to weigh their devotion to patients against service to the objectives of government or other third parties. Dual loyalty poses particular challenges for health professionals throughout the world when the subordination of the patient's interests to state or other purposes risks violating the patient's human rights.

There is a tendency to think of the "dual loyalty" problem in terms of health professionals working under repressive governments, where pervasive human rights abuses, combined with restrictions on freedom of expression, make it difficult to speak out and to report abuses. But, as touched on in the previous chapter, breaches of human rights under governmental policies can also take place in open societies in relation to particular groups of individuals.

The dual loyalty dilemma is most often raised in association with forensic psychiatry where the obligation to the justice system may conflict with the principles of beneficence and nonmaleficence (Robertson and Walter 2008). More broadly, the central issue is whether mental health practitioners (and in particular psychiatrists) should ever participate in non-therapeutic endeavours.

Critics of the coercive nature of psychiatry such as Thomas Szasz (1963, 1970, 2007) would argue that psychiatrists are fundamentally agents of the state not only in repressive states, but also in open societies, wherever some form of coercion is involved. Szasz writes (2005: 77) that "[p]sychiatry was founded and continues to function as a coercive apparatus of the State" on the basis that "[c]oercing the patient is the oldest, most enduring, and most characteristic feature of the psychiatrist's job."

His view (2005: 78) is that since World War II, psychologists have "embraced the prevailing principles and practices of psychiatrists" and that when psychologists treat individuals against their will, "they act as coercive agents of the State, regardless of what lies they tell themselves or what lies their superiors or professional organizations tell them."

Unlike those in the anti-psychiatry camp, Szasz is not opposed to the practice of psychiatry and psychology if such practice is non-coercive. If the relationship between mental health professional and client is a contractual service between consenting adults with no state involvement, then his view is that the mental health professions comply with ethical principles.

Rael Strous (2006: 34) suggests that "psychiatry, by nature, incorporates contemporary ideology into its approach to the individual and society." Writing about psychiatrists' involvement in Nazi Germany, he posits (2006: 34) that "this connection to contemporary ideology and its values – may have desensitized psychiatrists to the extermination process and to their role in it." He, therefore, sounds a warning for psychiatrists in the present day to abide by ethical principles in order "to protect society from the corruption of science in the name of political ideology" (2006: 36).

On this basis, providing evidence of risk in legal settings where a person's liberty is at stake may be viewed as a subset of unethical coercive practice. It is not aimed at helping the individual, but can be seen as serving government policies aimed at segregating certain groups of individuals on the basis of community protection. In the words of Gwen Adshead (1999: 326), mental health laws (and by analogy other laws relating to preventive detention) should not provide "a mandate for tidying away dangerous people."

More than two decades ago, Alan Stone (1984) started a debate in the United States about the ethics of forensic psychiatry, arguing that as a matter of individual ethical commitment, he could not justify himself giving evidence for the purposes of the criminal justice system. While he did not go so far as to say that psychiatrists should *never* testify in court, he pointed out that those who did so risked violating the ethics relevant to those whose primary duty was to treat individuals.

Three years later, Gary Melton, John Petrila, Norman Poythress, and Christopher Slobogin (1987: 204) argued that, in relation to risk assessment, there is "no specialized clinical knowledge that permits categorical, or even relative conclusions about dangerousness." As a result, they stated (1987: 205) that mental health practitioners "may decide that they cannot ethically offer prediction testimony."

More adamantly, Charles Ewing (1991: 162) has argued that "[t]he psychiatrist or psychologist who makes a prediction of dangerousness violates his or her ethical obligation to register judgments that rest on a scientific basis." Similarly, Eric Janus (2004b: 50) has stated that the indeterminacy of legal terms such as "likely" or "highly likely" require mental health practitioners to "make political judgments that determine the balance between public safety and individual liberty."

Refusing to engage in risk assessments for the purposes of the criminal justice system on the basis that it is unethical to do so is obviously an extreme action. Risk assessment not only informs decisions concerning the detention of offenders and the law relating to the civil commitment of individuals with mental illness, but it also informs child protection matters and detention to prevent the spread of infectious diseases. Paul Appelbaum (2008: 198) makes the point that where rights or liberty are at stake, it may be preferable to "have a decision-maker whose judgment [is] informed by the testimony of experts in the field rather than one who [is] forced to rely on his or her haphazard knowledge and entrenched prejudices."

In reality, only a few mental health practitioners will take this extreme ethical approach, but such a position does force mental health practitioners to consider whether and in what circumstances assessing risk and giving risk assessment testimony is justifiable.

There are different ways of finding the middle ground between the two extreme approaches of always assessing and testifying as to risk and never doing so. These approaches are explored in the next section. However, as will be argued, finding the middle ground in relation to preventive detention schemes that are primarily focused on community protection remains problematic.

Finding the Middle Ground

There are three possible approaches that may be viewed as finding an ethical "middle ground" between always engaging in risk assessment and giving risk testimony when legally required for the purposes of preventive detention and supervision schemes and never doing so. The first approach focuses on treatment, the second uses a "justice ethics" approach, and the third approach draws a distinction between risk assessment for treatment purposes and risk assessment for detention and supervision.

A focus on treatment

One approach to the issue of risk assessment and risk testimony is to extend the principle of acting for the benefit of the patient under traditional medical ethics so that it includes acting for the benefit of the individual who is subject to potential detention or supervision. In this scenario, mental health practitioners should assume when accepting a call for risk assessment by the courts or mental health tribunals that there is always some prospect of treatment or benefit available for the individual concerned. A focus on treatment may be a less than ideal approach, however, when it is known that adequate treatment is not available.

Another version of the focus on treatment approach is to extend existing medical ethics to act only where it is known that the individual concerned will indeed receive some form of health benefit. Thus, Alec Buchanan and Adrian Grounds (2011: 421) state that "it is inappropriate to comment on a defendant's risk unless psychiatric intervention is proposed or other benefit will result."

Going one step further, in relation to offenders, this could mean acting only on behalf of the individual rather than for the state. This, however, assumes that mental health practitioners will know when treatment is available and when it will be of benefit. It may also lead to a refusal to assess certain individuals who are not considered "treatable," thus depriving them of any form of expert evidence.

While there are difficulties with the focus on treatment approach in relation to the detention and supervision of offenders, a focus on treatment may provide an ethical way of approaching the detention and supervision of those with severe mental illness. Paul Appelbaum (1988: 780) states that "[p]sychiatrists point to treatment as the ultimate purpose of commitment, even if society — out of concern for limiting intrusions on autonomy — restricts the imposition of involuntary treatment to those who are dangerous to themselves or others." On this basis, detention in mental health facilities can be of direct benefit because "treatment" can include providing a safe haven away from societal pressures as well as enabling the more traditional notion of treatment through medical intervention. The dilemma here is when society expects psychiatrists "to assume responsibility for protecting victims of potentially violent persons in situations in which treatment is not possible" (Appelbaum 1988: 780). Gwen Adshead (2000: 304) describes the dilemma:

> At present, if an ordinary citizen makes threats to kill someone, the police may or may not act depending on whether they think the citizen has actually breached the relevant statute; however, if an individual with a history of mental illness makes a threat to kill, then it is sometimes claimed that psychiatrists should immediately detain that person indefinitely against his or her will.

The most straightforward ethical approach here would be for mental health practitioners to refuse to admit individuals to mental health facilities who do not require hospitalization for the purpose of treatment. Appelbaum (1988: 783) believes this approach maintains "clinical integrity" but notes that it is dependent on the majority of mental health practitioners taking the same approach to ensure a consistent ethical standard. This is doubtful from a practical perspective given that some mental health practitioners will take a cautious approach to the question of risk. Some mental health practitioners may see involuntary commitment as ethically justifiable in such circumstances "since the length of confinement is usually only a few days" (Leong 1989: 240). Nicholas Scurich and Richard John (2010: 429) have also stated that the shorter the time frame for detention, the lower the potential cost of a "false positive" in relation to risk assessment.

One of the theories behind modern preventive detention regimes explored in Chapter 2 was that of the "precautionary principle." As outlined in Chapter 2, this theory stems from environmental science and posits that where the risk of harm is both unpredictable and uncertain and where the damage wrought will be irreversible, any lack of scientific certainty in relation to the nature of the harm or its consequences should not prevent action being taken (Sunstein 2005). In relation to those with severe mental illness, there may thus be a perception that the duty to protect others from potential harm means that a precautionary approach should be taken and individuals thought to be at risk of harming others should be hospitalized solely for the purpose of preventing them from engaging in risky behaviour.

The fear of litigation if a person is not hospitalized and harm occurs may also result in overcautious mental health practice (Rangarajan and McSherry 2009). This may have the effect of creating a *de facto* "duty to detain," thereby affecting the way in which mental health practitioners interpret the purposes of the statutory provisions relating to detention and treatment embodied in mental health legislation. Associate Justice Santow pointed out in the New South Wales case of *Hunter Area Health Service v Presland* (2005: 123) that the consequence of imposing a legal duty to detain would be to distort the impartiality of the exercise of discretion under relevant mental health legislation by introducing a "detrimentally defensive frame of mind on the part of the decision maker" and "promoting a bias toward detention."

A focus on treatment may, therefore, offer one way of approaching the question of preventive detention for those with severe mental illness, although it is unlikely that all mental health practitioners will take this approach given the rise of the precautionary principle in practice. It may also be of some relevance to serious offenders provided that treatment is known to be available under preventive detention and supervision regimes.

Justice ethics

Another approach to the issue of risk assessment and giving evidence of risk is to use a different ethical framework for forensic psychiatry beyond that of medical ethics, which attaches such importance to treatment. The Royal College of Psychiatrists for the United Kingdom and the Republic of Ireland (2005) refers to this as "justice ethics", a term that appears to stem from Paul Appelbaum's work (1984, 1990, 1997, 2008) that forensic psychiatry should use a framework of ethics based on "truth" rather than "beneficence." This approach requires the fundamental value of truthtelling and respect for the individual, with the ultimate goal being to advance justice rather than to act for the benefit of the individual patient. The principle of truthtelling requires testifying as to what the mental health professional believes to be true, regardless of whether this advantages or disadvantages the particular individual concerned, but it also requires an accurate presentation of the scientific data available and the consensus of the field (Appelbaum 2008). In relation to testimony using actuarial scales, for example, this principle would require the mental health professional to outline the limitations of the scales used (Morse 2008).

The principle of respect for persons requires respect for the individual being assessed. In Appelbaum's words (2008: 197) this requires that mental health practitioners do not "engage in deception, exploitation, or needless invasion of the privacy of the people who we examine or about whom we testify."

Gwen Adshead and Sameer Sarkar (2005) have pointed out that the "justice ethics" approach dominates forensic psychiatry in the United States, whereas the "welfare paradigm," which emphasizes the traditional medical principles of beneficence and nonmaleficence, is the dominant force in forensic psychiatry in the United Kingdom. Similarly, the Royal College of Psychiatrists for the United Kingdom and the Republic of Ireland (2005: 77) has stated that "[f]orensic psychiatrists in the College consider themselves first and foremost as doctors and would not accept the forensicist position adopted in the USA."

In Canada, the Canadian Psychological Association's (2000) *Canadian Code of Ethics for Psychologists* also appears to take a welfare approach to psychological practice in general. It emphasizes four main principles: respect for the dignity of persons, responsible caring, integrity in relationships, and responsibility to society. The Canadian Code (2000: 2) sets out that the principle of responsibility to society should be given the lowest weight in the event that the principles conflict:

> This principle generally should be given the lowest weight of the four principles when it conflicts with one or more of them. Although it is necessary and important to consider responsibility to society in every ethical decision, adherence to this principle must be subject to and guided by Respect for the Dignity of Persons, Responsible Caring, and Integrity in

Relationships. When a person's welfare appears to conflict with benefits to society, it is often possible to find ways of working for the benefit of society that do not violate respect and responsible caring for the person. However, if this is not possible, *the dignity and well-being of a person should not be sacrificed to a vision of the greater good of society*, and greater weight must be given to respect and responsible caring for the person (emphasis added).

This welfare approach to forensic psychiatry may help explain why there was such dissent in England and Wales early this century about the government's proposal to allow the involuntary hospitalization of "dangerous people with severe personality disorders" solely for the purpose of managing problematic behaviour rather than for the purpose of treatment or because they had committed a crime (Seddon 2007, 2008). More than 50 organizations, including the Royal College of Psychiatry for the United Kingdom and the Republic of Ireland, formed the Mental Health Alliance to lobby against the proposed legislation (Appelbaum 2005), and many editions of the *British Medical Journal* and the *Psychiatric Bulletin* contained articles and letters condemning the proposal (see, for example, Mullen, 1999; Haddock *et al.* 2001; Birmingham 2002; Coid and Maden 2003). Some critics of the proposal raised the prospect of being agents of social control (Corbett and Westwood 2005) and "the civil liberty implications of creating a newly coercible group that was not being defined using recognised mental health criteria" (Buchanan and Grounds 2011: 421). Much of the debate derived from the principles of beneficence and nonmaleficence in emphasizing the duty of psychiatrists to treat individuals rather than control them.

This concerted opposition to the proposal at least forced the government to rethink its approach and to redraft its proposed legislation (Hebenton and Seddon 2009). The aim of the Dangerous and Severe Personality Disorders programme changed from one solely concerned with public protection to one focused on assessing and treating offenders. Dangerous and Severe Personality Disorders units and services were established, with around 300 beds being used in two secure hospitals and two prison sites in England and Wales (Taylor 2012). The cost of implementing the programme has been estimated to be £200 million (Buchanan and Grounds 2011).

The programme ended up being praised for providing effective mental health services to a group of offenders in dire need of such services (Mullen 2007). The Department of Health and National Offender Management Service Offender Personality Disorder Team (2011) has since signalled the reconfiguration of services for offenders with personality disorder and the gradual decommissioning of Dangerous Severe Personality Disorder units in National Health Service Secure Hospitals. Alec Buchanan and

Adrian Grounds (2011) have pointed out that this does not mean that individuals assessed to have a Dangerous Severe Personality Disorder will be left uncontrolled, but rather, that the existing programme will be diversified.

It would seem from the example of the Dangerous and Severe Personality Disorders experience, that there is more of an emphasis on the principle-based approach to ethics in forensic psychiatry in England and Wales than on a separate idea of justice ethics. Buchanan and Grounds (2011: 421) write in relation to the ethical challenges for forensic psychiatry in the United Kingdom:

> Just as clinical placement should seek the 'least restrictive alternative', so forensic mental healthcare should reflect the same principles and standards that are recognised elsewhere in psychiatry and medicine. The institutional cultures surrounding secure prisons and hospitals make this difficult and addressing these difficulties is an ethical obligation.

A major problem with the justice ethics approach is that it may lead to harm and even death to certain individuals where the law so dictates. Gregg Bloche (1999: 270) outlines a movement in the 1990s that saw any consequent harm upon expert evidence as irrelevant "when physicians serve the state or other third parties." That is, expert witnesses were seen as being justified in putting the justice system first and the individuals they assessed for it second. This view found some traction in a Report by the American Medical Association's Council on Ethical and Judicial Affairs (1995) on the involvement of physicians in death penalty cases. The Report concluded that physicians were ethically justified in testifying that individuals were competent for execution because physicians were assisting in the administration of justice in such circumstances. They were "acting as an advocate of justice, not as a source of punishment" (1995: 1). The ensuing death of the individual concerned was thus viewed as irrelevant to the assessment. As Michael Robertson and Garry Walter (2008: 229) describe this approach, "no distinction should be drawn between a psychiatric assessment that facilitates a financial penalty (or benefit), a custodial sentence or the death penalty."

On this reasoning, if the consequences of a psychiatric assessment are ignored, serving what "justice" dictates can ethically justify assessing individuals as fit for torture as well as for death. In the Soviet Union, from the 1960s to the mid-1980s, psychiatrists were called upon to use psychiatric hospitals as prisons in order to isolate political prisoners from the rest of society, discredit their views, and break them physically and mentally (Bloch and Reddaway 1984). If justice ethics is to be a viable approach, it must have limits and the ethical import of harm should be a consideration. Gregg Bloche (1999: 271) points out in this regard:

> Unreflective reliance on law is . . . deeply problematic. It abdicates the task of explaining why law should determine the ethical import of consequent harm. Moreover, it ignores an especially troublesome aspect of such harm from a medical perspective. To the extent that a medical hand is doing harm is evident, public confidence in medicine as a caring enterprise is put at risk.

In relation to risk assessment, Thomas Grisso and Paul Appelbaum (1992: 631) have argued that a mid-way point is to see predictive testimony as neither ethical or unethical in itself, but the *use* of the testimony may be ethical or unethical given the variability in the types of liberty restrictions involved. They write (1992: 631) that this approach:

> would encourage professional debate regarding the circumstances (e.g., degree and type of liberty restrictions associated with the legal question, types of benefits that may accrue) in which the various magnitudes of false-positive error resulting from risk probability testimony would be ethically acceptable or unacceptable in relation to the balance of consequences for the individual and society.

This may mean that the use of risk assessment to breach an individual's right to liberty (rather than for monitoring and treatment purposes for example) is unethical. This is explored further in the next section.

Drawing a Distinction Between the Purposes of Risk Assessment Testimony

Some mental health practitioners may consider that it is ethical to engage in risk assessment for the purposes of treatment, but that it is unethical to engage in risk assessment and giving risk assessment testimony for the specific purpose of post-sentence preventive detention. Geoffrey Leong (1989: 241) foreshadowed this:

> Given the current direction of legal changes that increasingly require psychiatrists to help remedy society's problems and show less concern for patients' welfare, psychiatrists could soon be placed in the untenable ethical position of becoming a direct extension of law enforcement agencies.

Danny Sullivan, Paul Mullen, and Michele Pathé (2005) are three psychiatrists who have questioned the ethics of requiring clinicians to assess risk for the purposes of continued detention or coercive supervision after sentence. They have pointed out that being required to give evidence for preventive detention and supervision schemes raises the spectre of mental health practitioners being "agents of supervision, social control and monitoring" rather than "independent clinicians" (2005: 320). Similarly, Eric Janus (2004b: 50) is of the view that mental health practitioners should not engage in giving testimony for sexually violent predator laws in the United States because such testimony involves what he terms "political judgments that determine the balance between public safety and individual liberty."

The Royal College of Psychiatrists for the United Kingdom and the Republic of Ireland held a seminar on the ethics of giving evidence for extended sentencing purposes in 2002. It published an overview of the discussion in the *Psychiatric Bulletin* in 2005 and stated that one view aired was that "it is not ethically part of medicine to assist the courts in increasing punishment and public protection by applying medical skills to such a purpose" (Royal College of Psychiatrists 2005: 75).

The Royal College of Psychiatrists (2005: 75) noted, however, that there "may be an ethical argument for ensuring that disagreements regarding mental disorder and risk are considered early on at the point of sentencing when the court, rather than doctors, can decide these issues." This suggests that it may be more ethically justifiable to give evidence for indeterminate detention and supervision schemes that operate at the time of sentence than preventive detention schemes that operate *after* the expiry of an individual's sentence as in Australia and the United States. Nevertheless, even at the sentencing stage, mental health practitioners may be viewed as using their expert knowledge to increase the punishment of the offender by lengthening his or her sentence. Gwen Adshead and Sameer Sarkar (2005: 1016) point out that the main ethical objection in relation to testimony that indirectly contributes to punishment is that "there is no good quality evidence base for an expert to share with the court in relation to risk of re-offending. Rather than contributing to the justice process, it might be seriously misleading and lead to a miscarriage of justice." As explored in Chapter 3, however, some mental health practitioners would argue that risk assessment techniques have developed to a standard that enables justice to be served, providing the limitations of such techniques are recognized.

The view that risk assessment testimony is unethical for the purpose of post-sentence preventive detention may run into the same problem in reality as that in relation to a complete refusal to engage in providing testimony for the criminal justice system – there will always be some mental health practitioners willing to engage with legislative requirements to provide assessments of risk. However, at the very least, this position does raise the issue of mental health practitioners being agents of social control and provides a starting point for distinguishing between the justifications for risk assessment for sentencing purposes within the criminal justice system as opposed to risk assessment for "civil" forms of detention outside of the criminal justice system.

PROFESSIONAL GUIDELINES ON FORENSIC ISSUES

If a treatment or justice ethics approach is accepted as justifying the giving of risk assessment testimony for the purpose of preventive detention and supervision schemes, certain professional guidelines may assist in circumscribing the scope of such testimony. This section sets out some of the key guidelines in specific jurisdictions in relation to giving testimony in courts and tribunals in general that may be relevant to risk assessment testimony. Mental health practitioners will also need to abide by the rules of the particular court or tribunal as to the giving of evidence, as explored in Chapter 6.

The Royal College of Psychiatrists for the United Kingdom and the Republic of Ireland (2008) has written a report entitled *Court Work* that makes a series of recommendations about giving testimony. Most relevantly, it states (2008: 8) that "psychiatrists involved in legal processes should be confident in their findings, reports and evidence, but must be clear about the limitations of their knowledge and expertise and avoid being tempted to answer questions, no matter how pressing, beyond their competence." It also sets out (2008: 10–11) that:

Ethical psychiatric experts will:

- not give evidence beyond their expertise
- undertake CPD [continuing professional development] to maintain their expertise
- have an awareness, when making their recommendations to the court, of the possibilities for the treatment or placement of those on whom they prepare reports
- declare any conflict of interests to the courts (e.g., if a recommendation is made for the placement of a person in an establishment in which the expert has an interest or the subject of the report is or has been their own patient)
- prepare a report based on their opinions from the evidence and their specialist knowledge, uninfluenced by the exigencies of the litigation and regardless of who commissioned the report.

Similar recommendations are set out in guidelines drafted by the Royal Australian and New Zealand College of Psychiatrists (1980, 2003).

The Canadian Medical Association's (1996) *Code of Ethics* has a section on "Responsibilities to society." Principle 30 refers to the medical profession's duty to "[a]ccept a share of the profession's responsibility to society in matters relating to public health, health education, environmental protection, legislation affecting the health or well-being of the community, and the need for testimony at judicial proceedings." Grainne Neilson (2002) has developed annotations to this Code of Ethics for psychiatrists and comments on this responsibility:

> The task of the psychiatric expert is to render credible and useful testimony to assist the court in its deliberations. Psychiatric experts must be comprehensive, honest, objective, and unbiased in their assessments and should declare openly to the court any factors that interfere with these aims. They should limit testimony to areas of actual expertise.

The emphasis on honesty and objectivity is also referred to in Part III of the Canadian Academy of Psychiatry and Law's (1998) *Ethics Guidelines for the Practice of Forensic Psychiatry* and in Part IV of the American Academy of Psychiatry and Law's (2005) *Ethics Guidelines for the Practice of Forensic Psychiatry*. The latter states:

> When psychiatrists function as experts within the legal process, they should adhere to the principle of honesty and should strive for objectivity. Although they may be retained by one party to a civil or criminal matter, psychiatrists should adhere to these principles when conducting evaluations, applying clinical data to legal criteria, and expressing opinions.

In its Commentary (2005) on this Guideline, the Academy points out:

> Psychiatrists practicing in a forensic role enhance the honesty and objectivity of their work by basing their forensic opinions, forensic reports and forensic testimony on all available data. They communicate the honesty of their work, efforts to attain objectivity, and the soundness of their clinical opinion, by distinguishing, to the extent possible, between verified and unverified information as well as among clinical "facts," "inferences," and "impressions."

In relation to forensic psychology, Terence Campbell (2003: 277) points out that "there is no shame in psychologists acknowledging the limits of [their] expertise" and many of the relevant professional guidelines also stress that acknowledging limitations is good ethical practice. For example, the standards set out in the American Psychological Association's *Speciality Guidelines for Forensic Psychology* (2011) are relevant in this regard. It sets the following standards:

- When conducting forensic examinations, forensic practitioners strive to be unbiased and impartial, and avoid partisan presentation of unrepresentative, incomplete, or inaccurate evidence that might mislead finders of fact (Standard 1.02).
- Forensic practitioners seek to provide opinions and testimony that are sufficiently based upon adequate scientific foundation, and reliable and valid principles and methods that have been applied appropriately to the facts of the case (Standard 2.05).

Honesty and objectivity are thus the keystone standards for the giving of expert evidence in relation to issues of risk. All these guidelines provide for minimum standards of practice and some mental health practitioners may not be persuaded that these standards justify the giving of evidence when human rights are breached.

CONCLUSION

This chapter started with the extreme example of how some psychiatrists in the late 1930s and early 1940s were subsumed within a regime that enabled the mass murder of those with mental and intellectual impairments. Rael Strous (2007b: 5) points out that "Germany possessed one of the most advanced and sophisticated code of medical ethics in the world in existence from 1931," yet some psychiatrists carrying out the "euthanasia" programme could justify their actions from a scientific and legal standpoint without regard to fundamental ethical principles concerning killing those with disabilities. The reasons why some psychiatrists took part in the mass killing of those with mental and intellectual impairments are obviously complex, but Strous (2007b: 5) makes an important point about the difference between ethics in theory and practice when he states that "'[e]thical mantras' have little value when they exist away from a context of a mature understanding and self-reflection that needs to precede good ethical judgment and professionalism."

It is important to learn from the transgressions of the past and to reflect on the ethical principles that should guide the practice of mental health practitioners in relation to preventive detention and supervision schemes.

In terms of alternative approaches to the question of risk assessment and giving testimony as to risk for courts and tribunals, this chapter has dismissed the first option that it is always ethical to engage in risk assessment and to give risk assessment testimony in the knowledge that it will lead to human rights breaches. It has also dismissed as impractical the second option that it is never ethical to engage in risk assessment where a person's liberty is at stake, given that many areas of practice require mental health practitioners to engage in such assessments, although some mental health practitioners may prefer to take this approach.

In trying to find a middle ground, a focus on treatment may be a useful guide to the question of preventive detention for those with severe mental illness and it may also be of some relevance to serious offenders provided that treatment is known to be available under preventive detention and supervision regimes.

A justice ethics approach may also help provide a workable ethical framework for assessing and testifying on risk issues. However, there is a danger in this approach giving licence to expert witnesses to putting the justice system first to the detriment of the individuals being assessed. Justice ethics needs to have limits and any consequential harms must be considered. In this regard, specific ethical guidelines may help circumscribe the limits of testimony in relation to risk.

It is clear that accepting government policies without question must be avoided. However, there is no definitive answer to the question as to whether or not it is ethical for mental health practitioners to provide evidence of risk for the deprivation of liberty. Some mental health practitioners may take the approach that it is unethical for them to engage in risk assessment and the giving of risk assessment testimony knowing that this may lead to breaches of human rights. Others may accept that this can be done ethically provided that certain key limitations are acknowledged and the standards of honesty and objectivity are followed. What is important is that there is further discussion about the ethics of such practices in order to avoid the potential for the abuses of the past to recur.

Part IV

CONCLUSION

9

CONCLUSION

INTRODUCTION: THE CURRENT SITUATION

This book has contended that legally sanctioned preventive detention regimes are not new. Certain groups of individuals have long been singled out for preventive detention. For example, the Australian Bushranger legislation outlined in Chapter 2 is now mirrored in current laws enabling the preventive detention of suspected terrorists. However, it is the growing reliance upon preventive detention and supervision regimes at both the pre-crime and post-sentence ends of the spectrum *in addition to* a growing emphasis on risk and precaution that forms an unprecedented shift in managing the fear of future harm.

Rory Brown (2011: 103) has posited in relation to the fear of suspected terrorists that "one very practical thing we can do to reduce the effect of terrorism on our lives is to worry about it less . . . the chance of dying in a terrorist attack is still very low." However, it is often difficult to override instinctive fear responses. Decision-making theories help explain why the prospect of certain types of harm bring about strong emotions such as fear, even when the likelihood of such harm occurring is remote. When fear of harm is accompanied, in Susan Fiske's (1998) words, by "gut level" prejudices towards sex offenders, individuals with severe mental illness, and suspected terrorists, it is little wonder that such individuals are singled out for legislative methods of control.

The growing reliance on preventive detention and supervision schemes in conjunction with the growing emphasis on risk and precaution can be viewed as the product of different, but coalescing trends. As explored in Chapter 2, these include the development of the "risk society"; the growth of "actuarial justice"; and the shift from managing risk towards the "precautionary principle" that necessitates taking "radical prevention" in curtailing liberty before harm results.

The risk of harm to others is a central element of the preventive detention and supervision schemes outlined in this book. It remains an important criterion for admission to mental health facilities, although in some jurisdictions, this criterion exists as an alternative to risk of harm to self or the need for treatment. The protection of the community also underlies preventive detention and supervision schemes relating to sex offenders and suspected terrorists. These laws have been tested through the courts that have set out the parameters of such schemes, with the majority being upheld as constitutional.

Similarly, the main justification for supervision and control orders is the prevention of future harm through monitoring the whereabouts of serious offenders and suspected terrorists and restricting their behaviour via certain conditions. Community treatment orders for those with severe mental illness are in a slightly different category in that they are concerned with continued treatment rather than supervision or control, but they may also have restrictions of liberty attached to them. Supervision, control, and community treatment orders are all considered to be constitutionally valid despite breaching human rights such as the right to liberty.

While preventive detention and supervision orders are thus "lawful," they raise issues concerning the balance between the use of state powers to protect the community and the infringement of human rights. As explored in Chapter 7, post-sentence preventive detention of sex offenders has been held by both the United Nations Human Rights Committee and the European Court of Human Rights to breach the right to liberty. Post-sentence preventive detention also violates the right to a fair trial as well as the rights not to be subject to double punishment and retrospective laws. Nevertheless, international declarations to this effect may be disregarded at the domestic level and it can be a slow process for human rights frameworks to be accepted by governments.

While the detention of those of "unsound mind" has been held by the European Court of Human Rights not to breach the right to liberty providing that certain minimum conditions are satisfied, this is now being challenged by recent interpretations of Article 14 of the Convention on the Rights of Persons with Disabilities. The preventive detention and control of suspected terrorists may also be lawful providing stringent conditions are applied.

The current situation thus enables the lawful detention and supervision of certain groups of individuals even where such restrictions breach human rights. The emphasis on risk means that mental health practitioners may be called upon to provide assessments for the purposes of preventive detention and supervision schemes. One of the main purposes of this book is to highlight the ethical concerns in this regard.

AN ETHICAL APPROACH TO RISK

While risk assessment is now a growth industry when it comes to managing offenders, the concept of risk is treated very differently when it comes to those with severe mental illness and suspected terrorists. That in itself raises questions as to whether actuarial risk instruments and/or structured professional judgment has a role to play in providing evidence of risk of these latter two groups.

One of the key questions posed throughout this book is how should mental health practitioners view their role in providing assessments of risk for legislative schemes that involve the deprivation of liberty? Whatever the conclusion reached on an individual basis, it is essential for mental health practitioners to reflect on the ethical principles that guide their practice in relation to preventive detention and supervision schemes.

In terms of alternative approaches to the question of risk assessment and giving testimony as to risk for courts and tribunals, the previous chapter dismissed the option that it is always ethical to engage in risk assessment and to give risk assessment testimony in the knowledge that it will lead to human rights breaches. There are already enough tragic examples of mental health practitioners becoming agents of state control to warrant unquestioning acceptance of current preventive detention and supervision schemes that breach human rights.

Some mental health practitioners may take the view that it is never ethical to engage in risk assessment where a person's liberty is at stake. However, given that many areas of practice require mental health professionals to engage in such assessments, it may be more appropriate to try to find a middle ground, where a focus on treatment becomes the paramount factor. The previous chapter explored how a justice ethics approach may help provide a workable ethical framework for assessing and testifying on risk issues, providing there are sufficient ethical guidelines in existence to help ensure that expert witnesses do not put the justice system first to the detriment of the individuals being assessed.

While there may be no definitive answer to the question as to whether or not it is ethical for mental health professionals to provide evidence of risk for the deprivation of liberty, it is important that discussions ensue in this regard.

PROVING RISK AND PROCEDURAL FAIRNESS

As explored in Chapter 3, actuarial risk assessment instruments and their use in courts have been widely criticized on numerous grounds, including the use of specific variables and the variable-based approach itself, problems associated with applying group data to the individual, differences in particular groups, and the prospect of unnecessary deprivation of liberty due to "false positives." In the context of decisions relating to the detention and supervision of individuals with severe mental illness, risk assessment is generally based on the treating clinicians' views, without recourse to any actuarial instruments. In comparison, risk assessment is currently not a focal point of the preventive detention of suspected terrorists, although this may be changing.

The developing field of structured professional judgment certainly seems to be an improvement on clinical judgment alone, but its purpose is to help with the management and treatment of offenders. It has not been developed with the primary aim of preventive detention and supervision. The limitations of risk assessment, therefore, need to be emphasized before courts and tribunals, rather than being held out as highly probative.

Expert evidence of risk may be admissible, but it is still up to the court or the tribunal to decide whether that evidence satisfies the requisite legal test. That is, judges have retained discretion as to how much weight to place upon it. In this regard, there is a role for better training of both judges and advocates as to some of the criticisms that have been made of risk assessment techniques.

Often evidence of risk is presented before courts and tribunals without sufficient and detailed analysis by either counsel or judges. Counter-evidence should be called by advocates for the individual concerned wherever possible. In relation to sex offenders, it is very concerning that expert testimony in court regarding preventive detention and supervision is generally accepted by judges without challenge. It is one thing to accept the admissibility of such evidence, but another thing entirely to fail to question its reliability and validity.

At present there is a lack of consistency in the type of proceedings, the standard of proof, and the evidentiary rules that apply to preventive detention and supervision schemes. While it may be unrealistic to believe that a consistent approach can ever be achieved across the different schemes, imposing a high standard of proof and strict compliance with the rules of procedural fairness and expert evidence may help ensure that evidence of risk is rigorously examined and people are not unnecessarily deprived of their liberty.

CONCLUSION

Marius Duker and Marijke Malsch (2012: 249) point out that the "wish for control has in many situations become the dominant response to both crime and risks for safety and security, and it has largely replaced a focus on rehabilitation and treatment." Preventive detention and supervision is one way for policymakers to control community fears of future harm by certain individuals. Detention in prison or special facilities has the advantage of removing the individual from the community, thereby making harm to others in the community impossible.

From a human rights perspective, however, the right to liberty is a core human right and needs to be carefully balanced against community protection. The law can go some way in ensuring sufficient checks and balances to ensure detention is not arbitrary, but it is important to see preventive detention as a last resort.

Perhaps the most important point to remember is that human rights exist for the benefit of *all* individuals. Even those who have committed brutal crimes possess human rights and any curtailment of the right to liberty must be carefully justified because, ultimately, the arbitrary denial of human rights for selected groups erodes the value of human rights for everyone.

REFERENCES

Adshead, G. (1999) Duties of Psychiatrists: Treat the Patient or Protect the Public?, *Advances in Psychiatric Treatment*, 5(5): 321–28.

Adshead, G. (2000) Care or Custody? Ethical Dilemmas in Forensic Psychiatry, *Journal of Medical Ethics*, 26(5): 302–304.

Adshead, G. and Sarkar, S.P. (2005) Justice and Welfare: Two Ethical Paradigms in Forensic Psychiatry, *Australian and New Zealand Journal of Psychiatry*, 39(11): 1011–1017.

Albrecht, H.-J. (2012) The Incapacitation of the Dangerous Offender: Criminal Policy and Legislation in the Federal Republic of Germany, in M. Malsch and M. Duker (eds) *Incapacitation: Trends and New Perspectives*, Farnham: Ashgate Publishing Ltd, 39–61.

Alen, A. and Melchior, M. (2002) in collaboration with Renauld, B., Meersschaut, F. and Courtoy, C., The Relations Between the Constitutional Courts and the Other National Courts, Including the Interference in this Area of the Action of the European Courts – XIIth Conference of the European Constitutional Courts, Brussels, 14–16 May 2002, General Report, *Human Rights Law Journal*, 23: 304–30.

Allan, A. and Dawson, D. (2002) *Developing a Unique Risk of Violence Tool for Australian Indigenous Offenders*, Canberra: Criminology Research Council. Available online at http://www.criminologyresearchcouncil.gov.au/reports/200001-06.pdf (accessed January 31, 2013).

Allderidge, P. (1979) Hospitals, Madhouses and Asylums: Cycles in the Care of the Insane, *British Journal of Psychiatry*, 134: 321–34.

Alpert, G.P. and Smith, W.C. (1994) How Reasonable is the Reasonable Man? Police and Excessive Force, *Journal of Criminal Law and Criminology*, 85(2): 481–501.

American Academy of Psychiatry and Law (2005) *Ethics Guidelines for the Practice of Forensic Psychiatry*. Available online at http://www.aapl.org/pdf/ETHICSGDLNS.pdf (accessed January 31, 2013).

American Medical Association Council on Ethical and Judicial Affairs (1995) *Report of the Council on Ethical and Judicial Affairs*, Chicago: American Medical Association. Available online at http://www.ama-assn.org/resources/doc/ethics/ceja_6a95.pdf (accessed January 31, 2013).

American Psychiatric Association (1974) *Clinical Aspects of the Violent Individual*, Washington, DC: American Psychiatric Association.

American Psychiatric Association (2010) *The Principles of Medical Ethics with Annotations Especially Applicable to Psychiatry*, Arlington, VA: American Psychiatric Association. Available online at http://www.psychiatry.org/practice/ethics/ resources standards (accessed January 31, 2013).

American Psychological Association (1978) Report of the Task Force on the Role of Psychology in the Criminal Justice System, *American Psychologist*, 33: 1099–113.

American Psychological Association (2003) *Ethical Principles of Psychologists and Code of Conduct*, Washington, DC: American Psychological Association http://www.apa. org/ethics/code/index.aspx (accessed January 31, 2013).

American Psychological Association (2011) *Specialty Guidelines for Forensic Psychology*, Washington, DC, American Psychological Association. Available online at http:// www.apa.org/practice/guidelines/forensic-psychology.aspx (accessed January 31, 2013).

Appelbaum, P.S. (1984) Psychiatric Ethics in the Courtroom, *Bulletin of the American Academy of Psychiatry and Law*, 12: 225–31.

Appelbaum, P.S. (1988) The New Preventive Detention: Psychiatry's Problematic Responsibility for the Control of Violence, *American Journal of Psychiatry*, 145(7): 779–85.

Appelbaum, P.S. (1990) The Parable of the Forensic Psychiatrist: Ethics and the Problem of Doing Harm, *International Journal of Law and Psychiatry*, 13(4): 249–59.

Appelbaum, P.S. (1997) A Theory of Ethics for Forensic Psychiatry, *Journal of the American Academy of Psychiatry and the Law*, 25: 233–47.

Appelbaum, P.S. (2005) Dangerous Severe Personality Disorders: England's Experiment in Using Psychiatry for Public Protection, *Psychiatric Services*, 56(4): 397–99.

Appelbaum, P.S. (2008) Ethics and Forensic Psychiatry; Translating Principles into Practice, *Journal of the American Academy of Psychiatry and the Law*, 36(2): 195–200.

Arnoldi, J. (2009) *Risk: An Introduction*, Cambridge: Polity Press.

Ashworth, A. (2009) Criminal Law, Human Rights and Preventative Justice, in B. McSherry, A. Norrie and S. Bronitt (eds) *Regulating Deviance: The Redirection of Criminalisation and the Futures of Criminal Law*, Portland: Hart, 87–108.

Ashworth, A., Gardner, J., Morgan, R., Smith, A., von Hirsch, A. and Wasik, M. (1998) Neighbouring on the Oppression: The Government's Anti-Social Behaviour Proposals, *Criminal Justice*, 16(1): 7–14.

Baderin, M.A. and Ssenyonjo, M. (2010) Development of International Human Rights Law Before and After the UDHR, in M.A. Baderin and M. Ssenyonyo (eds) *International Human Rights Law: Six Decades after the UDHR and Beyond*, Farnham: Ashgate Publishing Ltd, 3–27.

Barnett, M. and Hayes, R. (2008) Evaluating the Judicial Interpretation of Civil Commitment Schemes for Serious Sex Offenders, *University of Western Sydney Law Review*, 12(5): 39–72.

Barry, J. (1969) *The Courts and Criminal Punishments: Three Lectures*, Wellington: Government Printer.

Bartlett, B., Lewis, O. and Thorold, O. (2007) *Mental Disability and the European Convention on Human Rights*, Leiden: Martinus Nijhoff.

Bassiouni, M.C. (1999) International Terrorism, in M. Cherif Bassiouni (ed.) *International Criminal Law: Volume 1: Crimes*, 2nd edn, New York: Transnational, 765–801.

Bates, E. (2005) A "Public Emergency Threatening the Life of the Nation?", The United Kingdom's Derogation from the European Convention on Human Rights of 18 December 2001 and the "A" Case, *British Yearbook of International Law*, 245–336.

BBC News (2000) Paediatrician Attacks "Ignorant" Vandals, 30 August. Available online at http://news.bbc.co.uk/2/hi/uk_news/wales/901723.stm (accessed January 31, 2013).

Beauchamp, T.L. (2007) The "Four Principles" Approach to Health Care Ethics, in R.E. Ashcroft, A. Dawson, H. Draper and J.R. McMillan (eds) *Principles of Health Care Ethics*, 2nd edn, Chichester, UK: John Wiley and Sons, 3–10.

Beauchamp, T.L. and Childress, J.F. (2001) *Principles of Biomedical Ethics*, 5th edn, New York: Oxford University Press.

Beck, U. (1986) *Risikogesellschaft: Auf dem Weg in Eire Andere Moderne*, Frankfurt am Main: Suhrkamp.

Beck, U. (1992a) *Risk Society: Towards a New Modernity*, London: Sage.

Beck, U. (1992b) From Industrial Society to the Risk Society: Questions of Survival, Social Structure and Ecological Enlightenment, *Theory, Culture and Society*, 9(1): 97–123.

Beck, U. (1999) *World Risk Society*, Cambridge: Polity Press.

Beck, U. (2009) *World at Risk*, Cambridge: Polity Press.

Bergman, L.R. and Magnusson, D. (1997) A Person-Orientated Approach in Research on Developmental Psychopathology, *Development and Psychopathology*, 9(2): 291–319.

Berlin, F.S., Galbreath, N.W., Geary, B. and McGlone, G. (2003) The Use of Actuarials at Civil Commitment Hearings to Predict the Likelihood of Future Sexual Violence, *Sexual Abuse*, 15(4): 377–82.

Bernstein, D.E. (1995) The Science of Forensic Psychiatry and Psychology, *Psychiatry, Psychology and Law*, 2(1): 75–80.

Birmingham, L. (2002) Detaining Dangerous People with Mental Disorders: New Legal Framework is Open for Consultation, *British Medical Journal*, 325(7354): 2–3.

Blay, S. and Piotrowicz, R. (2000) The Awfulness of Lawfulness: Some Reflections on the Tension Between International Law and Domestic Law, *Australian Yearbook of International Law*, 21: 1–20.

Bloch, S. and Pargiter, R. (2009) Codes of Ethics in Psychiatry, in S. Bloch and S.A. Green (eds) *Psychiatric Ethics*, 4th edn, Oxford: Oxford University Press, 151–73.

Bloch, S. and Reddaway, P. (1984) *Soviet Psychiatric Abuse: The Shadow over World Psychiatry*, London: Gollancz.

Bloche, M.G. (1999) Clinical Loyalties and the Social Purposes of Medicine, *Journal of the American Medical Association*, 281(3): 269–74.

Boer, D.P., Hart, S.D., Kropp, P.R. and Webster, C.D. (1997) *Manual for the Sexual Violence Risk-20: Professional Guidelines for Assessing Risk of Sexual Violence*, Vancouver, BC: British Columbia Institute Against Family Violence.

Bowcott, O. (2008) CCTV Boom has Failed to Slash Crime, Say Police, *The Guardian*, 6 May. Available online at http://www.guardian.co.uk/uk/2008/may/06/ukcrime1 (accessed January 31, 2013).

Boxall, G.E. (1924) *History of the Australian Bushrangers*, 5th edn, Sydney: Cornstalk Publishing Company.

Brems, E. (2001) *Human Rights: Universality and Diversity*, The Hague: Kluwer Law International.

Bronitt, S. and McSherry, B. (2010) *Principles of Criminal Law*, 3rd edn, Prymont, NSW: Thomson Reuters.

Brooks, R.A. (2000) Official Madness: A Cross-Cultural Study of Involuntary Civil Confinement Based on Mental Illness, in J. Hubert (ed.) *Madness, Disability and Social Exclusion: The Archaeology and Anthropology of "Difference"*, New York: Routledge, 9–28.

Brophy, L. and McDermott, F. (2012) Using Social Work Theory and Values to Investigate the Implementation of Community Treatment Orders, *Australian Social Work*, DOI: 10.1080/0312407x.2011.651727.

Brophy, L.M., Reece, J.E. and McDermott, F. (2006) A Cluster Analysis of People on Community Treatment Orders in Victoria, Australia, *International Journal of Law and Psychiatry*, 29(6): 469–81.

Brown, K.J. (2012) "It is not as Easy as ABC": Examining Practitioners' Views on Using Behavioural Contracts to Encourage Young People to Accept Responsibility for Their Anti-Social Behaviour, *Journal of Criminal Law*, 76(1): 53–70.

Brown, R. (2011) *Fighting Monsters: British-American War-Making and Law-Making*, Oxford: Hart Publishing Ltd.

Bruckard, D. and McSherry, B. (2009) Mental Health Laws for those Compliant with Treatment, *Journal of Law and Medicine*, 17(1): 16–21.

Buchanan, A. and Grounds, A. (2011) Forensic Psychiatry and Public Protection, *British Journal of Psychiatry*, 198(6): 420–23.

Burdge, R. (2011) First "Risk of Sexual Harm Order" Used to Keep Perth Man from Young Girls, *The Courier*, April 12, 2011. Available online at http://www.thecourier.co.uk/News/Perthshire/article/12836/first-risk-of-sexual-harm-order-used-to-keep-perth-man-from-young-girls.html (accessed January 31, 2013).

Burns, T. and Dawson, J. (2009) Community Treatment Orders: How Ethical Without Experimental Evidence?, *Psychological Medicine*, 39(10): 1583–86.

Burns, T., Rugkôsa, J., Molodynski, A., Dawson, J., Yeeles, K., Vacques-Montes, M., Voysey, M., Sinclair, J. and Priebe, S. (2013) Community Treatment Orders for Patients with Psychosis (OCTET): A Randomised Controlled Trial, *The Lancet*, 381: 1–7, published online March 26, http://dx.doi.org/10.1016/50140–6736(13)60107-5 (accessed May 18, 2013).

Burton, W.W. (1834) *Opinion for Governor Bourke* in *Historical Records of Australia*, series 1, vol 17: Governors' Dispatches to and from England, 1788–1848: Sydney: Library Committee of the Commonwealth Parliament, 524–33.

Bush, S.S., Connell, M.A. and Denny, R.L. (2006) *Ethical Practice in Forensic Psychology: A Systematic Model for Decision Making*, Washington, DC: American Psychological Association.

Campbell, M.A., French, S. and Gendreau, P. (2009) The Prediction of Violence in Adult Offenders: A Meta-Analytic Comparison of Instruments and Methods of Assessment, *Criminal Justice and Behavior*, 36(6): 567–90.

Campbell, T.W. (2000) Sexual Predator Evaluations and Phrenology: Considering Issues of Evidentiary Reliability, *Behavioral Sciences and the Law*, 18(1): 111–30.

Campbell, T.W. (2003) Sex Offenders and Actuarial Risk Assessments: Ethical Considerations, *Behavioral Sciences and the Law*, 21(2): 269–79.

Canadian Academy of Psychiatry and Law (1998) *Ethics Guidelines for the Practice of Forensic Psychiatry*. Available online at http://capl-acpd.org/pages/ethical.html (accessed January 31, 2013).

Canadian Medical Association (1996) *Code of Ethics of the Canadian Medical Association: Approved by the CMA Board of Directors, October 15, 1996*, Ottawa: Canadian Medical Association. Available online at http://www.cma.ca/multimedia/CMA/Content_Images/Inside_cma/Ethics/Code-of-Ethics/1996.pdf (accessed January 31, 2013).

Canadian Medical Association (2010) Value of Community Treatment Orders Remains at Issue, *Canadian Medical Association Journal*, 182(8) May 18: E337–E38.

Canadian Psychological Association (2000) *Canadian Code of Ethics for Psychologists*, 3rd edn, Ontario: Canadian Psychological Association. Available online at http://www.cpa.ca/cpasite/userfiles/Documents/Canadian%20Code%20of%20Ethics%20for%20Psycho.pdf (accessed January 31, 2013).

Carney, T., Tait, D., Perry, J., Vernon, A. and Beaupert, F. (2011) *Australian Mental Health Tribunals: Space for Fairness, Freedom, Protection and Treatment?* Annandale, NSW: Federation Press.

Carroll, A., Lyall, M. and Forrester, A. (2004) Clinical Hopes and Public Fears in Forensic Mental Health, *Journal of Forensic Psychiatry and Psychology*, 15(3): 407–25.

Cavadino, M. (1998) Death to the Psychopath, *Journal of Forensic Psychiatry*, 9(1): 5–8.

Chamberlin, J. (2006) Foreword, in G. Thornicroft (ed.) *Shunned: Discrimination against People with Mental Illness*, Oxford: Oxford University Press, xi–xiii.

Churchill, R., Owen, G., Singh, S. and Hotopf, M. (2007) *International Experiences of Using Community Treatment Orders*, London: Institute of Psychiatry.

Clarke, M.J. (2008) *Report of the Inquiry into the Case of Mohamed Haneef*. Available online at http://pandora.nla.gov.au/pan/84427/20090121-0022/www.haneefcaseinquiry.gov.au/www/inquiry/haneefcaseinquiry.nsf/Page/Report.html (accessed January 31, 2013).

Cleland, A. (2005) Protection is Better than Care, *Scots Law Times*, 36: 201–205.

Code of Ethics Review Group (2002) *Code of Ethics for Psychologists Working in Aotearoa/New Zealand*. Available online at http://www.psychology.org.nz/cms_show_download.php?id=10 (accessed January 31, 2013).

Coid, J. and Maden, T. (2003) Should Psychiatrists Protect the Public? A New Risk Reduction Strategy, Supporting Criminal Justice, Could Be Effective, *British Medical Journal*, 326(7386): 406–407.

Conte, A. (2010) *Human Rights in the Prevention and Punishment of Terrorism: Commonwealth Approaches: United Kingdom, Canada, Australia and New Zealand*, Berlin: Springer.

Cooke, D. and Michie, C. (2010) Limitations of Diagnostic Precision and Predictive Utility in the Individual Case: A Challenge for Forensic Practice, *Law and Human Behavior*, 34(4): 259–74.

Cooke, D. and Michie, C. (2011) Violence Risk Assessment: Challenging the Illusion of Certainty, in B. McSherry and P. Keyzer (eds) *Dangerous People: Policy, Prediction and Practice*, New York: Routledge, 147–61.

Corbett, K. and Westwood, T. (2005) "Dangerous and Severe Personality Disorder": A Psychiatric Manifestation of the Risk Society, *Critical Public Health*, 15(2): 121–33.

Council of Australian Governments (2013) *Review of Counter-Terrorism Legislation*, Canberra: Commonwealth of Australia.

Coyle, I. (2011) The Cogency of Risk Assessments, *Psychiatry, Psychology and Law*, 18(2): 270–96.

Craig, L.A. and Beech, A. (2009) Best Practice in Conducting Actuarial Risk Assessments with Adult Sexual Offenders, *Journal of Sexual Aggression*, 15(2): 193–211.

Crenshaw, M. (1981) The Causes of Terrorism, *Comparative Politics*, 13: 379–99.

Crowden, A. (2003) Ethically Sensitive Mental Health Care: Is There a Need for a Unique Ethics for Psychiatry?, *Australian and New Zealand Journal of Psychiatry*, 37(2): 143–49.

Darbyshire, P. (2001) What Can We Learn from Published Jury Research? Findings from the Criminal Courts Review 2001, *Criminal Law Review*, 970–79.

Darjee, R. and Russell, K. (2011) The Assessment and Sentencing of High-Risk Offenders in Scotland, in B. McSherry and P. Keyzer (eds) *Dangerous People: Policy, Prediction and Practice*, New York: Routledge, 217–32.

Davis, M. and Ogloff, J. (2008) Risk Assessment, in K. Fritson and P. Wilson (eds) *Forensic Psychology and Criminology: An Australasian Perspective*, North Ryde, NSW: McGraw-Hill Australia, 141–50.

Dawson, J. (2005) *Community Treatment Orders: International Comparisons*, Otago: University of Otago.

Dawson, J. (2007) Factors Influencing the Rate of Use of Community Treatment Orders, *Psychiatry*, 6(2): 42–44.

Dawson, J. (2008) Community Treatment Orders and Human Rights, in B. McSherry (ed.) *International Trends in Mental Health Laws*, Annandale, NSW: Federation Press, 148–59.

Dawson, J. (2010) Compulsory Outpatient Treatment and the Calculus of Human Rights, in B. McSherry and P. Weller (eds) *Rethinking Rights Based Mental Health Laws*, Oxford: Hart, 327–54.

Dawson, J. and Szmukler, G. (2006) Fusion of Mental Health and Incapacity Legislation, *British Journal of Psychiatry*, 188: 504–509.

De Vogel, V., de Vries Robbé, M., de Ruiter, C. and Bouman, Y.H.A. (2011) Assessing Protective Factors in Forensic Psychiatric Practice: Introducing the SAPROF, *International Journal of Forensic Mental Health*, 10(3): 171–77.

De Vogel, V., de Ruiter, C., Bouman, Y.H.A. and de Vries Robbé, M. (2007) *Handleiding bij de SAPROF. Structured Assessment of Protective Factors for Violence Risk. Versie 1*, Utrecht: Forum Educatief.

Denney, D. (2005) *Risk and Society*, London: Sage.

Denney, D. (2008) Fear, Human Rights and New Labour Policy Post-9/11, *Social Policy and Administration*, 42(6): 560–75.

Department of Health and National Offender Management Service Offender Personality Disorder Team (2011) *Response to the Offender Personality Disorder Consultation*, London: Department of Health. Available online at http://www.dh.gov.uk/prod_consum_dh/groups/dh_digitalassets/documents/digitalasset/dh_130701.pdf (accessed January 31, 2013).

Derby Telegraph (2012) Derby School Sacks Worker Over Sex Messages to Pupil, 13, 2 February 2012. Available online at http://www.thisisderbyshire.co.uk/Derby-school-sacks-worker-sex-messages-pupil-13/story-15107284-detail/story.html (accessed January 31, 2013).

Dernevik, M., Beck, A., Grann, M., Hogue, T. and McGuire, J. (2009) The Use of Psychiatric and Psychological Evidence in the Assessment of Terrorist Offenders, *Journal of Forensic Psychiatry and Psychology*, 20(4): 508–15.

Di Furia, G. and Mees, H.L. (1963) Dangerous to be at Large: A Constructive Critique of Washington's Sexual Psychopath Law, *Washington Law Review*, 38(3), 531–37.

Domestic Intelligence (1835) *The Australian* no 157 vol III: 2. Available online at http://trove.nla.gov.au/ndp/del/article/42009917 (accessed January 31, 2013).

Donahue, D.E. (1980) Human Rights in Northern Ireland: Ireland v. the United Kingdom, *Boston College International and Comparative Law Review*, 3(2), 377–432.

Donaldson, K. (1976) *Insanity Inside Out*, New York: Crown Publishers.

Dong, J.Y.S., Ho, T.P. and Kan, C.K. (2005) A Case-Control Study of 92 Cases of In-Patient Suicides, *Journal of Affective Disorders*, 87(1): 91–99.

Donnelly, M. (2008) Community-Based Care and Compulsion: What Role for Human Rights?, *Journal of Law and Medicine*, 15(5), 782–93.

Donoghue, J. (2010) *Anti-Social Behaviour Orders: A Culture of Control?* New York: Palgrave Macmillan.

Donohue, L.K. (2001) *Counter-Terrorist Law and Emergency Powers in the United Kingdom, 1922–2000*, Dublin: Irish Academic Press.

Douglas, H. (2008) Post-Sentence Preventive Detention: Dangerous and Risky, *Criminal Law Review*, 11: 854–73.

Douglas, M. (1982) Environments at Risk, in B. Barnes and D. Edge (eds) *Science in Context: Readings in the Sociology of Science*, Maidenhead: Open University Press, 260–75.

Douglas, M. (1985) *Risk Acceptability According to the Social Sciences*, London: Routledge and Kegan Paul.

Douglas, M. (1992) *Risk and Blame: Essays in Cultural Theory*, London: Routledge.

Doyle, D.J. and Ogloff, J.R.P. (2009) Calling the Tune Without the Music: A Psycho-Legal Analysis of Australia's Post-Sentence Legislation, *Australian and New Zealand Journal of Criminology*, 42(2): 179–203.

Doyle, D.J., Ogloff, J.R.P. and Thomas, S.D.M. (2011) An Analysis of Dangerous Sexual Offender Assessment Reports: Recommendations for Best Practice, *Psychiatry, Psychology and Law*, 18(4): 537–56.

Drenkhahn, K., Morgenstern, C. and van Zyl Smit, D. (2012) What is in a Name? Preventive Detention in Germany in the Shadow of European Human Rights Law, *Criminal Law Review*, 3: 167–87.

Ducat, L., Thomas, S. and Blood, W. (2009) Sensationalising Sex Offenders and Sexual Recidivism: Impact of the Serious Sex Offender Monitoring Act 2005 on Media Reportage, *Australian Psychologist*, 44(3): 156–65.

Duker, M. and Malsch, M. (2012) Incapacitation: Trends and New Perspectives, in M. Malsch and M. Duker (eds) *Incapacitation: Trends and New Perspectives*, Farnham: Ashgate Publishing Ltd, 237–51.

Eigen, J.P. (1995) *Witnessing Insanity: Madness and Mad-Doctors in the English Court*, New Haven: Yale University Press.

Ellard, J. (1996) Personality Disorder or the Snark Still at Large, *Australasian Psychiatry*, 4(2): 58–64.

Elsea, J.K. (2010) *The Military Commissions Act of 2009: Overview and Legal Issues*, Washington, DC: Congressional Research Service. Available online at http://www.fas.org/sgp/crs/natsec/R41163.pdf (accessed January 31, 2013).

Ericson, R.V. (2007) *Crime in an Insecure World*, Cambridge: Polity Press.

Ericson, R.V. and Haggerty, K.D. (1997) *Policing the Risk Society*, Toronto: University of Toronto Press.

Ewald, F. (1993) Two Infinities of Risk, in B. Massumi (ed.) *The Politics of Everyday Fear*, Minneapolis: University of Minnesota Press, 221–29.

Ewald, F. (2002) The Return of Descartes's Malicious Demon: An Outline of a Philosophy of Precaution, in T. Baker and J. Simon (eds) *Embracing Risk: The Changing Culture of Insurance and Responsibility*, Chicago: Chicago University Press, 273–301.

Ewing, C. (1991) Preventive Detention and Execution: The Constitutionality of Punishing Future Crimes, *Law and Human Behavior*, 15(2): 139–63.

Farina, A. (1998) Stigma, in K.T. Meuser and N. Tarrier (eds) *Handbook of Social Functioning in Schizophrenia*, Boston: Allyn and Bacon, 247–79.

Farina, A. and Ring, K. (1965) The Influence of Perceived Mental Illness on Interpersonal Relations, *Journal of Abnormal Psychology*, 70(1): 47–51.

Farnham, F.R. and James, D.V. (2001) "Dangerousness" and Dangerous Law, *Lancet*, 358(9297): 1926.

Farrington, D.P. (ed.) (2005) *Integrated Development and Life Course Theories of Offending*, London: Transaction.

Feeley, M. and Simon, J. (1992) The New Penology: Notes on the Emerging Strategy of Corrections and its Implications, *Criminology*, 30(4): 449–74.

Feeley, M. and Simon, J. (1994) Actuarial Justice: The Emerging New Criminal Law, in D. Nelken (ed.) *The Futures of Criminology*, London: Sage, 173–201.

Fennell, P. (2010) Institutionalising the Community, in B. McSherry and P. Weller (eds) *Rethinking Rights-Based Mental Health Laws*, Oxford: Hart, 13–49.

Ferguson, G. (2000) Recent Developments in Canadian Criminal Law, *Criminal Law Journal*, 24(4): 248–63.

Finnane, M. and Donkin, S. (2013) Fighting Terror with Law? Some Other Genealogies of Pre-emption, *International Journal for Crime and Justice*, 2(1): 3–17.

Fiske, S.T. (1998) Stereotyping, Prejudice and Discrimination, in D.T. Gilbert, S.T. Fiske and G. Lindzey (eds) *The Handbook of Social Psychology*, 4th edn, Boston, MA: McGraw-Hill, 357–411.

Foucault, M. (1965) *Madness and Civilization: A History of Insanity in an Age of Reason*, New York: Pantheon Books.

Foucault, M. (1991) Governmentality, in G. Burchell, C. Gordon and P. Miller (eds) *The Foucault Effect: Studies in Governmentality*, London: Harvester Wheatsheaf, 87–104.

Freckelton, I. (2005) Distractors and Distressors in Involuntary Status Decision-Making, *Psychiatry, Psychology and Law*, 12(1), 88–102.

Freckelton, I. (2008) Expert Evidence, in K. Fritzon and P. Wilson (eds) *Forensic Psychology and Criminology: An Australasian Perspective*, North Ryde, NSW: McGraw-Hill Australia, 203–17.

Freckelton, I. (2010) Extra-Legislative Factors in Involuntary Status Decision-Making, in B. McSherry and P. Weller (eds) *Rethinking Rights-Based Mental Health Laws*, Oxford: Hart, 204–30.

Freckelton, I. and Keyzer, P. (2010) Case Commentary: Indefinite Detention of Sex Offenders and Human Rights: The Intervention of the Human Rights Committee of the United Nations, *Psychology, Psychiatry and Law*, 17(3): 345–54.

Freckelton, I. and Selby, H. (2009) *Expert Evidence: Law, Practice, Procedure and Advocacy*, 4th edn, Pyrmont, NSW: Lawbook Co.

Freiberg, A. and Carson, W.G. (2010) The Limits of Evidence-Based Policy: Evidence, Emotion and Criminal Justice, *Australian Journal of Public Administration*, 69(2): 152–64.

Furedi, F. (1997) *Culture of Fear: Risk Taking and the Morality of Low Expectation*, London: Continuum.

Furedi, F. (2002) *Culture of Fear: Risk Taking and the Morality of Low Expectation*, rev edn, London: Continuum.

Furedi, F. (2008) Fear and Security: A Vulnerability-Led Policy Response, *Social Policy and Administration*, 42(6): 645–61.

Fyfe, I. and Gailey, Y. (2011) The Scottish Approach to High-Risk Offenders, in B. McSherry and P. Keyzer (eds) *Dangerous People: Policy, Prediction and Practice*, New York: Routledge, 201–16.

Gani, M. and Mathew, P. (eds) (2008) *Fresh Perspectives on the "War on Terror"*, Canberra: Australian National University ePress.

Garland, D. (1985) *Punishment and Welfare: A History of Penal Strategies*, Aldershot: Gower.

Garland, D. (1996) Limits of the Sovereign State: Strategies of Crime Control in Contemporary Society, *British Journal of Criminology*, 36(4): 445–71.

Garland, D. (2001) *The Culture of Control: Crime and Social Order in Contemporary Society*, Chicago: The University of Chicago Press.

Garland, D. (2003) Penal Modernism and Postmodernism, in T. Blomberg and S. Cohen (eds) *Punishment and Social Control: Essays in Honor of Sheldon Messinger*, 2nd edn, New York: Aldine de Gruyter, 45–73.

Giddens, A. (1990) *Consequences of Modernity*, Cambridge: Polity Press.

Giddens, A. (1991) *Modernity and Self-Identity: Self and Society in the Late Modern Age*, Oxford: Polity Press.

Giddens, A. (1998) Risk Society: The Context of British Politics, in J. Franklin (ed.) *The Politics of Risk Society*, Cambridge: Polity Press, 23–34.

Gigerenzer, G. (2006) Out of the Frying Pan into the Fire: Behavioral Reactions to Terrorist Attacks, *Risk Analysis*, 26(2): 347–51.

Glazebrook, S. (2010) Risky Business: Predicting Recidivism, *Psychiatry, Psychology and Law*, 17(1): 88–120.

Gleb, C. (1991) Washington's Sexually Violent Predator Law: The Need to Bar Unreliable Psychiatric Predictions of Dangerousness from Civil Commitment Proceedings, *UCLA Law Review*, 39(1), 213–50.

Gledhill, K. (2011) Preventive Sentences and Orders: The Challenges of Due Process, *Journal of Commonwealth Criminal Law*, 1: 78–104.

Goffman, E. (1963) *Stigma: Notes on the Management of Spoiled Identity*, Englewood Cliffs, NJ: Prentice-Hall.

Golder, B. and Williams, G. (2004) What is "Terrorism"? Problems of Legal Definition, *University of New South Wales Law Journal*, 27(2): 270–95.

Gordon, D. (2007) History and Development of Social Exclusion and Policy, in D. Abrams, J. Christian and D. Gordon (eds) *Multidisciplinary Handbook of Social Exclusion Research*, Chichester: John Wiley and Sons, 193–210.

Gostin, L. and Gable, L. (2004) The Human Rights of Persons with Mental Disabilities: A Global Perspective on the Application of Human Rights Principles to Mental Health, *Maryland Law Review*, 63: 20–121.

Grattan, M. (2005) War in Iraq Raised Terror Risk, Say 66%, *The Age*, 3 August, 1, 2.

Greig, D. (1997) Professions and the Risk Society, *Psychiatry, Psychology and Law*, 4(2): 231–40.

Grisso, T. and Appelbaum, P.S. (1992) Is It Unethical to Offer Predictions of Future Violence?, *Law and Human Behavior*, 16(6): 621–33.

Grounds, A. (2004) Forensic Psychiatry and Political Controversy, *Journal of the American Academy of Psychiatry and the Law*, 32(2): 192–96.

Grove, W.M. and Meehl, P.E. (1996) Comparative Efficiency of Informal (Subjective, Impressionistic) and Formal (Mechanical, Algorithmic) Prediction Procedures: The Clinical-Statistical Controversy, *Psychology, Public Policy and Law*, 2(2): 293–323.

Gudjonsson, G.H. (2009) The Assessment of Terrorist Offenders: A Commentary on the Dernevik et al. Article and Suggestions for Future Directions, *Journal of Forensic Psychiatry and Psychology*, 20(4): 516–19.

Gutheil, T.G. (2005) The History of Forensic Psychiatry, *Journal of the American Academy of Psychiatry and the Law*, 33(2): 259–62.

Haddock, A.W., Snowden, P.R., Dolan, M., Parjer, J. and Rees, H. (2001) Managing Dangerous People with Severe Personality Disorder: A Survey of Forensic Psychiatrists' Opinions, *Psychiatric Bulletin*, 25(8): 293–96.

Hale, C. and Fitzgerald, M. (2007) Social Exclusion and Crime, in D. Abrams, J. Christian and D. Gordon (eds) *Multidisciplinary Handbook of Social Exclusion Research*, Chichester: John Wiley and Sons, 137–58.

Hanks, P., Keyzer, P. and Clarke, J. (2004) *Australian Constitutional Law: Materials and Commentary*, 7th edn, Sydney: Lexis Nexis Butterworths.

Hanson, R.K. (1997) *The Development of a Brief Actuarial Scale for Sex Offender Recidivism 1997–04*, Ottawa: Department of the Solicitor General of Canada. Available online at http://www.publicsafety.gc.ca/res/cor/rep/_fl/199704-dbarssor-eng.pdf (accessed January 31, 2013).

Hanson, R.K. (2003) Who is Dangerous and When are They 'Safe? Risk Assessment with Sex Offenders, in B. Winick and J. La Fond (eds) *Protecting Society from Sexually Dangerous Offenders: Law, Justice and Therapy*, Washington, DC: American Psychological Association, 63–74.

Hanson, R.K. and Harris, A. (2000) *The Sex Offender Need Assessment Rating (SONAR): A Method for Measuring Change in Risk Levels 2000–1*, Ottawa: Department of the Solicitor General of Canada. Available online at http://www.publicsafety.gc.ca/res/cor/rep/_fl/sonar-eebds-eng.pdf (accessed January 31, 2013).

Hanson, R.K., Harris, A.J.R., Scott, T. and Helmus, L. (2007) *Assessing the Risk of Sexual Offenders on Community Supervision: The Dynamic Supervision Project 2007-05*, Ottawa: Public Safety Canada. Available online at http://www.publicsafety.gc.ca/res/cor/rep/_fl/crp2007-05-en.pdf (accessed January 31, 2013).

Hanson, R.K. and Howard, P. (2010) Individual Confidence Intervals Do Not Inform Decision-Makers About the Accuracy of Risk Assessment Evaluations, *Law and Human Behavior*, 34(4): 275–81.

Hanson, R.K. and Thornton, D. (1999) *Static-99: Improving Actuarial Risk Assessments for Sex Offenders: 2000–01*, Ottawa: Department of the Solicitor General of Canada.

Hanson, R.K. and Thornton, D. (2003) *Notes on the Development of Static-2002: 2003–01*, Ottawa: Department of the Solicitor General of Canada. Available online at http://www.publicsafety.gc.ca/res/cor/rep/_fl/2003-01-not-sttc-eng.pdf (accessed January 31, 2013).

Hardy, K. (2011) Bright Lines and Open Prisons: The Effect of a Statutory Human Rights Instrument on Control Order Regimes, *Alternative Law Journal*, 36(1): 4–9.

Hare, R.D. (1991) *The Hare Psychopathy Checklist: Revised*, Toronto: Multi-Health Systems.

Hare, R.D. (2002) Psychopathy and Risk for Recidivism and Violence, in N. Gray, J. Laing and L. Noaks (eds) *Criminal Justice, Mental Health and the Politics of Risk*, London: Cavendish, 27–47.

Hare, R.D. and Neumann, C.S. (2010) The Role of Antisociality in the Psychopathy Construct: Comment on Skeem and Cooke, *Psychological Assessment*, 22(2), 446–54.

Harris, A. (1847) *Settlers and Convicts, or, Recollections of Sixteen Years' Labor in the Australian Backwoods by An Emigrant Mechanic* (1964 edn), Melbourne: Melbourne University Press.

Harris, A.J. and Lobanov-Rostovsky, C. (2010) Implementing the Adam Walsh Act's Sex Offender Registration and Notification Provisions: A Survey of the States, *Criminal Justice Policy Review*, 21(2): 202–22.

Harris, G.T., Rice, M.E. and Quinsey, V.L. (1993) Violent Recidivism of Mentally Disordered Offenders: The Development of a Statistical Prediction Instrument, *Criminal Justice and Behavior*, 20(4): 315–35.

Hart, S.D. and Cooke, D.J. (2013) Another Look at the (Im-)Precision of Individual Risk Estimates Made Using Actuarial Risk Assessment Instruments, *Behavioral Sciences and the Law*, 31: 81–102.

Hart, S.D., Kropp, P.R. and Laws, D.R. with Klaver, J., Logan, C. and Watt, K.A. (2003) *The Risk for Sexual Violence Protocol (RSVP): Structured Professional Guidelines for Assessing Risk of Sexual Violence*, Burnaby, BC: Simon Fraser University Mental Health, Law and Policy Institute.

Hart, S.D., Michie, C. and Cooke, D.J. (2007) Precision of Actuarial Risk Asessment Instruments: Evaluating the "Margins of Error" of Group v. Individual Predictions of Violence, *British Journal of Psychiatry*, 190(s 49): s60–s65.

Hassan, P. (1973) The International Covenant on Civil and Political Rights: Background and Perspective on Article 9(1), *Denver Journal of International Law and Policy*, 3(2): 153–83.

Hassenfeld, I.N. (2002) Doctor-Patient Relations in Nazi Germany and the Fate of Psychiatric Patients, *Psychiatric Quarterly*, 73(3): 183–94.

Hebenton, B. and Seddon, T. (2009) From Dangerousness to Precaution: Managing Sexual and Violent Offenders in an Insecure and Uncertain Age, *British Journal of Criminology*, 49(3): 343–62.

Hebenton, B. and Thomas, T. (1996a) Sexual Offenders in the Community: Reflections of Problems of Law, Community and Risk Management in the USA, England and Wales, *International Journal of the Sociology of Law*, 24(4): 427–43.

Hebenton, B. and Thomas, T. (1996b) "Tracking" Sex Offenders, *Howard Journal of Criminal Justice*, 35(2): 97–112.

Heilbrun, K., Ogloff, J.R.P. and Picarello, K. (1999) Dangerous Offender Statutes in the United States and Canada: Implications for Risk Assessment, *International Journal of Law and Psychiatry*, 22(3–4): 393–415.

Hewitt, J. (2008) Dangerousness and Mental Health Policy, *Journal of Psychiatric and Mental Health Nursing*, 151(3): 186–94.

Hiday, V.A. (2003) Coerced Community Treatment: International Trends and Outcomes, in K. Diesfeld and I. Freckelton (eds) *Involuntary Detention and Therapeutic Jurisprudence: International Perspectives on Civil Commitment*, Aldershot: Ashgate Publishing Ltd, 435–53.

Hogg, R. (2007) Criminology, Crime and Politics Before and After 9/11, *Australian and New Zealand Journal of Criminology*, 40(1): 83–105.

Home Office (2011) *Review of Counter-Terrorism and Security Powers: Review Findings and Recommendations*, London: Home Office. Available online at https://p10.secure. hostingprod.com/@spyblog.org.uk/ssl/spyblog/images/roctp/review-findings-and-rec.pdf (accessed January 31, 2013).

Home Office (2012) *Putting Victims First: More Effective Responses to Anti-Social Behaviour*, London: Home Office. Available online at http://www.official-documents.gov.uk/document/cm83/8367/8367.asp (accessed January 31, 2013).

Howard, J. (2007) Quoted in S. Smiles and C. Marriner, "PM Defiant: No Visa and No Apology", *The Age*, 31 July, http://www.theage.com.au/articles/2007/07/30/1185647828688.html (accessed January 31, 2013).

Hudson, B. (2003) *Justice in the Risk Society: Challenging and Re-Affirming Justice in Late Modernity*, London: Sage.

International Dual Loyalty Working Group (2002) *Dual Loyalty and Human Rights in Health Professional Practice: Proposed Guidelines and Institutional Mechanisms*, Cape Town: University of Cape Town. Available online at https://s3.amazonaws.com/PHR_Reports/dualloyalties-2002-report.pdf (accessed January 31, 2013).

Ion, R.M. and Beer, M.D. (2003) Valuing the Past: The Importance of an Understanding of the History of Psychiatry for Healthcare Professionals, Service Users and Carers, *International Journal of Mental Health Nursing*, 12(4): 237–42.

Janus, E.S. (2003) Minnesota's Sex Offender Commitment Program: Would an Empirically-Based Prevention Policy be More Effective?, *William Mitchell Law Review*, 29(4): 1083–133.

Janus, E.S. (2004a) Closing Pandora's Box: Sexual Predators and the Politics of Sexual Violence, *Seton Hall Law Review*, 34(4):1233–53.

Janus, E.S. (2004b) Sexually Violent Predator Laws: Psychiatry in Service to a Morally Dubious Enterprise, *Lancet*, 364: 50–51.

Janus, E.S. (2004c) The Preventive State, Terrorists and Sexual Predators: Countering the Threat of a New Outsider Jurisprudence, *Criminal Law Bulletin*, 40(6): 576–98.

Janus, E.S. (2006) *Failure to Protect: America's Sexual Predator Laws and the Rise of the Preventive State*, Ithaca: Cornell University Press.

Janus, E.S. (2011) Sexual Violence, Gender Politics, and Outsider Jurisprudence: Lessons from the American Experience in Prevention, in B. McSherry and P. Keyzer (eds) *Dangerous People: Policy, Prediction and Practice*, New York: Routledge, 73–82.

Janus, E.S. and Prentky, R.A. (2003) Forensic Use of Actuarial Risk Assessment with Sex Offenders: Accuracy, Admissibility and Accountability, *American Criminal Law Review*, 40: 1443–99.

Johnson, B. (2005) Prophecy with Numbers: Prospective Punishment for Predictable Human Behaviour?, *University of Technology Sydney Law Review*, 7: 117–33.

Jost, J.T. and Banaji, M.R. (1994) The Role of Stereotyping in System-Justification and the Production of False Consciousness, *British Journal of Social Psychology*, 33(1): 1–27.

Junginger, J., Claypole, K., Laygo, R. and Cristiani, A. (2006) Effects of Serious Mental Illness and Substance Abuse on Criminal Offenses, *Psychiatric Services*, 57(6): 879–82.

Kaczorowska, A. (2010) *Public International Law*, 4th edn, London: Routledge.

Kahneman, D. (2011) *Thinking, Fast and Slow*, New York: Farrar, Straus and Giroux.

Kahneman, D. and Tversky, A. (1979) Prospect Theory: An Analysis of Decisions under Risk, *Econometrica*, 47(2): 263–91.

Kämpf, A., McSherry, B., Ogloff, J. and Rothschild, A. (2009) *Confidentiality for Mental Health Professionals: A Guide to Ethical and Legal Principles*, Bowen Hills, Qld: Australian Academic Press.

Kemshall, H. (2003) *Understanding Risk in Criminal Justice*, Maidenhead: Open University Press.

Kemshall, H. and Wood, J. (2008) Risk and Public Protection: Responding to Involuntary and "Taboo" Risk, *Social Policy & Administration*, 42(6): 611–29.

Kemshall, H., Mackenzie, G., Wood, J., Bailey, R. and Yates, R. (2005), *Strengthening Multi-Agency Protection Arrangements (MAPPAs)*, London: Home Office. Available online at http://www.nacro.org.uk/data/files/nacro-2005112202-513.pdf (accessed January 31, 2013).

Keyzer, P. (2009) The "Preventive Detention" of Serious Sex Offenders: Further Consideration of the International Human Rights Dimensions, *Psychiatry, Psychology and Law*, 30(1): 262–70.

Keyzer, P. and Blay, S. (2006) Double Punishment? Preventive Detention Schemes Under Australian Legislation and their Consistency with International Law: The Fardon Communication, *Melbourne Journal of International Law*, 7(2): 407–24.

Keyzer, P., Pereira, C. and Southwood, S. (2004) Pre-Emptive Imprisonment for Dangerousness in Queensland under the *Dangerous Prisoners (Sexual Offenders) Act* 2003: The Constitutional Issues, *Psychiatry, Psychology and Law*, 11(2): 244–53.

Kittichaisaree, K. (2001) *International Criminal Law*, New York: Oxford University Press.

Knapp, S.J. and VandeCreek, L.D. (2003) *A Guide to the 2002 Revision of the American Psychological Association's Ethics Code*, Sarasota, FLA: Professional Resource Press/ Professional Resource Exchange.

Koocher, G.P. and Keith-Spiegel, P. (2008) *Ethics in Psychology and the Mental Health Professions: Standards and Cases*, 3rd edn, New York: Oxford University Press.

Kroner, D.G., Mills, J.F. and Reddon, J.R. (2005) A Coffee Can, Factor Analysis, and Prediction of Antisocial Behavior: The Structure of Criminal Risk, *International Journal of Law and Psychiatry*, 28(4): 360–74.

Kurzban, R. and Leary M.R. (2001) Evolutionary Origins of Stigmatization: The Functions of Social Exclusion, *Psychological Bulletin*, 12(2): 187–208.

La Fond, J.Q. (1992a) Washington's Sexually Violent Predator Law: A Deliberate Misuse of the Therapeutic State for Social Control, *University of Puget Sound Law Review*, 15: 655–708.

La Fond, J.Q. (1992b) Washington's Violent Predator Statute: Law or Lottery? A Response to Professor Brooks, *University of Puget Sounds Law Review*, 15: 755–59.

La Fond, J.Q. (1998) The Costs of Enacting a Sexual Predator Law, *Psychology, Public Policy and Law*, 4(1): 468–504.

La Fond, J.Q. (2005) *Preventing Sexual Violence: How Society Should Cope with Sex Offenders*, Washington, DC: American Psychological Association.

La Fond, J.Q. (2008) Sexually Violent Predator Laws and the Liberal State: An Ominous Threat to Individual Liberty, *International Journal of Law and Psychiatry*, 31(2): 158–71.

La Fond, J.Q. (2011) Sexual Offender Commitment Laws in the USA: The Inevitable Failure of Misusing Civil Commitment to Prevent Future Sex Crimes, in B. McSherry and P. Keyzer (eds) *Dangerous People: Policy, Prediction and Practice*, New York: Routledge, 51–61.

Large, M.M., Ryan, C.J., Nielssen, O.B. and Hayes, R.A. (2008) The Danger of Dangerousness: Why We Must Remove the Dangerousness Criterion from our Mental Health Acts, *Journal of Medical Ethics*, 34(12): 877–81.

Lawton-Smith, S. (2008) Community Treatment Orders are Not a Good Thing, *British Journal of Psychiatry*, 193(2): 96–97.

Lenoir, R. (1974) *Les Exclus Un Français Sur Dix*, Paris: Seuil.

Leong, G. (1989) The Expansion of Psychiatric Participation in Social Control, *Hospital and Community Psychiatry*, 40(3): 240–42.

Lifton, R.J. (1986) *The Nazi Doctors: Medical Killing and the Psychology of Genocide*, New York: Basic Books.

Light, E., Kerridge, I., Ryan, C. and Robertson, M. (2012) Community Treatment Orders in Australia: Rates and Patterns of Use, *Australasian Psychiatry*, published online, November 6, 2012, DOI: 10.1177/1039856212466159.

Lloyd, Lord (1996) *Inquiry into Legislation against Terrorism*, London: Stationery Office.

Lorimer, J. (2008) Super ASBOs, *New Law Journal*, 158: 56.

Lupton, D. (1999) *Risk*, London: Routledge.

Lussier, P. and Davies, G. (2011) A Person-Oriented Perspective on Sexual Offenders, Offending Trajectories, and Risk of Recidivism: A New Challenge for Policymakers, Risk Assessors, and Actuarial Prediction?, *Psychology, Public Policy and Law*, 17(4): 530–61.

Lussier, P., Tzoumakis, S., Cale, J. and Amirault, J. (2010) Criminal Trajectories of Adult Sex Offenders and the Age Effect: Examining the Dynamic Aspect of Offending in Adulthood, *International Criminal Justice Review*, 20(2): 147–68.

Lynch, A. (2005) We Have Not Been Bombed Back to the Dark Ages by Terrorism, *The Age*, August 4, 15.

Macken, C. (2005) Preventive Detention and the Right of Personal Liberty and Security under the International Covenant on Civil and Political Rights, 1966, *Adelaide Law Review*, 26(1): 1–28.

Macken, C. (2011) *Counter-Terrorism and the Detention of Suspected Terrorists: Preventive Detention and Human Rights Law*, London: Routledge.

Maguire, M., Kemshall, H., Noaks, L., Wincup, E. and Sharpe, K. (2001) *Risk Management of Sexual and Violent Offenders: The Work of Public Protections Panels*,

London: Home Office. Available online at http://webarchive.nationalarchives.gov.
uk/20110218135832/http://rds.homeoffice.gov.uk/rds/prgpdfs/prs139.pdf
(accessed January 31, 2013).

Major, B. and Eccleston, C.P. (2005) Stigma and Social Exclusion, in D. Abrams,
M.A. Hogg and J.M. Marques (eds) *The Social Psychology of Inclusion and Exclusion*,
New York: Psychology Press, 63–87.

Malsch, M. and Duker, M. (2012) Introduction, in M. Malsch and M. Duker
(eds) *Incapacitation: Trends and New Perspectives*, Farnham: Ashgate Publishing Ltd,
1–13.

McAuley, F. (1993) *Insanity Psychiatry and Criminal Responsibility,* Dublin: Round Hall
Press.

McBeth, A., Nolan, J. and Rice, S. (2011) *The International Law of Human Rights*,
South Melbourne: Oxford University Press.

McCallum, D. (2001) *Personality and Dangerousness: Genealogies of Antisocial Personality
Disorder*, Cambridge: Cambridge University Press.

McGarrity, N. (2012) From Terrorism to Bikies: Control Orders in Australia,
Alternative Law Journal, 37(3): 166–70.

McMaster, K. and Wells, A. (2006) From Uncertainty to Certainty: Is it Possible?,
in K. McMaster and L. Bakker (eds) *Will They Do It Again? Assessing and Managing
Risk*, Lytellton, New Zealand: Hall McMaster and Associates, 7–23.

McSherry, B. (2004) Terrorism Offences in the Criminal Code: Broadening the
Boundaries of Australian Criminal Laws, *University of New South Wales Law Journal*,
27(2): 354–72.

McSherry, B. (2005) Indefinite and Preventive Detention Legislation: From Caution
to an Open Door, *Criminal Law Journal*, 29(2): 94–110.

McSherry, B. (2008) The United Nations Convention on the Rights of Persons with
Disabilities, *Journal of Law and Medicine*, 16(1): 17–20.

McSherry, B. (2011) The Preventive Detention of Suspected Terrorists: Better Safe
than Sorry?, in B. McSherry and P. Keyzer (eds) *Dangerous People: Policy, Prediction
and Practice*, New York: Routledge, 97–107.

McSherry, B. (2012) Post-Sentence Incapacitation of Sex Offenders and the Ethics of
Risk Assessment, in M. Malsch and M. Duker (eds) *Incapacitation*, Aldershot:
Ashgate Publishing Ltd, 77–96.

McSherry, B. and Keyzer, P. (2010) *Sex Offenders and Preventive Detention: Politics, Policy
and Practice*, Annandale, NSW: Federation Press.

McSherry, B. and Weller, P. (eds) (2010) *Rethinking Rights-Based Mental Health Laws*,
Oxford: Hart.

Meacham, S. (2007) Family Urges New Ben Hall Inquest, *The Age*, March 31.
Available online at http://www.theage.com.au/news/national/family-urges-new-
ben-hall-inquest/2007/03/30/1174761754719.html (accessed January 31, 2013).

Melton, G.B., Petrila, J., Poythress, N.G. and Slobogin, C. (1987) *Psychological
Evaluations for the Courts: A Handbook for Mental Health Professionals and Lawyers*,
New York: Guilford Press.

Melton, G.B., Petrila, J., Poythress, N.G. and Slobogin, C. (with Lyons, P.M., Jr. and
Otto, R.) (2007) *Psychological Evaluations for the Courts: A Handbook for Mental
Health Professionals and Lawyers*, 3rd edn, New York: Guilford Press.

Mental Health Review Board of Victoria (2006) *Members Manual*, 2nd edn, Melbourne:
Mental Health Review Board.

Mercado, C.C. and Ogloff, J.R.P. (2007) Risk and the Preventive Detention of Sex Offenders in Australia and the United States, *International Journal of Law and Psychiatry*, 30(1): 49–59.

Meyer, J.-E. (1988) The Fate of the Mentally Ill in Germany During the Third Reich, *Psychological Medicine*, 18(3): 575–81.

Meyerson, D. (2009) Risks, Rights, Statistics and Compulsory Measures, *Sydney Law Review*, 31(4): 507–35.

Michaelsen, C. (2012) "From Strasbourg with Love": Preventive Detention Before the German Federal Constitutional Court and the European Court of Human Rights, *Human Rights Law Review*, 12(1): 148–67.

Millar, J. (2007) Social Exclusion and Social Policy Research: Defining Exclusion, in D. Abrams, J. Christian and D. Gordon (eds) *Multidisciplinary Handbook of Social Exclusion Research*, Chichester: John Wiley and Sons, 1–15.

Miller, C.T. and Kaiser, C.R. (2001) Implications of Mental Models of Self and Others for the Targets of Stigmatization, in M.R. Leary (ed.) *Interpersonal Rejection*, New York: Oxford University Press, 189–212.

Minkel, J.R. (2010) Fear Review: Critique of Forensic Psychopathy Scale Delayed 3 Years by Threat of Lawsuit, *Scientific American*, June 17. Available online at http://www.scientificamerican.com/article.cfm?id=critique-of-forensic-psychopathy-scale-delayed-by-lawsuit (accessed January 31, 2013).

Moloney, T. (2010) Sexual Offences Prevention Orders, Foreign Travel Orders and Risk of Sexual Harm Orders, in P. Rook and R. Ward (eds) *Rook and Ward on Sexual Offences Law and Practice*, 4th edn, London: Thomson Reuters, 1105–26.

Monahan, J. (1981) *The Clinical Prediction of Violent Behavior*, Northvale, NJ: Jason J. Aronson.

Monahan, J. (2002) The MacArthur Studies of Violence Risk, *Criminal Behaviour and Mental Health*, 12(s1): s67–s72.

Monahan, J. (2008) Structured Risk Assessment of Violence, in R. Simon and K. Tardiff (eds) *Textbook of Violence Assessment and Management*, Washington, DC: American Psychiatric Publishing, 17–33.

Monahan, J. (2012) The Individual Risk Assessment of Terrorism, *Psychology, Public Policy and Law*, 18(2): 167–205.

Monahan, J., Steadman, H.J., Robbins, P.C., Appelbaum, P., Banks, S., Grisso, T., Heilbrun, K., Mulvey, E.P., Roth, L. and Silver, E. (2005) An Actuarial Model of Violence Risk Assessment for Persons With Mental Disorders, *Psychiatric Services*, 56(7): 810–15.

Monahan, J., Steadman, H.J., Robbins, P.C., Silver, E., Appelbaum, P.S., Grisso, T., Mulvey, E.P. and Roth, L.H. (2000) Developing a Clinically Useful Actuarial Tool for Assessing Violence Risk, *British Journal of Psychiatry*, 176(4): 312–19.

Monahan, J., Steadman, H.J., Silver, E., Appelbaum, P.S., Robbins, P.C., Mulvey, E.P., Roth, L.H., Grisso, T. and Banks, S. (2001) *Rethinking Risk Assessment: The MacArthur Study of Mental Disorder and Violence*, Oxford: Oxford University Press.

Morris, G.H. (1999) Defining Dangerousness: Risking a Dangerous Definition, *Journal of Contemporary Legal Issues*, 10: 61–101.

Morse, S.J. (2008) The Ethics of Forensic Practice: Reclaiming the Wasteland, *The Journal of the American Academy of Psychiatry and the Law*, 36: 206–17.

Mossman, D. and Selke, T. (2007) Avoiding Errors about "Margins of Error", *British Journal of Psychiatry*, 191(6): 561.

Mullen, P.E. (1999) Dangerous People with Severe Personality Disorder, *British Medical Journal*, 319: 1146–47.

Mullen, P.E. (2001) Dangerousness, Risk and the Prediction of Probability, in M. Gelder, J.J. Lopez-Ibor and N. Andersen (eds) *New Oxford Textbook of Psychiatry*, Oxford: Oxford University Press, 2066–78.

Mullen, P.E. (2007) Dangerous and Severe Personality Disorder and in Need of Treatment, *British Journal of Psychiatry*, 190(s 49): s3–s7.

Mullen, P.E., Burgess, P., Wallace, C., Palmer, S. and Ruschena, D. (2000) Community Care and Criminal Offending in Schizophrenia, *Lancet*, 355(9204): 614–17.

Mulvey, E.P. and Lidz, C.W. (1985) Back to Basics: A Critical Analysis of Dangerousness Research in a New Legal Environment, *Law and Human Behavior*, 9(2): 209–19.

Murphy, T. and Whitty, N. (2009) Is Human Rights Prepared? Risk, Rights and Public Health Emergencies, *Medical Law Review*, 17(2): 219–44.

Neighbour, S. (2006) The Convert, ABC Television, *Four Corners* Program Transcript, February 27. Available online at http://www.abc.net.au/4corners/content/2006/s1580223.htm (accessed January 31, 2013).

Neilson, G. (2002) *The 1996 CMA Code of Ethics Annotated for Psychiatrists*. Available online at http://www.ftsr.ulaval.ca/ethiques/CMApsy.pdf (accessed January 31, 2013).

Neuberg, S.L., Smith, D.M. and Asher, T. (2000) Why People Stigmatize: Toward a Biocultural Framework, in T.F. Heatherton, R.E. Kleck, M.R. Hebk and J.G. Hull (eds) *The Social Psychology of Stigma*, New York: Guilford Press, 31–61.

Norko, M.A. and Baranoski, M.V. (2005) The State of Contemporary Risk Assessment Research, *Canadian Journal of Psychiatry*, 50(1): 18–26.

Oaks, D.W. (2011) The Moral Imperative for Dialogue with Organizations of Survivors of Coerced Psychiatric Human Rights Violations, in T.W. Kallert, J.E. Mezzich and J. Monahan, (eds) *Coercive Treatment in Psychiatry*, Chichester: Wiley-Blackwell, 185–211.

O'Connor, P.A., Freckelton, I.R. and Sallman, P. (2006) *Practice Manual for Tribunals*, Melbourne: Council of Australasian Tribunals.

O'Malley, P. (1991) Legal Networks and Domestic Security, *Studies in Law, Politics and Society*, 11: 165–84.

O'Malley, P. (2001a) Discontinuity, Government and Risk: A Response to Rigakos and Hadden, *Theoretical Criminology*, 5(1): 85–92.

O'Malley, P. (2001b) Risk, Crime, and Prudentialism Revisited, in K. Stenson and R. Sullivan (eds) *Crime, Risk and Justice*, Cullompton: Willan, 89–103.

O'Malley, P. (2004) *Risk, Uncertainty and Government*, London: GlassHouse.

O'Malley, P. (2010) *Crime and Risk*, London: Sage.

Perlin, M. (2000) *The Hidden Prejudice: Mental Disability on Trial*, Washington, DC: American Psychological Association.

Perlin, M. (2012) *International Human Rights and Mental Disability Law: When the Silenced Are Heard*, New York: Oxford University Press.

Petersen, J.K., Skeem, J.L., Hart, E., Vidal, S. and Keith, F. (2012) Comparing the Offense Patterns of Offenders with and without Mental Disorder: Exploring the Criminalization Hypothesis, *Psychiatric Services*, 61(12): 1217–22.

Petrila, J. (2004) Emerging Issues in Forensic Mental Health, *Psychiatric Quarterly*, 75: 3–19.

Petrila, J. (2010) Rights-Based Legalism and the Limits of Mental Health Law: The United States's Experience, in B. McSherry and P. Weller (eds) *Rethinking Rights-Based Mental Health Laws*, Oxford: Hart, 357–78.

Picken, A. (2009) Better Than Cure, *Solicitors Journal*, 153(21): 14.

Pokorny, A.D. (1983) Prediction of Suicide in Psychiatric Patients: Report of a Prospective Study, *Archives of General Psychiatry*, 40(3), 249–57.

Poythress, N. and Petrila, J.P. (2010) PCL-R Psychopathy: Threats to Sue, Peer Review, and Potential Implications for Science and Law: A Commentary, *International Journal of Forensic Mental Health*, 9(1): 3–10.

Pratt, J. (1995) Dangerousness, Risk and Technologies of Power, *Australian and New Zealand Journal of Criminology*, 28: 1–73.

Pratt, J. (1998) *Governing the Dangerous: Dangerousness, Law and Social Change*, Annandale: The Federation Press.

Pratt, J. (2000a) Emotive and Ostentatious Punishment: Its Decline and Resurgence in Modern Society, *Punishment and Society*, 2(4): 417–39.

Pratt, J. (2000b) The Return of the Wheelbarrow Men: or, The Arrival of Postmodern Penality?, *British Journal of Criminology*, 40(1): 127–45.

Pressman, D.E. (2009) *Risk Assessment Decisions for Violent Extremism*, Ottawa: Canadian Centre for Security and Intelligence Studies.

Prins, H. (1996) Risk Assessment and Management in Criminal Justice and Psychiatry, *Journal of Forensic Psychiatry*, 7(1): 42–62.

Pryce, T. (2008) "Crasbos": Criminal Antisocial Behaviour Orders: An Analysis, *Scottish Criminal Law*, March, 275–82.

Quinsey, V.L., Harris, G.T., Rice, M.E. and Cormier, C.A. (1998) *Violent Offenders: Appraising and Managing Risk*, Washington, DC: American Psychological Association.

Radden, J. (2002) Notes Towards a Professional Ethics for Psychiatry, *Australian and New Zealand Journal of Psychiatry*, 36(1): 52–59.

Radden, J. (2004) The Debate Continues: Unique Ethics for Psychiatry, *Australian and New Zealand Journal of Psychiatry*, 38(3): 115–18.

Ramsay, P. (2009) The Theory of Vulnerable Autonomy and the Legitimacy of Civil Preventative Orders, in B. McSherry, A. Norrie and S. Bronitt (eds) *Regulating Deviance: The Redirection of Criminalisation and the Futures of Criminal Law*, Oxford: Hart, 109–39.

Rangarajan, S. and McSherry, B. (2009) To Detain or Not to Detain: A Question of Public Duty?, *Psychiatry, Psychology and Law*, 16(2): 288–302.

Reed, A. and Aquino, K.F. (2003) Moral Identity and the Expanding Circle of Moral Regard Toward Out-Groups, *Journal of Personality and Social Psychology*, 84(6): 1270–86.

Richardson, G. (2010) Rights-Based Legalism: Some Thoughts from the Research, in B. McSherry and P. Weller (eds) *Rethinking Rights-Based Mental Health Laws*, Oxford: Hart, 181–201.

Rigakos, G.S. (2001) On Continuity, Risk and Political Economy: A Response to O'Malley, *Theoretical Criminology*, 5(1): 93–100.

Rigakos, G.S. and Hadden, R.W. (2001) Crime, Capitalism and the "Risk Society": Towards the Same Olde Modernity?, *Theoretical Criminology*, 5(1): 61–84.

Risk Management Authority (2007) *Risk Assessment Tools Evaluation Directory: RATED Version 2*, Paisley: Risk Management Authority. Available online at http://www. rmascotland.gov.uk/files/5512/7306/6150/riskAssessmentToolsEvaluation Directory.pdf (accessed January 31, 2013).

Risk Management Authority (2011) *Annual Report and Accounts 2010/11*. Available online at http://www.rmascotland.gov.uk/files/6713/1410/2788/RMA_Annual_ Report_and_Accounts_2010-11.pdf (accessed January 31, 2013).

Robertson, M.D. and Walter, G. (2008) Many Faces of the Dual-Role Dilemma in Psychiatric Ethics, *Australian and New Zealand Journal of Psychiatry*, 42(3): 228–35.

Robinson, N. (2007) Jack Thomas Order Relaxed, *The Australian*, 24 August. Available online at http://www.theaustralian.com.au/news/nation/jack-thomas-order-relaxed/story-e6frg6nf-1111114256511 (accessed January 31, 2013).

Roelcke, V., Hohendorf, G. and Rotzoll, M. (2001) Psychiatric Research and "Euthanasia": The Case of the Psychiatric Department at the University of Heidelberg, 1941–1945, *Psychoanalytic Review*, 88(2): 275–94.

Rose, N. (1998) Governing Risky Individuals: The Role of Psychiatry in New Regimes of Control, *Psychiatry, Psychology and Law*, 5(2): 177–95.

Rose, N. (2000) Government and Control, *British Journal of Criminology*, 40(2): 321–39.

Royal Australian and New Zealand College of Psychiatrists (1980) *Guide to Ethical Principles on Medico-Legal Reports: Ethical Guideline #1*. Available online at http:// www.ranzcp.org/Files/ranzcp-attachments/Resources/College_Statements/ Ethical_Guidelines/eg01-pdf.aspx (accessed January 31, 2013).

Royal Australian and New Zealand College of Psychiatrists (2003) *Ethical Guidelines for Independent Medical Examination and Report Preparation by Psychiatrists: Ethical Guideline #9*. Available online at http://www.ranzcp.org/getattachment/Resources/ Statements-Guidelines/Ethical-Guidelines/9_EG-2003.pdf.aspx (accessed January 31, 2013).

Royal College of Psychiatrists for the United Kingdom and the Republic of Ireland (2005) The Psychiatrist, Courts and Sentencing: The Impact of Extended Sentencing on the Ethical Framework of Forensic Psychiatry: Council Report CR129, June 2004, *Psychiatric Bulletin*, 29(2): 73–77.

Royal College of Psychiatrists for the United Kingdom and the Republic of Ireland (2008) *Court Work: Final Report of a Scoping Group*, London: Royal College of Psychiatrists. Available online at http://www.rcpsych.ac.uk/files/pdfversion/cr147. pdf (accessed January 31, 2013).

Ruschena, D. (2003) Determining Dangerousness: Whatever Happened to the Rules of Evidence?, *Psychiatry, Psychology and Law*, 10(1): 122–39.

Ryan, C.J. (2011) Capacity as a Determinant of Non-Consensual Treatment of the Mentally Ill in Australia, *Psychiatry, Psychology and Law*, 18(2): 248–62.

Ryan, C., Callaghan, S. and Large, M. (2012) Better Laws for Coercive Psychiatric Treatment: Lessons from the Waterlow Case, *Australasian Psychiatry*, DOI: 10.1177/1039856212449668.

Salekin, R.T., Rogers, R. and Sewell, K.W. (1996) A Review and Meta-Analysis of the Psychopathy Checklist and Psychopathy Checklist-Revised: Predictive Validity of Dangerousness, *Clinical Psychology: Science and Practice*, 3(3): 203–15.

Santow, E. and Williams, G. (2012) Terrorism Threat Assessments: Problems of Constitutional Law and Government Accountability, *Public Law Review*, 23(1): 33–49.

Savage, C., Glaberson, W. and Lehren, A.N. (2011) Classified Files Offer New Insight into Detainees, *New York Times*, April 24, p. A1. Available online at http://www.nytimes.com/2011/04/25/world/guantanamo-files-lives-in-an-american-limbo.html?pagewanted=3&_r=1&ref=andrewwlehren (accessed January 31, 2013).

Schleuter, D. (2008) *Military Criminal Justice: Practice and Procedure*, 7th edn, Newark, NJ: Matthew Bender.

Scottish Executive (2000) *Report of the Committee on Serious Violent and Sexual Offenders (the MacLean Committee)*, Edinburgh: Scottish Executive. Available online at http://www.sccjr.ac.uk/documents/files/79392b9f6a8cfc305b0f559b9a5f744e.pdf (accessed January 31, 2013).

Scottish Executive (2001) *Serious Violent and Sexual Offenders Criminal Justice*, Edinburgh: Scottish Executive. Available online at http://www.scotland.gov.uk/Resource/Doc/158912/0043171.pdf (accessed January 31, 2013).

Scurich, N. and John, R. (2010) The Normative Threshold for Psychiatric Civil Commitment, *Jurimetrics*, 50(4): 425–52.

Seddon, T. (2007) *Punishment and Madness: Governing Prisoners with Mental Health Problems*, New York: Routledge-Cavendish.

Seddon, T. (2008) Dangerous Liaisons: Personality Disorder and the Politics of Risk, *Punishment and Society*, 10(3): 301–17.

Seeman, M.V. (2005) Psychiatry in the Nazi Era, *Canadian Journal of Psychiatry*, 50(4): 218–24.

Serious Organised Crime Agency (2012) The Long Arm of the Serious Crime Prevention Order, 15 February. Available online at http://www.soca.gov.uk/news/400-the-long-arm-of-the-serious-crime-prevention-order (accessed January 31, 2013).

Shute, S. (2004) The Sexual Offences Act 2003: (4) New Civil Preventative Orders: Sexual Offences Prevention Orders; Foreign Travel Orders; Risk of Sexual Harm Orders, *Criminal Law Review*, 417–40.

Sidanius, J. and Pratto, F. (1993) The Inevitability of Oppression and the Dynamics of Social Dominance, in P. Sniderman, P.E. Tetlock and E.G. Carmines (eds) *Prejudice, Politics, and the American Dilemma*, Stanford: Stanford University Press.

Silver, E. and Miller, L.L. (2002) A Cautionary Note on the Use of Actuarial Risk Assessment Tools for Social Control, *Crime and Delinquency*, 48(1): 138–61.

Simester, A.P. and von Hirsch, A. (2006) Regulating Offensive Conduct Through Two-Step Prohibition, in A. von Hirsch and A.P. Simester (eds) *Incivilities: Regulating Offensive Behaviour*, Oxford: Hart, 173–94.

Simon, J. (1988) The Ideological Effects of Actuarial Practices, *Law and Society Review*, 22(4): 771–800.

Simon, J. (1993) *Poor Discipline: Parole and the Social Control of the Underclass, 1890–1990*, Chicago: University of Chicago Press.

Simon, J. (1998) Managing the Monstrous: Sex Offenders and the New Penology, *Psychology, Public Policy and Law*, 4(1/2): 452–67.

Simon, J. (2012) Total Incapacitation: The Penal Imaginary and the Rise of an Extreme Penal Rationale in California in the 1970s, in M. Malsch and M. Duker (eds) *Incapacitation: Trends and New Perspectives*, Farnham: Ashgate Publishing Ltd, 15–37.

Simon, J. and Feeley, M.M. (2003) The Form and Limit of the New Penology, in T.G. Blomberg and S. Cohen (eds) *Punishment and Social Control*, enlarged 2nd edn, New York: Aldine de Gruyter, 75–116.

Skeem, J.L. and Cooke, D.J. (2010a) Is Criminal Behavior a Central Component of Psychopathy? Conceptual Directions for Resolving the Debate, *Psychological Assessment*, 22(2), 433–45.

Skeem, J.L. and Cooke, D.J. (2010b) One Measure Does Not a Construct Make: Directions Toward Reinvigorating Psychopathy Research: Reply to Hare and Neumann (2010), *Psychological Assessment*, 22(2): 455–59.

Skeem, J.L. and Monahan, J. (2011) *Current Directions in Violence Risk Assessment*, Virginia Public Law and Legal Theory Research Paper No 2011-03, University of Virginia Law School. Available online at http://ssrn.com/abstract=1793193 (accessed January 31, 2013).

Skeem, J.L., Petersen J. and Silver, E. (2011) Toward Research-Informed Policy for High-Risk Offenders with Severe Mental Illnesses, in B. McSherry and P. Keyzer (eds) *Dangerous People: Policy, Prediction, and Practice*, New York: Routledge, 111–21.

Skelton, A., Riley, D., Wales, D. and Vess, J. (2006) Assessing Risk for Sexual Offenders in New Zealand: Development and Validation of a Computer-Scored Risk Measure, *Journal of Sexual Aggression*, 12(3): 277–86.

Slobogin, C. (2003) Jurisprudence of Dangerousness, *Northwestern University Law Review*, 98(1): 1–62.

Slobogin, C. (2006) *Minding Justice: Laws that Deprive People with Mental Disability of Life and Liberty*, Cambridge, MA: Harvard University Press.

Slobogin, C. (2007) *Proving the Unprovable: The Role of Science, and Speculation in Adjudicating Culpability and Dangerousness*, Oxford: Oxford University Press.

Slobogin, C. (2011a) Legal Limitations on the Scope of Preventive Detention, in B. McSherry and P. Keyzer (eds) *Dangerous People: Policy, Prediction, and Practice*, New York: Routledge, 37–47.

Slobogin, C. (2011b) Prevention as the Primary Goal of Sentencing: The Modern Case for Indeterminate Dispositions in Criminal Cases, *San Diego Law Review*, 1127–71.

Slobogin, C. (2012a) Preventive Detention in Europe, the United States, and Australia, *Vanderbilt Public Law Research Paper* No. 12–27; *Vanderbilt Law and Economics Research Paper* No. 12–20. Available online at http:ssrn.com/abstract= 2094358 (accessed January 31, 2013).

Slobogin, C. (2012b) Risk Assessment, in J. Petersilia and K.R. Reitz (eds) *Oxford Handbook of Sentencing and Corrections*, Oxford: Oxford University Press, 196–214.

Squires, P. (2008) Introduction: Why "Anti-social Behaviour?", Debating ASBOs in P. Squires (ed.) *ASBO Nation: The Criminalisation of Nuisance*, Bristol: Policy Press, 1–33.

Squires, P. and Stephen, D.E. (2005) *Rougher Justice: Anti-Social Behaviour and Young People*, Cullompton: Willan.

Stankove, L., Higgins, D., Saucier, G. and Kneževié, G. (2010) Contemporary Militant Extremism: A Linguistic Approach to Scale Development, *Psychological Assessment*, 22(2): 246–58.

Stary, R. (2011) Anti-Terror Laws Cost Us Dearly, *National Times*, 9 September. Available online at http://www.nationaltimes.com.au/opinion/society-and-culture/antiterror-laws-cost-us-dearly-20110908-1jzsc.html (accessed January 31, 2013).

Steadman, H.J. (2000) From Dangerousness to Risk Assessment of Community Violence: Taking Stock at the Turn of the Century, *Journal of the American Academy of Psychiatry and the Law*, 28(3): 265–71.

Steadman, H.J. and Cocozza, J.J. (1974) *Careers of the Criminally Insane: Excessive Social Control of Deviance*, Lexington, MA: Lexington Books.

Stone, A.A. (1984) The Ethical Boundaries of Forensic Psychiatry: A View from the Ivory Tower, *Bulletin of the American Academy of Psychiatry and the Law*, 12(3): 209–19.

Stout, C.E. (ed.) (2004) *Psychology of Terrorism: Coping with the Continuing Threat*, Westport, CT: Praeger.

Strous, R.D. (2006) Hitler's Psychiatrists: Healers and Researchers Turned Executioners and its Relevance Today, *Harvard Review of Psychiatry*, 14(1): 30–37.

Strous, R.D. (2007a) Commentary: Political Activism: Should Psychologists and Psychiatrists Try to Make a Difference?, *Israel Journal of Psychiatry and Related Sciences*, 44(1): 12–17.

Strous, R.D. (2007b) Psychiatry During the Nazi Era: Ethical Lessons for the Modern Professional, *Annals of General Psychiatry*, DOI:10.1186/1744-859X-6-8.

Strous, R.D. (2011) Historical Injustice in Psychiatry with Examples from Nazi Germany and Others: Ethical Lessons for the Modern Professional, in T.W. Kallert, J.E. Mezzich and J. Monahan (eds), *Coercive Treatment in Psychiatry: Clinical, Legal and Ethical Aspects*, London: John Wiley and Sons, 161–73.

Sullivan, D.H., Mullen, P.E. and Pathé, M.T. (2005) Legislation in Victoria on Sexual Offenders: Issues for Health Professionals, *Medical Journal of Australia*, 183(6): 318–20.

Sunstein, C. (2005) *Laws of Fear: Beyond the Precautionary Principle*, Cambridge: Cambridge University Press.

Swartz, M.S. and Swanson, J.W. (2004) Involuntary Outpatient Commitment, Community Treatment Orders, and Assisted Outpatient Treatment: What's in the Data?, *Canadian Journal of Psychiatry*, 49(9): 585–91.

Szasz, T. (1963) *Law, Liberty and Psychiatry: An Inquiry into the Social Uses of Mental Health Practices*, New York: Macmillan.

Szasz, T. (1970) *Ideology and Insanity: Essays on the Psychiatric Dehumanization of Man*, Garden City, NY: Anchor Books.

Szasz, T. (2005) Should Psychologists Be Coercive Agents of the State?, *Current Psychology*, 24(2): 77–79.

Szasz, T. (2007) *Coercion as Cure: A Critical History of Psychiatry*, New Brunswick, NJ: Transaction Publishers.

Szmukler, G. and Rose, N. (2013) Risk Assessment in Mental Health Care: Values and Costs, *Behavioral Sciences and the Law*, 31: 125–40.

Szmukler, G., Daw, R. and Dawson, J. (2010) A Model Law Fusing Incapacity and Mental Health Legislation, *Journal of Mental Health Law*, 11–22.

Tajfel, H. and Turner, J.C. (1986) The Social Identity Theory of Intergroup Behavior, in S. Worchel and W.G. Austin (eds) *The Psychology of Intergroup Relations*, 2nd edn, Chicago, IL: Nelson-Hall, 7–24.

Taylor, P. (2012) Severe Personality Disorder in the Secure Estate: Continuity and Change, *Medicine, Science and the Law*, 125–27.

Third Session of the Ad Hoc Committee on the UN Convention on the Rights of Persons with Disabilities (2004) *Daily Summary of Discussion Related to Article 10:*

Liberty and Security of the Person, 26 May. Available online at http://www.un.org/esa/socdev/enable/rights/ahc3sum10.htm (accessed January 31, 2013).

Thomas, D.A. (2011) Sentencing: Sexual Offence Prevention Orders: General Guidance, *Criminal Law Review*, 12: 967–74.

Thomas, T. (2011) *The Registration and Monitoring of Sex Offenders: A Comparative Study*, New York: Routledge.

Thomson, L. (2011) The Role of Forensic Mental Health Services in Managing High-Risk Offenders, in B. McSherry and P. Keyzer (eds) *Dangerous People: Policy, Prediction and Practice*, New York: Routledge, 165–81.

Thornberry, T.P. and Krohn, M.D. (2003) *Taking Stock of Delinquency: An Overview of Findings from Contemporary Longitudinal Studies*, New York: Kluwer/Plenum Press Publishers.

Thornicroft, G. (2006) *Shunned: Discrimination Against People with Mental Illness*, Oxford: Oxford University Press.

Thornton, D., Mann, R., Webster, S., Blud, L., Travers, R., Friendship, C. and Erikson, M. (2003) Distinguishing and Combining Risks for Sexual and Violent Recidivism, *Annals of the New York Academy of Sciences*, 989(1): 225–35.

Tonry, M. (2004) *Thinking About Crime: Sense and Sensibility in American Penal Culture*, Oxford: Oxford University Press.

Tonry, M. (2010) The Costly Consequences of Populist Posturing: ASBOs, Victims, 'Rebalancing' and Dimunition in Support for Civil Liberties, *Punishment & Society*, 12(4): 387–413.

Tulloch, J. and Lupton, D. (2003) *Risk and Everyday Life*, London: Sage.

Tversky, A. and Kahneman, D. (1973) Availability: A Heuristic for Judging Frequency and Probability, *Cognitive Psychology*, 5(2): 207–32.

United Nations Committee on the Rights of Persons with Disabilities (2011a) *Consideration of Reports Submitted by States Parties under Article 35 of the Convention: Concluding Observations of the Committee on the Rights of Persons with Disabilities: Tunisia*. UN Doc CRPD/C/TUN/Co/1.

United Nations Committee on the Rights of Persons with Disabilities (2011b) *Consideration of Reports Submitted by States Parties under Article 35 of the Convention: Concluding Observations of the Committee on the Rights of Persons with Disabilities: Spain*. Un Doc CRPD/C/ESP/CO/1. Available online at http://www.ohchr.org/EN/HRBodies/CRPD/Pages/Session6.aspx (accessed January 31, 2013).

United Nations Human Rights Council (2009) *Annual Report of the United Nations High Commissioner for Human Rights and Reports of the Office of the High Commissioner and the Secretary–General: Thematic Study by the Office of the United Nations High Commissioner for Human Rights on Enhancing Awareness and Understanding of the Convention on the Rights of Persons with Disabilities: Summary*. UN Doc A/HRC/10/48. Available online at http://www2.ohchr.org/english/bodies/hrcouncil/docs/10session/A.HRC.10.48.pdf (accessed January 31, 2013).

United Nations Human Rights Council (2013) *Report of the Special Rapporteur on Torture and Other Cruel, Inhuman or Degrading Treatment or Punishment*, Juan E. Méndez, A/HRC/22/53 (1 February).

United Nations Office of the High Commissioner for Human Rights (1982) *General Comment No. 08: Right to Liberty and Security of Persons (Art 9): 06/30/1982*. Available online at http://www.unhchr.ch/tbs/doc.nsf/0/f4253f9572cd4700c1256 3ed00483bec?Opendocument (accessed January 31, 2013).

Vaughan, G.M. and Hogg, M.A. (2011) *Social Psychology*, 6th edn, Frenchs Forest, NSW: Pearson Australia.

Vess, J. and Eccleston, L. (2009) Extended Supervision of Sexual Offenders in Australia and New Zealand: Differences in Implementation Across Jurisdictions, *Psychiatry, Psychology and Law*, 16(2): 271–87.

Victorian Law Reform Commission (2011) *Sex Offenders Registration: Final Report*, Melbourne: Victorian Law Reform Commission. Available online at http://www.lawreform.vic.gov.au/sites/default/files/SOR_Final%20Report_Full%20text.pdf (accessed January 31, 2013).

Victoroff, J. (2005) The Mind of the Terrorist: A Review and Critique of Psychological Approaches, *Journal of Conflict Resolution*, 49(1): 3–42.

Walker, C. (2011) *Terrorism and the Law*, Oxford: Oxford University Press.

Walker, C. and Horne, A. (2012) The Terrorism Prevention and Investigations Measures Act 2011: One Thing But Not Much the Other?, *Criminal Law Review*, 6: 421–38.

Wallace, C., Mullen, P.E. and Burgess, P. (2004) Criminal Offending in Schizophrenia over a 25 Year Period Marked by Deinstitutionalization and Increasing Prevalence of Comorbid Substance Use Disorders, *American Journal of Psychiatry*, 161(4) 716–27.

Wallace, C., Mullen, P., Burgess, P., Palmer, S., Ruschena, D. and Browne, C. (1998) Serious Criminal Offending and Mental Disorder, *British Journal of Psychiatry*, 172(6): 477–84.

Ward, T. and Eccleston, L. (2000) The Assessment of Dangerous Behaviour: Research and Clinical Issues, *Behaviour Change*, 17(2): 53–68.

Ward, T. and Syversen, K. (2009) Human Dignity and Vulnerable Agency: An Ethical Framework for Forensic Practice, *Aggression and Violent Behavior*, 14(2): 94–105.

Watchirs, H. (2005) Human Rights Audit of Mental Health Legislation: Results of an Australian Pilot, *International Journal of Law and Psychiatry*, 28(2): 99–125.

Webster, C.D., Eaves, D., Douglas, K.S. and Wintrup, A. (1995) *The HCR-20 Scheme: The Assessment of Dangerousness and Risk*, Burnaby, BC: Simon Fraser University Mental Health, Law, and Policy Institute, and Forensic Psychiatric Services Commission of British Columbia.

Webster, C.D., Douglas, K.S., Eaves, D. and Hart, S.D. (1997) *HCR-20: Assessing Risk for Violence*, version 2, Burnaby, BC: Simon Fraser University Mental Health, Law and Policy Institute.

Webster, C., Martin, M., Brink, J. and Middleton, C. (2004) *Short-term Assessment of Risk and Treatability*, Hamilton, ON: St. Josephs Healthcare and Forensic Psychiatric Services Commission.

Weisstub, D.N. and Arboleda-Flórez, J. (2000) An International Perspective on Mental Health Law Reform, in A. Okasha, J. Arboleda-Flórez and N. Sartorius (eds) *Ethics, Culture, and Psychiatry: International Perspectives*, Washington, DC: American Psychiatric Press, 189–209.

Weller, P. (2013) *New Law and Ethics in Mental Health Advance Directives: The Convention on the Rights of Persons with Disabilities and the Right to Choose*, London: Routledge.

White House Office of the Press Secretary (2011) *Statement by the President on H.R. 1540*. Available online at http://www.whitehouse.gov/the-press-office/2011/12/31/statement-president-hr-1540 (accessed January 31, 2013).

Wills, T.A. (1981) Downward Comparison Principles in Social Psychology, *Psychological Bulletin*, 90(2): 245–71.

Wilson, P. (2008) Terrorism in Australia, in K. Fritzon and P. Wilson (eds) *Forensic Psychology and Criminology: An Australian Perspective*, North Ryde: McGraw-Hill Australia.

Winick, B. (2003) A Therapeutic Jurisprudence Model for Civil Commitment, in K. Diesfeld and I. Freckelton (eds) *Involuntary Detention and Therapeutic Jurisprudence: International Prespectives on Civil Committment*, Aldershot: Ashgate Publishing Ltd, 23–54.

Winick, B. and La Fond, J. (2003) *Protecting Society from Sexually Dangerous Offenders: Law Justice and Therapy*, Washington, DC: American Psychological Association.

Wise, S. (2012) *Inconvenient People: Lunacy, Liberty and the Mad-Doctors in Victorian England*, London: The Bodley Head.

Yang, M., Wong, S. and Coid, J. (2010) The Efficacy of Violence Prediction: A Meta-Analytic Comparison of Nine Assessment Tools, *Psychological Bulletin*, 136(5): 740–67.

Zedner, L. (2007) Pre-Crime and Post-Criminology?, *Theoretical Criminology*, 11(2): 261–81.

Zedner, L. (2009) *Security*, New York: Routledge.

Zuckerberg, J. (2010) Mental Health Law and Its Discontents: A Reappraisal of the Canadian Experience, in B. McSherry and P. Weller (eds) *Rethinking Rights-Based Mental Health Laws*, Oxford: Hart, 299–326.

INDEX